AAT
INTERACTIVE TEXT

Technician Unit 15

Cash Management and Credit Control

In this May 2000 edition

- Layout designed to be easier on the eye - and easy to use
- Icons to guide you through a 'fast track' approach if you wish
- Numerous activities throughout the text to reinforce learning
- Thorough reliable updating of material to 1 May 2000

FOR 2000 AND 2001 DEVOLVED ASSESSMENTS

BPP Publishing
May 2000

First edition 1998
Third edition May 2000

ISBN 0 7517 6221 0 (Previous edition 0 7517 6165 6)

British Library Cataloguing-in-Publication Data
A catalogue record for this book
is available from the British Library

Published by

BPP Publishing Limited
Aldine House, Aldine Place
London W12 8AW

www.bpp.com

Printed by in Great Britain by Ashford Colour Press, Gosport, Hants

All our rights reserved. No part of this publication may be reproduced, stored in a retrieval system or transmitted, in any form or by any means, electronic, mechanical, photocopying, recording or otherwise, without the prior written permission of BPP Publishing Limited.

We are also grateful to the Lead Body for Accounting for permission to reproduce extracts from the Standards of Competence for Accounting, and to the AAT for permission to reproduce extracts from the mapping and Guidance Notes.

©
BPP Publishing Limited
2000

Contents

Page

INTRODUCTION (v)
How to use this Interactive Text – Technician Qualification Structure – Unit 15 Standards of Competence – Assessment Strategy

PART A: CASH MANAGEMENT

1	Cash and cash flows	3
2	Forecasting cash flows	23
3	Cash budgeting techniques	49
4	The banking system and the economic context	71
5	Dealing with banks	89
6	Raising finance	103
7	Investing money	121

PART B: CREDIT CONTROL

8	Credit control: policies and procedures	149
9	Assessing creditworthiness	173
10	Managing debtors	205
11	Remedies for bad debts	227

LIST OF KEY TERMS 255

INDEX 256

ORDER FORM

REVIEW FORM & FREE PRIZE DRAW

HOW TO USE THIS INTERACTIVE TEXT

Aims of this Interactive Text

> To provide the knowledge and practice to help you succeed in devolved assessments for Technician Unit 15 *Cash Management and Credit Control*.

To pass the devolved assessment you need a thorough understanding in all areas covered by the standards of competence.

> To tie in with the other components of the BPP Effective Study Package to ensure you have the best possible chance of success.

Interactive Text
This covers all you need to know for devolved assessment for Unit 15 *Cash Management and Credit Control*. Icons clearly mark key areas of the text. Numerous activities throughout the text help you practise what you have just learnt.

Devolved Assessment Kit
When you have understood and practised the material in the Interactive Text, you will have the knowledge and experience to tackle the Devolved Assessment Kit for Unit 15. This aims to get you through the devolved assessment, whether in the form of the AAT simulation or in the workplace. It contains the AAT's sample simulation for Unit 15 plus other simulations.

Recommended approach to this Interactive Text

- To achieve competence in Unit 15 (and all the other units), you need to be able to do **everything** specified by the standards. Study the text very carefully and do not skip any of it.

- Learning is an **active** process. Do **all** the activities as you work through the text so you can be sure you really understand what you have read.

- After you have covered the material in the Interactive Text, work through the **Devolved Assessment Kit**.

- Before you take the devolved assessment, check that you still remember the material using the following quick revision plan for each chapter.

    o Read through the **chapter learning objectives**. Are there any gaps in your knowledge? If so, study the section again.

    o Read and learn the **key terms**.

    o Look at the **assessment alerts**. These show the sort of things that are likely to come up.

    o Read and learn the **key learning points**, which are a summary of the chapter.

    o Do the **quick quiz** again. If you know what you're doing, it shouldn't take long.

    This approach is only a suggestion. You college may well adapt it to suit your needs.

Remember this is a **practical** course.

- Try to relate the material to your experience in the workplace or any other work experience you may have had.

- Try to make as many links as you can to your study of the other Units at Technician level.

- Keep this Text - (hopefully) you will find it invaluable in your everyday work too!

TECHNICIAN QUALIFICATION STRUCTURE

The competence-based Education and Training Scheme of the Association of Accounting Technicians is based on an analysis of the work of accounting staff in a wide range of industries and types of organisation. The Standards of Competence for Accounting which students are expected to meet are based on this analysis.

The Standards identify the **key purpose** of the accounting occupation, which is **to operate, maintain and improve systems to record, plan, monitor and report on the financial activities of an organisation**, and a number of **key roles** of the occupation. Each key role is subdivided into **units of competence**, which are further divided into **elements of competences**. By successfully completing assessments in specified units of competence, students can gain qualifications at NVQ/SVQ levels 2, 3 and 4, which correspond to the AAT Foundation, Intermediate and Technician stages of competence respectively.

Whether you are competent in a Unit is demonstrated by means of:

- *Either* a Central Assessment (set and marked by AAT assessors)
- *Or* a Devolved Assessment (where competence is judged by an Approved Assessment Centre to whom responsibility for this is devolved)
- Or *both* Central *and* Devolved Assessment

On the following two pages, we set out the overall structure of the Technician (NVQ/SVQ Level 4) stage, indicating how competence in each Unit is assessed. In the next two sections, there is more detail about the Standards of Competence and the Devolved Assessment for Unit 15.

Technician qualification structure

NVQ/SVQ Level 4 - Technician

Units 8, 9 and 10 are compulsory. You can choose one out of Units 11-14, and then three out of Units 15-19.

Unit of competence

Elements of competence

Unit 8 Contributing to the management of costs and the enhancement of value
- 8.1 Collect, analyse and disseminate information about costs
- 8.2 Make recommendations to reduce costs and enhance value

Central Assessment *only*

Unit 9 Contributing to the planning and allocation of resources
- 9.1 Prepare forecasts of income and expenditure
- 9.2 Produce draft budget proposals
- 9.3 Monitor the performance of responsiblity centres against budgets

Central Assessment *only*

Unit 10 Managing accounting systems
- 10.1 Co-ordinate work activities within the accounting environment
- 10.2 Identify opportunities to improve the effectiveness of an accounting system
- 10.3 Prevent fraud in an accounting system

Devolved Assessment *only*

Unit 22 Monitor and maintain a healthy, safe and secure workplace (ASC)
- 22.1 Monitor and maintain health and safety within the workplace
- 22.2 Monitor and maintain the security of the workplace

Devolved Assessment *only*

Unit 11 Drafting financial statements (Accounting Practice, Industry and Commerce)
- 11.1 Interpret financial statements
- 11.2 Draft limited company, sole trader and partnership year end financial statements

Central Assessment *only*

Unit 12 Drafting financial statements (Central Government)
- 12.1 Interpret financial statements
- 12.2 Draft central government financial statements

Central Assessment *only*

Unit 13 Drafting financial statements (Local Government)
- 13.1 Interpret financial statements
- 13.2 Draft local authority financial statements

Central Assessment *only*

Technician qualification structure

Unit of competence

Elements of competence

Unit 14	Drafting financial statements (National Health Service)

Central Assessment *only*

14.1	Interpret financial statements
14.2	Draft NHS accounting statements and returns

Unit 15	Operating a cash management and credit control system

Devolved Assessment *only*

15.1	Monitor and control cash receipts and payments
15.2	Manage cash balances
15.3	Grant credit
15.4	Monitor and control the collection of debts

Unit 16	Evaluating current and proposed activities

Devolved Assessment *only*

16.1	Prepare cost estimates
16.2	Recommend ways to improve cost ratios and revenue generation

Unit 17	Implementing auditing procedures

Devolved Assessment *only*

17.1	Contribute to the planning of an audit assignment
17.2	Prepare capital allowances computations
17.3	Prepare related draft reports

Unit 18	Preparing business taxation computations

Devolved Assessment *only*

18.1	Adjust accounting profit and losses for trades and professions
18.2	Prepare capital allowances computations
18.3	Prepare Capital gains tax
18.4	Account for Advance Corporation tax and Income tax payable or recoverable by a company
18.5	Prepare Corporation tax computations and returns

Unit 19	Preparing personal taxation computations

Devolved Assessment *only*

19.1	Calculate income from employment
19.2	Prepare computations of property and investment income
19.3	Prepare Capital Gains Tax computations
19.4	Prepare personal tax returns

UNIT 15 STANDARDS OF COMPETENCE

The structure of the Standards for Unit 15

The Unit commences with a statement of the **knowledge and understanding** which underpin competence in the Unit's elements.

The Unit is then divided into **elements of competence** describing activities which the individual should be able to perform.

Each element includes the following.

- A set of **performance criteria** which define what constitutes competent performance.

- A **range statement.** This defines the situations, contexts, methods etc in which competence should be displayed.

- **Evidence requirements.** These state that competence must be demonstrated consistently, over an appropriate time scale with evidence of performance being provided from the appropriate sources.

- **Sources of evidence.** These are suggestions of ways in which you can find evidence to demonstrate that competence. These fall under the headings: 'observed performance; work produced by the candidate; authenticated testimonies from relevant witnesses; personal account of competence; other sources of evidence.' They are reproduced in full in our Devolved Assessment Kit for Unit 15.

The elements of competence for Unit 15: *Operating a Cash Management and Credit Control System* are set out below. Knowledge and understanding required for the unit as a whole are listed first, followed by the performance criteria and range statements for each element. Performance criteria and range statements are cross-referenced below to chapters in this Unit 15 *Cash Management and Credit Control* Interactive Text.

Unit 15: Cash management and credit control

Unit 15 is concerned with the management of cash and credit. The unit involves the management of cash balances as well as the granting of credit and the collection of outstanding debts.

Elements contained within the unit are:
Element: 15.1   Monitor and control cash receipts and payments
Element: 15.2   Manage cash balances
Element: 15.3   Grant credit
Element: 15.4   Monitor and control the collection of debts

Knowledge and understanding

The business environment

- A clear understanding of the main types of cash receipts and payments: regular revenue receipts and payments; capital receipts and payments; drawings/dividends and disbursements; exceptional receipts and payments (Element 15.1)

- The basic structure of the banking system and the money market in the UK. The relationships between financial institutions (Element 15.2)

- An understanding of bank overdrafts and loans; terms and conditions; legal relationship between bank and customer (Element 15.2)

- Types of marketable security (Bills of exchange, certificates of deposit, government securities, local authority short term loans); terms and conditions; risks (Element 15.2)

- A basic understanding of Government monetary policies (Element 15.2)

- Legal issues: basic contract; terms and conditions of contracts relating to the granting of credit; Data Protection Act and credit control information (Element 15.3)

- Sources of credit status information (Element 15.3)

- External sources of information: banks, credit agencies and official publications (Element 15.3)

- Legal issues: remedies for breach of contract (Element 15.4)

- Legal and administrative procedures for the collection of debts (Element 15.4)

- The effect of bankruptcy and insolvency on organisations (Element 15.4)

Accounting techniques

- Form and structure of cash budgets (Element 15.1)

- Lagged receipts and payments (Element 15.1)

- Basic statistical techniques for estimating future trends: moving averages, allowance for inflation (Element 15.1)

- Computer models to assess the sensitivity of elements in the cash budget to change (eg price, wage rate changes) (Element 15.1)

- Managing risk and exposure (Element 15.2)

- Discounts for prompt payment (Element 15.3)

- Interpretation and use of credit control information (Element 15.3 & 15.4)

- Methods of collection (Element 15.4)

- Factoring arrangements (Element 15.4)

- Debt insurance (Element 15.4)

- Methods of analysing information on debtors: age analysis of debtors; average periods of credit given and received; incidence of bad and doubtful debts (Element 15.4)

- Evaluation of different collection methods (Element 15.4)

Accounting principles and theory

- Cash flow accounting and its relationship to accounting for income and expenditure (Element 15.1)

- Liquidity management (Elements 15.2, 15.3 & 15.4)

Unit 15 Standards of competence

The organisation

- Understanding that the accounting systems of an organisation are affected by its organisational structure, its administrative systems and procedures and the nature of its business transactions (Elements 15.1, 15.2, 15.3 & 15.4)
- Understanding that recording and accounting practices may vary in different parts of the organisation (Elements 15.1 & 15.4)
- An understanding that practice in this area will be determined by an organisation's specific financial regulations, guidelines and security procedures (Element 15.2)
- An understanding that in public sector organisations there are statutory and other regulations relating to the management of cash balances (Element 15.2)
- Understanding that practice in this area will be determined by an organisation's credit control policies and procedures (Element 15.3)
- An understanding of the organisation's relevant policies and procedures (Elements 15.1, 15.3 and 15.4).

Element 15.1 Monitor and control cash receipts and payments

	Performance criteria	Chapters in this Text
1	Cash receipts and payments are monitored and controlled against budgeted cash flow	1
2	Appropriate staff are consulted to determine the likely pattern of cash flows over the accounting period and to anticipate any exceptional receipts or payments	2
3	Forecasts of future cash payments and receipts are in accord with known income and expenditure trends	2
4	Cash budgets are prepared in the approved format and clearly indicate net cash requirements	2
5	Significant deviations from the cash budget are identified and corrective action is taken within defined organisational policies	2

Range statement

1	Cash flows to be monitored: regular revenue receipts and payments; capital receipts and payments; drawings or dividends and disbursements; exceptional receipts and payments	1

Element 15.2 Manage cash balances

	Performance criteria	Chapters in this Text
1	Overdraft and loan facilities are arranged in anticipation of requirements and on the most favourable terms available	6
2	Surplus funds are invested in marketable securities within defined financial authorisation limits	7
3	The organisation's financial regulations and security procedures are observed	6, 7
4	Account is taken of trends in the economic and financial environment in managing cash balances	4
5	An adequate level of liquidity is maintained in line with cash forecasts	7

Unit 15 Standards of competence

Range statement	Chapters in this Text
1 Marketable securities: bills of exchange; certificates of deposit; government securities; local authority short term loans	7

Element 15.3 Grant credit

Performance criteria	Chapters in this Text
1 Credit terms are agreed with customers in accordance with the organisation's policies	9
2 Internal and external sources of information are identified and used to evaluate the current credit status of customers and potential customers	9
3 New accounts are opened for those customers with an established credit status	9
4 The reasons for refusing credit are discussed with customers in a tactful manner	10
Range statement	
1 Internal information derived from: analysis of the accounts; colleagues in regular contact with current or potential customers or clients	9
2 External information derived from: credit rating agencies; supplier references; bank references	9

Element 15.4 Monitor and control the collection of debts

Performance criteria	Chapters in this Text
1 Information relating to the current state of debtors' accounts is regularly monitored and appropriate action taken	10
2 Information regarding significant outstanding accounts and potential bad debts is promptly sent to relevant individuals within the organisation	10, 11
3 Discussions and negotiations with debtors are conducted courteously and achieve the desired outcome	11
4 Debt recovery methods used are appropriate to the circumstances of individual cases and are in accordance with the organisation's procedures	11
5 Recommendations to write off bad and doubtful debts are based on a realistic analysis of all known factors	11
Range statement	
1 Information on debtors: age analysis of debtors; average periods of credit given and received; incidence of bad and doubtful debts	10, 11
2 Appropriate action: information and recommendations for action passed to appropriate individual within own organisation; debtor contacted and arrangements made for the recovery of the debt	10, 11

ASSESSMENT STRATEGY

This unit is assessed by **devolved assessment**.

Devolved assessment is a means of collecting evidence of your ability to carry out **practical activities** and to **operate effectively in the conditions of the workplace** to the standards required. Evidence may be collected at your place of work or at an Approved Assessment Centre by means of simulations of workplace activity, or by a combination of these methods.

If the Approved Assessment Centre is a **workplace,** you may be observed carrying out accounting activities as part of your normal work routine. You should collect documentary evidence of the work you have done, or contributed to, in an **accounting portfolio**. Evidence collected in a portfolio can be assessed in addition to observed performance or where it is not possible to assess by observation.

Where the Approved Assessment Centre is a **college or training organisation**, devolved assessment will be by means of a combination of the following.

- Documentary evidence of activities carried out at the workplace, collected by you in an **accounting portfolio**.

- Realistic **simulations** of workplace activities. These simulations may take the form of case studies and in-tray exercises and involve the use of primary documents and reference sources.

- **Projects and assignments** designed to assess the Standards of Competence.

If you are unable to provide workplace evidence you will be able to complete the assessment requirements by the alternative methods listed above.

More detail on assessment can be found in the Devolved Assessment Kit for Unit 15.

Part A
Cash management

Chapter 1 Cash and cash flows

Chapter topic list

1. The cash flow cycle
2. Types of cash transaction
3. Profits and cash flow
4. The focus of cash and credit management
5. Cash accounting and accruals accounting
6. Treasury management

Learning objectives

On completion of this chapter you will be able to:

	Performance criteria	Range statement
monitor and control receipts and payments against budgeted cash flow	15.1.1	
understand clearly the main types of cash receipts and payments	15.1	15.1.1
understand the management of liquidity	15.2, 15.3, 15.4	

Part A: Cash management

1 THE CASH FLOW CYCLE

ASSESSMENT ALERT

You will probably already have learned about cash and credit, for example in earlier studies. For AAT Unit 14 however, you need to have familiarity with the planning aspects of cash and credit, and how cash and credit are inter-related.

1.1 A business which fails to make profits will go under in the long term. However, a business which runs out of cash, even for a couple of months, will fail, despite the fact that it is basically profitable. Why might this be so? Take the following example.

1.2 David Ltd, a small business, has won a contract worth £1m from Goliath, which will be repaid in equal annual instalments of £200,000 over five years at the end of each year. David Ltd has a maximum bank overdraft of £200,000. The work on the contract is completed at the end of year 2: a total of £750,000 was incurred on expenses, £200,000 in year 1 and £550,000 in year 2.

	Year 1 £	2 £	3 £	4 £	5 £
Brought forward (surplus/overdraft)	-	-	(200,000)	(150,000)	50,000
Received from Goliath	200,000	200,000	200,000	200,000	200,000
Payments to creditors	(200,000)	(400,000)	(150,000)	-	-
Cash surplus/(overdraft)	-	(200,000)	(150,000)	50,000	250,000
Creditors outstanding		150,000	-		

1.3 We can see that at the end of year 2, David Ltd is in trouble. David Ltd has run up the maximum overdraft, but some creditors have to wait over a year - until the end of year 3 - in order to get paid. Many will be unwilling to wait that long. David Ltd cannot pay its bills on time, and creditors can sue for the business to be wound up. Furthermore if the bank overdraft lasts for long enough, the bank may take a similar view, although the overdraft will have been paid off by the end of year 4. The bank may worry about the length of exposure.

1.4 David Ltd could have avoided this demise if it had planned things differently. Although the contract is profitable, the timing of cash outflows and inflows are differently timed.

(a) Suppliers will refuse to supply goods until they are paid for previous supplies. This will prevent the business functioning at all.

(b) Employees who are not paid can sue for breach of contract. They might also find alternative employment.

1.5 It sometimes helps to view the management of cash, debtors and creditors as a **cycle**, a flow of funds in and out of the business. This is a way of describing the organisation's use of **working capital**.

KEY TERM

Working capital is the net difference between **current assets** (mainly stocks, debtors and cash) and **current liabilities** (such as trade creditors and a bank overdraft).

(a) **Current assets** are items which are either cash already, or which will soon lead to the receipt of cash. Stocks will be sold to customers and create debtors; and debtors will soon pay in cash for their purchases.

(b) **Current liabilities** are items which will soon have to be paid for with cash. Trade creditors will have to be paid and bank overdraft is usually regarded as a short-term borrowing which may need to be repaid fairly quickly (or on demand, ie immediately).

1.6 In balance sheets, the word 'current' is applied to stocks, debtors, short-term investments and cash (current assets) and amounts due for payment within one year's time (current liabilities).

Working capital and trading operations

1.7 Current assets and current liabilities are a necessary feature of a firm's trading operations. There is a repeated cycle of buying and selling which is carried on all the time. For example, suppose that on 1 April a firm has the following items.

	£
Stocks	3,000
Debtors	0
Cash	2,000
	5,000
Creditors	0
Working capital	5,000

1.8 It might sell all the stocks for £4,500, and at the same time obtain more stock from suppliers at a cost of £3,500. The balance sheet items would now be:

	£
Stocks	3,500
Debtors	4,500
Cash	2,000
	10,000
Creditors	(3,500)
Working capital	6,500

(The increase in working capital to £6,500 from £5,000 is caused by the profit of £1,500 on the sale of the stocks.)

1.9 The debtors for £4,500 will eventually pay in cash and the creditors for £3,500 must also be paid. This would give us:

	£
Stocks	3,500
Debtors	0
Cash (2,000 + 4,500 – 3,500)	3,000
	6,500
Creditors	0
Working capital	6,500

1.10 However, if the stocks are sold on credit for £5,500 and further purchases of stock costing £6,000 are made, the cycle of trading will continue as follows:

	£
Stocks	6,000
Debtors	5,500
Cash	3,000
	14,500
Creditors	(6,000)
Working capital (boosted by further profit of £2,000)	8,500

Part A: Cash management

From this basic example you might be able to see that working capital items are part of a continuous flow of trading operations. Purchases add to stocks and creditors at the same time, creditors must be paid and debtors will pay for their goods. The cycle of operations always eventually comes back to cash receipts and cash payments.

The operating cycle

1.11 The **operating cycle** is a term used to describe the connection between working capital and cash movements in and out. The cycle is usually measured in days or months. It is sometimes, somewhat confusingly, called the **cash cycle**, although the movement of cash is only one element in the operating cycle.

1.12 A firm buys raw materials, probably on credit. The raw materials might be held for some time in stores before being issued to the production department and turned into an item of finished goods. The finished goods might be kept in a warehouse for some time before they are eventually sold to customers. By this time, the firm will probably have paid for the raw materials purchased. If customers buy the goods on credit, it will be some time before the cash from the sales is eventually received.

1.13 The operating cycle measures the period of time between the time cash is paid out for raw materials and the time cash is received in from debtors for goods sold. This cycle of repeating events in the cash flow cycle may be shown diagrammatically.

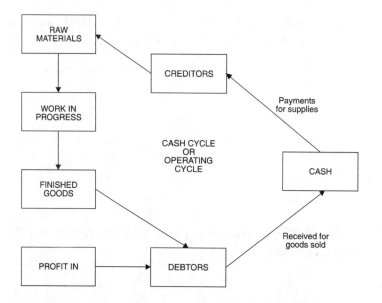

1.14 Suppose that a firm buys raw materials on 1½ months' credit, holds them in store for 1 month and then issues them to the production department. The production cycle is very short, but finished goods are held for 1 month before they are sold. Debtors take two months' credit. The operating cycle would be as follows.

	Months
Raw material stock turnover period	1.0
Less: credit taken from suppliers	(1.5)
Finished goods stock turnover period	1.0
Debtor's payment period	2.0
Cash cycle	2.5

There would be a gap of 2½ months between paying cash for raw materials and receiving cash (including profits) from debtors.

1.15 A few dates might clarify this point. Suppose the firm purchases its raw materials on 1 January. The sequence of events would then be as follows:

	Date
Purchase of raw materials	1 Jan
Issue of materials to production (one month after purchase)	1 Feb
Payment made to suppliers (1½ months after purchase)	15 Feb
Sale of finished goods (one month after production begins)	1 Mar
Receipt of cash from debtors (two months after sale)	1 May

The operating cycle is the period of 2½ months from 15 February, when payment is made to suppliers, until 1 May, when cash is received from debtors.

Activity 1.1

Farmer Giles has just bought a tractor for use on the farm. The tractor will last many years. 'It's just what I need, a little capital expenditure to help me work. And I didn't have to borrow, either. I saved up the subsidy I get from the European Union every month. I suppose you accountants would call this working capital?'

Is he right?

Different types of business

1.16 Different types of business have their own operating cycle characteristics. There are three main elements.

(a) Holding stocks (from their purchase from external suppliers, through the production and warehousing of finished goods, up to the time of sale)

(b) Taking time to pay suppliers and other creditors

(c) Allowing customers (debtors) time to pay

1.17 In a **retailing business**, most sales are for cash or by credit card and debit card, and the company therefore receives most of its cash income at the time of sale. Large supermarket chains which sell goods within a few days of purchase might not pay their suppliers until *after* the goods have been sold and the cash received.

1.18 In a **manufacturing business**, many sales will be on credit, as will many purchases. The operating cycle will therefore be more conventional, with payments preceding receipts.

1.19 Sometimes the operating cycle can be analysed into two elements.

(a) A **trading cycle**, identifying when a firm acquired goods and when it sold them

(b) A **cash cycle** identifying the movements of cash: when was the stock actually paid for? When was cash received from debtors?

Activity 1.2

(a) What are the three main elements in the cash cycle?
(b) Why do you think retailers (such as a supermarket) have a short cash cycle time?
(c) Lengthening the cash cycle will improve the cash balance for most companies. True or false?

Part A: Cash management

2 TYPES OF CASH TRANSACTION

2.1 In the previous section, we concentrated on **working capital**, in other words cash or near-cash aspects of a business's trading operations.

2.2 There are many types of cash transaction. They can be distinguished by their purpose (ie what they are for), their form (how they are implemented), and their frequency. Sometimes the following distinctions are made.

(a) **Capital** and **revenue** items

(i) Capital items relate to the long-term functioning of the business, such as raising money from shareholders, or acquiring fixed assets.

(ii) Revenue items relate to day-to-day operations, as in the operating cycle, including other matters such as overdraft interest.

(b) **Exceptional** and **unexceptional** items

(i) Exceptional items are unusual. An example would be the costs of closing down part of a business.

(ii) Unexceptional items include everything else. You have to be careful using this distinction, as the phrase 'exceptional item' has a precise meaning in the preparation of a company's financial statements.

(c) **Regular** and **irregular** items

(i) Regular items occur at predictable intervals. Such intervals might be frequent such as the payment of wages every week or month, or relatively infrequent, such as the disbursement of interim and final dividends twice a year. A capital item might be the regular repayment of principal and interest on leased property. Annual disbursements are sums of money paid at yearly intervals.

(ii) Irregular items do not occur at regular intervals.

2.3 **Cash outflows** can occur for a number of reasons. Here are some examples.

(a) Payments to:
   (i) Suppliers for goods purchased
   (ii) Employees for wages

This is **revenue expenditure**. Bonuses although paid infrequently are also revenue expenditure.

(b) Payments to government for taxes owing. The payment of corporation tax may be an **annual disbursement**. Regular payments are made for PAYE ('Pay as you earn' tax on employees.

(c) Payments to suppliers of finance:
   (i) Dividends to shareholders
   (ii) Interest to debentureholders, bondholders, banks

The regularity of these payments will vary. Dividends are normally paid twice a year, a smaller interim dividend during the year and a final dividend at the end of the year.

(d) Payments to cover the purchase cost of fixed assets, such as buildings, equipment. These are **capital payments** in that they are purchased for long-term use in the business. They may be irregular. On the other hand, paying of the principal of a long-term loan or lease instalments might be considered capital items.

(e) Payments to acquire investments:

(i) New businesses or to takeover companies (capital)
(ii) Short-term financial instruments to use surplus cash to turn a quick profit

(f) Purchases of foreign currency for trading overseas.

2.4 **Cash inflows** also come in many kinds.

(a) Cash received for sales:

(i) Immediately from customers
(ii) From debtors for sales made on credit

These are **revenue receipts**.

(b) Long-term grants from government institutions or from the European Commission. The use of such 'exceptional' receipts will depend on the terms of the grant.

(c) Cash received from providers of finance:

(i) Equity share capital invested in the business
(ii) Long-term loans provided by banks and other financial institutions

These are generally regarded as **capital receipts**, as they are for long-term investment in the business. Only rarely do companies raise share capital.

(d) Cash received as a result of:

(i) Sale of fixed assets after their useful life
(ii) The liquidation (ie conversion into cash) of short-term investments

2.5 Cash can be received and disbursed in a number of ways, for example:

(a) Notes and coin
(b) Cheques, bills of exchange and promissory notes
(c) Automated payment systems (such as BACS, which we explain later in this *Interactive Text*)

2.6 From the point of view of the accountant it may not matter too much how cash is received. The main considerations are the security and certainty of payment. However, the timings of cash payments and receipts must be harmonised if possible.

2.7 It is the job of accounts and treasury staff to monitor these cash flows.

(a) Exceptional items, such as proceeds from share issues, should be planned for in advance. There should be a short-term plan for investing the money before it is disbursed on other things.

(b) Accounts and treasury staff should monitor the activity in the cash account so as to:

(i) Ensure that any unexpected receipts are properly accounted for

(ii) Ensure that any unexpected outflows are investigated and, if appropriate, corrected

The point is that errors happen, and should be chased up. No bank is perfect.

(c) These two objectives require the accountant to have a number of contacts.

(i) Unexpected payments should be cleared with the bank and the purchase ledger.

(ii) Unexpected receipts should be discussed with the bank and the sales ledger at first instance.

Part A: Cash management

2.8 Cash flows, unlike profit and loss accounts and balance sheets, are not easily 'coloured' by **window dressing** and **creative accounting**. With some exceptions (for small companies and some wholly owned subsidiaries), UK companies must now present a **cash flow statement**, in a standard format (as laid down by FRS 1), as part of their published accounts.

Net cash flow

2.9 **Net cash flow** is the net change in the cash position between the beginning and the end of the period. For example, there has been a change in cash held by X Ltd from £5,000 at 31 December of Year 1 to £3,300 at 31 December of Year 2, giving a negative net cash flow of £1,700. Net cash flow is of little information value, however, unless its **component elements** or causes are analysed. A **categorised cash flow** sets out the entire cash flows of the business, not just cash flows from trading operations. The categories will be chosen to suit the requirements for analysis. In this example, they might be:

	£
Cash flow from sales	17,000
Cash paid for purchases	(10,300)
Cash paid for wages, etc	(4,000)
Interest payments	(400)
Fixed asset expenditure	(10,000)
Bank loan	4,000
Issue of shares	2,000
Net cash flow	(1,700)

A categorised cash flow gives the component elements of net cash flow.

2.10 Another method of categorisation that might be preferred gives four groupings: operational, priority, discretionary and financial.

(a) **Operational cash flows** derive from normal trading operations, in other words cash receipts from sales, payment for supplies, perhaps interest charges, too.

(b) **Priority cash flows** are payments for non-trading cash payments that must be made to keep the company afloat, and have priority over other non-operational payments. These priority items are all cash outflows. They include **interest payments** and **tax payments**.

(c) **Discretionary cash flows** are cash payments or receipts that do not have to be made. Discretionary cash payments could be deferred if necessary and some discretionary income could be earned if required. They include the following.

  (i) Discretionary outflows: capital expenditures, payments for acquisitions, the purchase of financial investments, payout of ordinary dividend and preference dividend. Some might be more urgent than others.

  (ii) Discretionary inflows: the sale of fixed assets, the sale of subsidiaries and the sale of financial investments.

(d) **Financial cash flows** arise from variations in long-term capital. **Financial inflows** include cash from the issue of shares, or from new loans. **Financial outflows** include the repayment of a long-term loan.

Operational cash flows: the cash tank and the cascade effect

2.11 Priority cash flows have to be met by cash inflows from at least one of the other three sources:

(a) Operational cash flows

(b) Net inflows from discretionary items
(c) Net inflows from long-term financing sources

2.12 Operational cash flows will often be the source of cash from which all or most other cash payments can be made, in a descending order of priority. It might be helpful to think of operational cash flows as water going into and out of a water tank. The tank represents the company's operations.

(a) The tank must be kept full of water, so that cash inflows are sufficient to meet cash outflows.

(b) If operational cash flow is positive, and cash inflows exceed outflows, the tank will overflow.

(c) The surplus water (cash) falls into a tray beneath the water tank, representing priority cash flows. When these have been paid, and the priority cash outflow tray is full, the surplus will overflow again into a lower tray, representing discretionary cash outflows.

2.13 It could be described as a cascade effect, with the surplus cash outflows at one level and moving down to the next level for cash outflows.

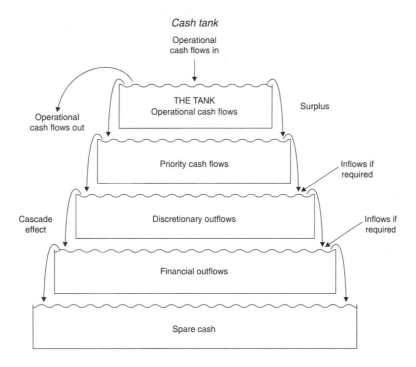

2.14 When operational cash flows are insufficient, a 'top-up' of cash will be needed from discretionary or financial sources (or by using existing cash in hand). These situations will occur, in particular when a company is expanding its operations rapidly, when it wishes to finance a large capital expenditure or acquisition, or when it must repay the principal on a large debt.

2.15 When a company has high profit margins, and its sales turnover is either stable or growing slowly, there should normally be very few operational cash flow problems. The company should have enough cash coming in to meet the payments it must make.

2.16 Operational cash flow problems are much more likely to occur when the company is making only small profits, or trading at a loss. Problems can also occur when the company is growing too fast and is **overtrading** (discussed further later).

Activity 1.3

Cash flows can be classified between regular revenue receipts and payments and infrequent or irregular receipts and disbursements.

Give an example of each of the following.

(a) A regular revenue receipt
(b) An exceptional payment
(c) A capital payment
(d) An annual disbursement

3 PROFITS AND CASH FLOW

3.1 It is important to recognise that a company can make losses but still have a net cash income from trading. (This is the opposite of the situation which we described earlier of the profitable business which runs out of cash.) A company can also make profits but have a net cash deficit on its trading operations. **Trading profits** and **cash flows** are different.

(a) Cash may be obtained from a transaction which has nothing to do with profit or loss. For example, an issue of shares or loan stock for cash has no effect on profit (except for subsequent interest charges on a loan) but is obviously a source of cash. Similarly, an increase in bank overdraft provides a source of cash for payments, but it is not reported in the profit and loss account.

(b) Cash may be paid for the purchase of fixed assets, but the charge in the profit and loss account is depreciation, which is only a part of an asset's cost.

(c) When a fixed asset is sold there is a profit or loss on sale equal to the difference between the sale proceeds and the 'net book value' of the asset in the balance sheet at the time it is sold.

(d) One reason is changes in the amount of the company's stocks, debtors and creditors. **Profit** is sales minus the cost of sales. **Operational cash flow** is the difference between cash received and cash paid from trading. Cash received differs from sales because of changes in the amount of debtors. Cash paid differs from the cost of sales because of changes in the amount of stocks and creditors. Operational cash flow therefore differs from profit because of changes in the amount of debtors, stocks and creditors between the start and end of a period.

  (i) The profit and loss account reports the total value of sales in a year. If goods are sold on credit, the cash receipts will differ from the value of sales as debtors will pay after the year end (excluding increases or decreases in the provision for doubtful debts and writing-off bad debts).

	£
Debtors owing money at the start of the year	X
Sales during the year	X
Total money due from customers	X
Less debtors owing money at the end of the year	(X)
Cash receipts from debtors during the year	X

  (ii) Similarly, the profit and loss account reports the cost of goods sold during the year, but some goods are purchased on credit, and some remain in stock over the year end.

  The relationship between the cost of materials in the materials cost of sales and cash payments for materials purchased is as follows:

	£
Opening stocks (at the start of the year)	X
Add purchases during the year	X
	X
Less closing stocks at the end of the year	(X)
Equals materials cost in the cost of sales	X

	£
Payments still owing to creditors at the start of the year	X
Add materials cost in the cost of sales	Y
	X
Less payments still owing to creditors at the end of the year	(X)
Equals cash payments to creditors during the year	X

3.2 A simple illustration helps to make this point. Suppose that a company buys and resells products. Gross profit from trading and operational cash flows from trading can be compared as follows.

Profit	*Operational cash flow*	*Notes*
Sales		
	Cash in	Cash in = Sales + Opening debtors – Closing debtors
– Cost of sales		Purchases = Cost of sales + Closing stock – Opening stock
	– Cash out	Cash out = Purchases + Opening creditors – Closing creditors
= Profit	= Operational cash flow	

Activity 1.4

Assume that Beta achieved sales turnover in a particular year of £200,000 and the cost of sales was £170,000. Stocks were £12,000, creditors £11,000 and debtors £15,000 at the start of the year. At the end of the year, stocks were £21,000, creditors were £14,000 and debtors £24,000.

Required

Find out the profits and the operational cash flow resulting from the year's trading.

3.3 A company that trades profitably should earn cash surpluses, at least in the longer term. However, a profitable company can also suffer from negative cash flows.

(a) It might spend cash on fixed asset purchases and extra working capital investments.

(b) It might use cash to pay for business acquisitions.

(c) High inflation rates might force a company to increase its funding of business assets in money terms, even when there is no real growth in the business.

(d) Dividends might exceed profits for the year. In recession, for example, profits fall but there will be pressure from shareholders to maintain or increase the dividend.

(e) There could be inefficient management of working capital. For example, there could be a build-up of excess stock, which has to be paid for, but earns no profit until it is used or sold.

3.4 The difference between profit and cash flow has important implications.

(a) If a company is profitable but short of cash, one reason could be an increase in the other elements of working capital. If a company were to seek credit from a bank to finance the growth in working capital, the bank might ask the management whether **operational cash flows could be improved** by squeezing working capital, and:

(i) Reducing debtors
(ii) Reducing stocks, or
(iii) Taking more trade credit from suppliers

Better control over working capital could remove the need to borrow.

(b) If a company is making losses, it could try to maintain a positive operational cash flow by taking more credit (ie by increasing its creditors and so reducing working capital). The credit managers of supplier companies should then consider whether to give the extra credit required, or whether to refuse because the risk would be too great.

Negative operational cash flows: implications

3.5 **Negative cash flows** from operations would normally be an indicator of **financial distress**, unless the company is in a period of rapid (and profitable) growth and is having to invest heavily in additional working capital (stocks and debtors). If a company has negative cash flows from operations for at least two of the previous three years, it will probably be safe to conclude that its financial position is deteriorating significantly.

Activity 1.5

Write brief notes on why the reported profit figure of a business for a period does not normally represent the amount of cash generated in that period.

4 THE FOCUS OF CASH AND CREDIT MANAGEMENT

4.1 In general terms, cash and credit management are concerned with **profitability**, **liquidity** and **safety** (or **security**).

Profitability

4.2 Normally speaking, **profitability** refers to a surplus of income over expenditure. In the context of cash management; profitability relates specifically to how the firm manages its cash in order to minimise costs and maintain a return.

4.3 EXAMPLE: PROFITABILITY

At the end of month 1, Bloggs Ltd finds it has cash balances surplus to requirements of £1,000, for which it has no conceivable use at the moment.

(a) It can leave it in the bank current account, where it will earn no interest.

(b) It can invest it in a deposit account where it will earn interest of £20 in month 2, provided the bank is given a *week's* notice should Bloggs require the money.

(c) It can buy shares in Gamma Ltd. At the beginning of the month they were worth £1,000: at the end, they were worth £1,040.

(d) It can go to the stock market and buy some shares in Delta Ltd for a month. The value of a share can go down as well as up. (*Tutorial note.* In practice a company could invest in government securities, which are detailed in a later chapter of this Interactive Text.)

It costs £10 in total to buy and sell the shares. At the beginning of the month the shares were worth £1,000: at the end they were worth £995.

Which is the best use of funds?

4.4 SOLUTION

	Current account (a) £	Deposit account (b) £	Gamma (c) £	Delta (d) £
Cash invested	(1,000)	(1,000)	(1,000)	(1,000)
Interest	-	20	-	-
Principal/sale proceeds	1,000	1,000	1,040	995
Transaction costs	-	-	(10)	(10)
Profit/(loss)	None	20	30	(15)

Gamma is the most profitable, but shares are more risky than the current or deposit accounts, as the example of Delta demonstrated.

Bloggs would be foolish simply to let the cash pile up and earn no money, even if investing is not the company's main business. At the same time, it must be careful to balance the risk of a course of action, such as investing in shares, with the profit. Although (a) earns nothing, the cash will be on hand **immediately** if needed.

Liquidity

4.5 We have touched on liquidity at the beginning of the chapter. *Liquidity* is the ability of a company to pay its creditors on time. A company can maintain its liquidity:

(a) If it ensures that its own credit customers pay on time

(b) By ensuring that it has investments that are easily convertible into cash, if need be

(c) By planning for its financial needs and setting up arrangements with the bank to ensure it can pay its debts, if this means borrowing from the bank

4.6 Liquidity also refers to the ease with which something can be converted into cash for use. Cash is the most 'liquid' asset of all. A short-term investment can be sold. Some accounts require notice. Buildings and property might be very illiquid, in that they are difficult to sell and convert into cash.

Safety

4.7 Cash and credit transactions should not involve the company in any undue risk.

(a) Notes and coin should be secure from theft.

(b) Cheques etc and electronic systems should be secure from fraud.

(c) Short-term investments should be such that the firm does not stand to risk heavy losses through falls in value. The example in Paragraph 3.4 indicated that shares can fall in price. As a short-term investment they are perhaps risky, whereas none of the principal was lost in the bank deposit account.

4.8 There is a relationship between **risk** and **return**. Generally speaking safer investments offer lower rewards. As far as a company is concerned:

(a) The risk needs to be spread

Part A: Cash management

(b) The loss of principal can be a severe loss

4.9 Credit control is a way of controlling the risk of debts going bad. (Bear in mind that a bad debt is equivalent to a firm giving away the goods to the customer for free.)

Activity 1.6

What are the three main issues underlying the management of cash and the control of credit? Would you say that one of them was always more important than the others?

The issue of risk

4.10 In general, the issues of **cash** and **credit** risk cannot be considered apart. Credit is 'near-cash'. Offering credit to a customer is more risky than asking for cash up front. The diagram below represents the context in which a firm's policies operate.

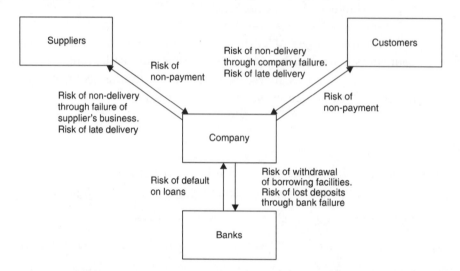

5 CASH ACCOUNTING AND ACCRUALS ACCOUNTING

5.1 The distinction between profits and cash flow has been a theme of this chapter so far. It is very important to grasp the principle, which is applied in nearly all businesses' accounts, that **accounts** are not prepared on a **cash basis** but on an **accruals (or earnings) basis**. That is, a sale or purchase is dealt with in the year in which it is made, even if cash changes hands in a later year. Most businesses, even if they do not sell on credit, make purchases on credit. If cash accounting is used, then accounts do not present a true picture of the business's activities in any given period. Accountants call this convention an application of the **accruals concept**. This is explained briefly by means of the example below.

5.2 EXAMPLE: ACCRUALS CONCEPT

Brenda has a business importing and selling model Corgi dogs. In May 19X7 she makes the following purchases and sales.

Invoice date	Numbers bought/sold	Amount £	Date paid
Purchases			
7.5.X7	20	100	1.6.X7
Sales			
8.5.X7	4	40	1.6.X7
12.5.X7	6	60	1.6.X7
23.5.X7	10	100	1.7.X7

What is Brenda's profit for May?

5.3 SOLUTION

	£
Cash basis	
Sales	0
Purchases	0
Profit/loss	0
Accruals basis	
Sales (£40 + £60 + £100)	200
Purchases	(100)
Profit	100

5.4 Obviously, the accruals basis gives a 'truer' picture than the cash basis. Brenda has no cash to show for her efforts until June but her customers are legally bound to pay her and she is legally bound to pay for her purchases.

5.5 This accruals concept states that, in **computing profit**, revenue earned must be matched against the expenditure incurred in earning it. This is illustrated in the example of Brenda; profit of £100 was computed by matching the revenue (£200) earned from the sale of 20 Corgis against the cost (£100) of acquiring them.

5.6 If, however, Brenda had only sold 18 Corgis, it would have been incorrect to charge her profit and loss account with the cost of 20 Corgis, as she still has two Corgis in stock. If she intends to sell them in June she is likely to make a profit on the sale. Therefore, only the purchase cost of 18 Corgis (£90) should be matched with her sales revenue, leaving her with a profit of £90.

5.7 Her balance sheet would therefore look like this.

	£
Assets	
Stock (at cost, ie 2 × £5)	10
Debtors (18 × £10)	180
	190
Liabilities	
Creditors	(100)
Net assets	90
Proprietor's capital (profit for the period)	90

5.8 In this example, the concepts of **going concern** and accruals are linked. Because the business is assumed to be a going concern it is possible to carry forward the cost of the unsold Corgis as a charge against profits of the next period.

5.9 If Brenda decided to give up selling Corgis, how would the two Corgis in the balance sheet be valued?

5.10 If Brenda decided to give up selling Corgis, then the going concern concept would no longer apply and the value of the two Corgis in the balance sheet would be a break-up valuation rather than cost. Similarly, if the two unsold Corgis were now unlikely to be sold at more than their cost of £5 each (say, because of damage or a fall in demand) then they should be recorded on the balance sheet at their net realisable value (ie the likely eventual sales price less any expenses to be incurred to make them saleable, eg paint) rather than cost.

Part A: Cash management

The accruals concept defined

> **KEY TERM**
>
> The **accruals concept** or **matching concept** is described in SSAP 2 as follows.
>
> 'Revenues and costs are accrued (that is, recognised as they are earned or incurred, not as money is received or paid), matched with one another so far as their relationship can be established or justifiably assumed, and dealt with in the profit and loss account of the period to which they relate ... Revenue and profits dealt with in the profit and loss account of the period are matched with associated costs and expenses by including in the same account the costs incurred in earning them (so far as these are material and identifiable)'.

5.11 Company legislation gives legal recognition to the accruals concept, stating that: 'all income and charges relating to the financial year to which the accounts relate shall be taken into account, without regard to the date of receipt or payment'. This has the effect, as we have seen, of requiring businesses to take account of sales and purchases when made, rather than when paid for, and also to carry unsold stock forward in the balance sheet rather than to deduct its cost from profit for the period.

Relevance of the accruals concept to cash control

5.12 The accruals concept is to do with **financial reporting**. In other words it is a way of letting investors know how much profit a business has made by matching income and expenditure. It has **no relevance whatsoever** to day-to-day cash management. Assume you have purchased a fixed asset for £1m: in the financial accounts it is an asset and it is depreciated over 5 years. This does not alter the fact that £1m has left your bank account, and that funds have to cover this expenditure. Certainly, over the life of the asset, it will generate positive cash flows. But it is important to remember that liquidity is a much more short-term consideration than profit.

The importance of cash flow information

5.13 Survival in business depends on the ability to generate cash. **Cash flow information** directs attention towards this critical issue. Cash flow is a more comprehensive concept than 'profit' which is dependent on accounting conventions and concepts.

5.14 Advantages of cash flow accounting being employed in financial reporting are as follows.

(a) Creditors (long and short-term) will be more interested in an entity's ability to repay them than in its profitability. Whereas 'profits' might indicate that cash is likely to be available, cash flow accounting is more direct with its message.

(b) Cash flow reporting satisfies the needs of other financial report users better.

(i) For management, it provides the sort of information on which decisions should be taken: (in management accounting, 'relevant costs' to a decision are future cash flows); traditional profit accounting does not help much with decision-making.

(ii) For shareholders and auditors, cash flow accounting can provide a satisfactory basis for stewardship accounting.

(c) Cash flow forecasts are easier to prepare, as well as more useful, than profit forecasts.

1: Cash and cash flows

6 TREASURY MANAGEMENT

6.1 In small companies, the financial director or chief accountant will be responsible for all the various accounting and financial activities of the firm.

6.2 As companies increase in size however, specialist personnel are employed to deal with financial and budgetary issues. Different firms have different ways of organising the finance function, but a suggestion is provided in the **diagram below**. Note the following.

(a) The credit control department, responsible for offering credit to customers and collecting debts, might be part of the sales function, and not report directly to the finance director. The credit control staff might alternatively report to the financial controller.

(b) To manage cash (funds) and foreign currency efficiently, many large companies have set up a separate treasury department.

(c) Cash forecasting and budgeting is likely to be a joint exercise between the management accounting department and treasury department. The management accountants will collate sales and production data, from which a cash budget is derived. The treasury department's job is to ensure that operations are financed.

6.3 Clearly, the various departments must co-operate, in the exchange and co-ordination of information and in financial planning.

> **KEY TERM**
>
> **Treasury management** can be defined as 'the corporate handing of all financial matters, the generation of external and internal funds for business, the management of currencies and cash flows, and the complex strategies, policies and procedures of corporate finance' (*Association of Corporate Treasurers*).

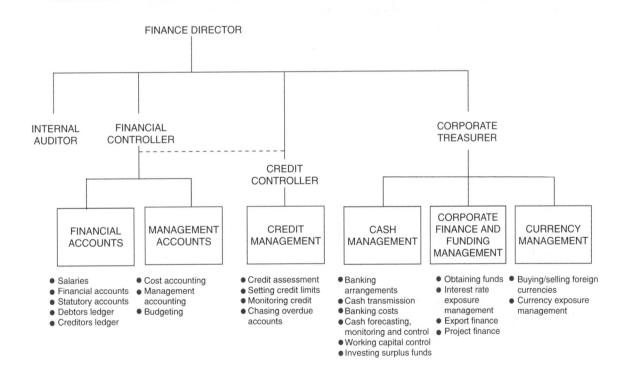

Part A: Cash management

Key learning points

- The **operating cycle** measures the period of time between cash outflows for materials and so on, and cash inflows from sales or debtors.

- **Working capital** is the difference between a firm's current assets and current liabilities. These are assets or liabilities which are, or can be turned into, cash.

- **Cash flow** can be defined in many ways.
    - Net cash flow is the *total* change in a company's cash balances over a period of time.
    - Operational cash flow is the net cash flow arising over a period from trading operations.
    - Priority cash flows do not relate to trade, but are vital to keep the company afloat.

- **Operational flows** can be improved by better management of stocks, debtors and creditors (eg fewer stocks, collecting money earlier, paying it later).

- **Cash** and **credit** are interrelated. A firm with poor cash flow is likely to be a high credit risk.

- Cash and credit management are concerned with **profitability, liquidity** and **safety** (or **security**).

- Accounts showing **trading profits** - calculated on an **earnings** (**accruals**) basis - are not the same as statements of **cash flow.**

- **Cash budgets** are not prepared according to the accruals concept, which tries to ensure income and expenditure are matched. Instead they are prepared on a cash (receipts and payments) basis.

- **Treasury management** in a modern enterprise covers various areas.

Quick quiz

1. What is generally understood by working capital?
2. What period of time is measured by the operating cycle?
3. What is the difference between 'capital' and 'revenue' flows?
4. What are priority cash flows?
5. Why are profits and cash flows different?
6. Name the three main focuses of cash and credit management.
7. What is the accruals concept?
8. Under what headings do the functions of a treasurer fall?

Answers to quick quiz

1. Current assets (stocks, debtors, cash) less current liabilities (creditors, overdraft).

2. The time between payment of cash for raw materials and receipt of cash from debtors.

3. Capital items relate to long-term functioning of the business; revenue items relate to day-to-day operations.

4. Non-trading payments, eg interest and tax payments, which are necessary to keep the enterprise going.

5. Profits are calculated using various non-cash items.

6. Profitability, liquidity and security/safety.

7. The matching of revenues and costs to the period to which they relate.

8. Cash management; corporate finance; funding management; currency management.

1: Cash and cash flows

Answers to activities

Answer 1.1

The tractor is a fixed asset investment. It doesn't matter how it was financed: it is not working capital in the sense we have discussed it here.

Answer 1.2

(a) *Items in the cash cycle*

    (i) Stocks held for use in the production process or resale
    (ii) Taking time to pay suppliers
    (iii) Receiving cash from sales

(b) A supermarket receives cash (or cash equivalents such as cheques, credit card or debit card payments) at the time of sale, and probably does not pay its suppliers until some time after.

(c) False.

Answer 1.3

(a) *A regular revenue receipt*
Examples might include cash sales, investment income (bank interest or dividends).

(b) *An exceptional payment*
Examples might include costs of closing redundant capacity.

(c) *A capital payment*
Examples might include purchase of fixed assets or the purchase of a new business.

(d) *An annual disbursement*
Examples might include payments to the Inland Revenue, a final dividend to shareholders, a bonus to the directors.

Answer 1.4

	Profit £	Operational cash flow £
Sales	200,000	200,000
Opening debtors (∴ received in year)		15,000
Closing debtors (outstanding at year end)		(24,000)
Cash in		191,000
Cost of sales	170,000	170,000
Closing stock (bought, but not used, in year)		21,000
Opening stock (used, but not bought, in year)		(12,000)
Purchases in year		179,000
Opening creditors (∴ paid in year)		11,000
Closing creditors (outstanding at year end)		(14,000)
Cash out		176,000
Profit/operational cash flow	30,000	15,000

Answer 1.5

The principal reasons why profit will not equal cash flow are as follows.

(a) The 'matching concept' means that costs and revenues do not equal payments and receipts. Revenue is recognised in the profit statement when goods are sold, and any revenue not received is recorded as a debtor. Similarly, costs are incurred when a resource is acquired or subsequently used, not when it happens to be paid for.

Part A: Cash management

(b) Some items appearing in the profit statement do not affect cash flow. For example, depreciation is a 'non-cash' deduction in arriving at profit.

(c) Similarly, items may effect cash flow but not profit. Capital expenditure decisions (apart from depreciation) and stock level adjustments are prime examples.

Answer 1.6

The three issues underlying the management of cash and the control of credit are as follows.

(a) *Profitability* relates to maintaining a surplus of income over expenditure, for example obtaining the best return on an investment. However, some cash management activities incur costs (eg interest payments, discount allowed) which are incurred as expenses necessary in the course of business: a discount may be offered to secure a sale, for example. These costs should be minimised.

(b) *Liquidity* refers to a business's ability to pay its debts as they fall due. A firm must have access to cash in order to pay its creditors. A failure of liquidity can lead to insolvency, in which case the firm will go out of business.

(c) *Safety* involves minimising the risk that, for example, a debt will not be collected, cash will be stolen, or that an 'investment' will turn out to be worthless.

All are equally important, but in different ways and over different timescales. As the example of Barings showed, unacceptable risk (a safety issue) can lead to insolvency. However, insolvency may only be a short-term problem. In the long term, a failure to be profitable can lead to collapse.

Chapter 2 Forecasting cash flows

Chapter topic list

1. The purpose of forecasts
2. Cash budgets in receipts and payments format
3. Cleared funds cash forecasts
4. Cash forecasts based on financial statements
5. Control and corrective action

Learning objectives

On completion of this chapter you will be able to:

	Performance criteria	Range statement
• consult appropriate staff to determine the likely pattern of cash flows over the accounting period and anticipate any exceptional receipts of payments	15.1.2	
• ensure that forecasts of future cash payments and receipts are in accord with known income and expenditure trends	15.1.3	
• prepare cash budgets in the approved format and clearly indicate net cash requirements	15.1.4	
• identify significant deviations from the cash budget and take corrective action within organisational policies	15.1.5	
• understand the form and structure of cash budgets including lagged receipts and payments	15.1	
• understand cash flow accounting and its relationship to income and expenditure	15.1	

Part A: Cash management

1 THE PURPOSE OF FORECASTS

1.1 **Cash forecasting** ensures that sufficient funds will be available when they are needed to sustain the activities of an enterprise, at an acceptable cost. Forecasts provide an early warning of liquidity problems, by estimating:

(a) How much cash is required
(b) When it is required
(c) How long it is required for
(d) Whether it will be available from anticipated sources

A company must know **when** it might need to borrow and for how long, not just **what amount** of funding could be required.

1.2 **Banks** have increasingly insisted that customers provide cash forecasts (or a business plan that includes a cash forecast) as a precondition of lending. A newly established company wishing to open a bank account will also normally be asked to supply a **business plan**. The cash and sales forecasts will also allow the bank to monitor the progress of the new company, and control its lending more effectively.

Deficiencies

1.3 Any forecast **deficiency** of cash will have to be funded.

(a) **Borrowing**. If borrowing arrangements are not already secured, a source of funds will have to be found. If a company cannot fund its cash deficits it could be wound up.

(b) The firm can make arrangements to **sell any short-term financial investments** to raise cash.

(c) The firm can delay payments to creditors, or pull in payments from customers. This is sometimes known as **leading and lagging**.

1.4 Because cash forecasts cannot be entirely accurate, companies should have **contingency funding**, available from a surplus cash balance and liquid investments, or from a bank facility. The approximate size of contingency margin will vary from company to company, according to the cyclical nature of the business and the approach of its cash planners.

1.5 Forecasting gives management time to arrange its funding. If planned in advance, instead of a panic measure to avert a cash crisis, a company can more easily choose when to borrow, and will probably obtain a lower interest rate.

Forecasting a cash surplus

1.6 Many cash-generative businesses are less reliant on high quality cash forecasts. If a cash surplus is forecast, having an idea of both its size and how long it will exist could help decide how best to invest it.

1.7 In some cases, the amount of interest earned from surplus cash could be significant for the company's earnings. The company might then need a forecast of its interest earnings in order to indicate its prospective earnings per share to stock market analysts and institutional investors.

Activity 2.1

Give examples of unforeseen changes which may affect cash flow patterns.

Types of forecast

1.8 There are two broad types of cash forecast.

(a) Cash flow based forecasts (or cash budgets) in **receipts and payments format**
(b) **Balance sheet and financial statement based** forecasts

We discuss these later on in this chapter, but some introductory points are in order here.

ASSESSMENT ALERT

Development of a cash forecast using one of the above methods is a typical assessment task for Unit 14. Alternatively you might be expected to analyse a cash forecast which is presented to you.

Receipts and payments forecasts

1.9 **Cash flow based forecasts** (**receipts** and **payments**) are forecasts of the amount and timing of cash receipts and payments, net cash flows and changes in cash balances, for each time period covered by the forecast. Cash flow based forecasts include cash budgets up to a year or so ahead and short-term forecasts of just a few days.

KEY TERM

A **cash budget** (or **cash flow budget**) is a detailed forecast of expected cash receipts, payments and balances over a **budget period**.

1.10 The cash budget is formally adopted as a planning target for the budget period. It is part of the annual master budget and is usually prepared by taking a profits budget for the period and adjusting the figures for sales, and costs of sales, into cash flows (receipts and payments). In companies that use cash flow reporting for control purposes, there will probably be:

(a) A cash budget divided into monthly or quarterly periods
(b) A statement comparing actual cash flows against the monthly or quarterly budget
(c) A revised cash forecast
(d) A statement comparing actual cash flows against a revised forecast

1.11 Revised forecasts should be prepared to keep forecasts relevant and up-to-date. Examples would be a revised three-month forecast every month for the next three-month period, or a revised forecast each month or each quarter up to the end of the annual budget period.

1.12 A **rolling forecast** is a forecast that is **continually updated**. When actual results are reported for a given time period (say for one month's results within an annual forecast period) a further forecast period is added and forecasts for intermediate time periods are updated. A rolling forecast can therefore be a 12-month forecast which is updated at the end of every month, with a further month added to the end of the forecast period and with figures for the intervening 11 months revised if necessary.

Part A: Cash management

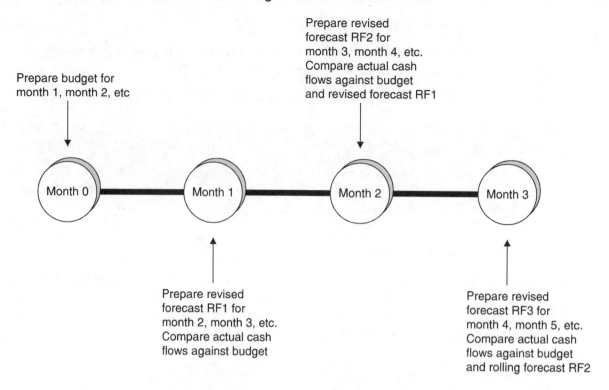

Cash flow control with budgets and revised forecasts

Balance sheet based forecasts

1.13 Balance sheet based forecasts are more suitable for strategic forecasts, in which a 'cash surplus' or 'funds deficit' is the **balancing item** after a forecast has been made for *all* the *other* items in the balance sheet.

For example, if a firm increases its credit period offered, leading to an increase in debtors, and intends to purchase fixed assets, what will be its requirements for cash. Such plans express the company's or group's likely future balance sheet as a consequence of adopting certain strategies. Strategic plans should consider:

(a) The amount of funds required to pursue the chosen strategies
(b) The sources of those funds, including internally generated cash flows
(c) The strategy's potential consequences for liquidity and financial gearing

Guidelines to preparing a forecast

1.14 The cash flow forecast should be broken down into the shortest time periods for which reasonably accurate information can be assembled.

(a) For short-term cash forecasts of up to one month or so, weekly periods are appropriate. In the very short term, up to one week or so, daily cash forecasts may be requested.

(b) For longer-term cash forecasts, periods of a month, a quarter or longer will be suitable. The more distant the time horizon becomes, the longer the time periods in the forecast should be.

1.15 Even fairly predictable items of income and spending (eg salary payments, and NI/tax deductions) cannot usually be forecast with **total** accuracy. Any forecast should therefore include a clear statement of the **assumptions** on which the figures are based. With clearly stated assumptions, a forecast can be tested for reasonableness. For example, cash receipts from sales and debtors might be forecast on the assumption that sales will be a certain level, and debtors will take a certain time to pay.

2 CASH BUDGETS IN RECEIPTS AND PAYMENTS FORMAT

2.1 As stated in the previous section, a **cash budget** (or **cash flow budget**) is a detailed forecast of expected cash receipts, payments and cash balances over a planning period. It is prepared from budgets and capital funding and spending programmes. A budget normally covers one year, and is divided into shorter time periods of a month or a quarter.

2.2 In broad terms, a cash budget is prepared by taking the budgets for sales, costs of sales and profit, and converting the income and expenditure items in these budgets into cash flows by allowing for credit periods, prepayments, accruals and so on. Adjustments are then made:

(a) For cash flow items *not* appearing in the profit and loss account, or
(b) For items in the profit and loss account which do not have a cash effect

2.3 A broad guideline to the preparation of a cash budget is shown below.

Steps in the preparation of a cash budget

Step 1

Sort out cash receipts from debtors.

- Establish budgeted sales month by month.
- Establish the credit period(s) taken by debtors.
- From (a) and (b), calculate when the budgeted sales revenue will be received as cash. Deduct any discount allowed for early payment.
- Establish when the outstanding debtors at the start of the budget period will pay.

Step 2

Establish whether any other cash income will be received, and when. Put these sundry items of cash receipts into the budget.

Step 3

Sort out cash payments to suppliers.

- Establish purchase quantities each month.
- Establish the credit period(s) taken from suppliers.
- From (a) and (b), calculate when the cash payments to suppliers will be made.
- Establish when the outstanding creditors at the start of the budget period will be paid.

Step 4

Establish other cash payments in the month.

These will include:

- Payments of wages and salaries.
- Payments for sundry expenses.
- Other one-off expenditures, such as fixed asset purchases, tax payments.

Items of cost not involving cash payments (eg depreciation) must be excluded. Payments should be scheduled into the month when they will actually occur. For example, rental costs of £120,000 per annum might be charged to the profit and loss account at £10,000 per month. The cash budget should identify in which month or months the £120,000 will actually be paid.

Part A: Cash management

Step 5

Set out the cash budget month by month. A commonly used general layout is as follows.

Receipts	X
Less payments	(X)
Net cash flow in month	X
Opening cash balance	X or (X)
Closing cash balance	X or (X)
Unused borrowing facilities	X

The closing cash balance in one month becomes the opening cash balance the next month.

Selecting components for the forecast

2.4 The starting point in the design of a cash flow forecast is to decide what items should be included. One approach is to look at the **nominal ledger**, which provides a list of all the items of income or expenditure for the company (as nominal ledger accounts). Cash receipts or payments in the forecast can be associated directly with an individual account (or group of accounts) within the company's accounting system. For example, payments to suppliers can be associated with the Purchases Account.

2.5 A second approach is to duplicate the items of revenue and cost in the profit and loss account, so that the contents and format of the cash budget are similar to those of the profit and loss account. Several **adjustments** will have to be made, however (ie depreciation).

2.6 For forecasting purposes, it is useful to separate **exceptional** or **occasional** cash flows from regular trading cash flows (eg wages).

Assumptions

2.7 For each item of cash inflows or outflows, assumptions must be made about the quantity and timing of the flows. (Existing assumptions about receipts and payments and timing patterns should be checked regularly.) The total amount of receipts and payments will be derived from other budgets, such as the company's operating budgets and capital expenditure budget. Assumptions will already have been made for these to prepare the profit or loss budget. Assumptions about the time to pay must be introduced for cash forecasting.

2.8 The forecasting method can be either one or a combination of the following.

- Identifying a particular cash flow, and scheduling when it will be received or paid
- Projecting future trends and seasonal cycles in business activity and cash flows
- Analysing historical payment patterns of regular repeat payments

ASSESSMENT ALERT
A list of the assumptions, once made, should be included with any cash forecast you prepare in an assessment.

Cash payments

2.9 **Assumptions about payments** are easier to make than assumptions about income. Assumptions about payments to suppliers can take account of:

2: Forecasting cash flows

(a) The credit terms given by suppliers (or groups of suppliers), company policy on purchase orders and the administration of cheque payments, etc

(b) Any **specific** supply arrangements, (such as a delivery once every two months, with payment for each delivery at the end of the following month)

(c) Past practice (eg the proportion of invoices (by value) paid in the month of supply and invoice, the proportion paid in the month following, and so on)

(d) The predictable dates for certain payments, such as payments for rent, business rates, telephones, electricity and corporation tax

As a guideline, assumptions about payments should lean towards caution, ie if in doubt, budget for earlier payments.

Fixed cost expenditures

2.10 Some items of expenditure will be regarded as **fixed costs** in the operating budget. Salaries, office expenses and marketing expenditure are three such items. With fixed costs, it could be assumed that there will be an equal monthly expenditure on each item, with cash payment in the month of expenditure perhaps, or in the month following.

2.11 An approach that might be more appropriate in *some* cases would be to identify particular months in which spending on 'fixed' costs is higher than in others. Clearly, if annual building rental is payable quarterly in advance, the budget should plan for payments on the specific dates.

Receipts

2.12 **Assumptions about receipts** might be more difficult to formulate than assumptions about payments.

(a) For a company that depends almost entirely on consumer sales by cash, credit card and debit card, the major uncertainty in the cash flow forecast will be the **volume of sales**. The timing of receipts from a large proportion of those sales will be predictable (payment with sale).

(b) Companies that have a mixture of cash and credit sales must attempt to estimate the proportion of each in the total sales figure, and then formulate assumptions for the timing pattern of receipts from credit sales.

(c) There are several ways of estimating when receipts will occur.

  (i) If the company has specific credit terms, such as a requirement to pay within 15 days of the invoice date, it could assume that:

   (1) Invoices will be sent out at the time of sale

   (2) A proportion, say 25%, will be paid within 15 days (1/2 month)

   (3) A proportion, say 65%, will be paid between 16 days and 30 days (one month after invoice)

   (4) A proportion (say 9%) will pay in the month following

   (5) There will be some bad debts (say 1%, a proportion that should be consistent with the company's budgeted expectations)

  (ii) If there is a policy of cash discounts for early payment, the discounts allowed should be provided for in the forecasts of receipts.

Part A: Cash management

(iii) The time customers take to pay can be estimated from past experience. Care should be taken to allow for seasonal variations and the possibility that payments can be slower at some times of the year than at others (for example, delays during holiday periods).

(iv) Payment patterns can also vary from one country to another. Companies in France and Italy for example will often take several months after the invoice date to pay amounts due.

Calendar variations

2.13 Assumptions could be required to take account of calendar variations.

(a) **Days-in-the-month effect**. It could be assumed that receipts will be the same on every day of the 20th/21st/22nd/23rd etc working day each month. Alternatively, it could be assumed that receipts will be twice as high in the first five days of each month. Assumptions should generally be based on past experience.

(b) **Days-in-the-week effect**. Where appropriate, assumptions should be made about the cash inflows on each particular day of the week, with some days regularly producing higher cash inflows than other days. Such forecasts should be based on historical analysis.

2.14 Receipts for some companies, particularly retailers, follow a regular weekly pattern (with some variations for holidays and seasons of the year). Companies should be able to estimate total weekly takings in cash (notes and coins), cheques and credit card vouchers, the number of cheques and credit card vouchers handled and the deposit spread (for each day, the percentage of the total takings for the week, eg 10% on Monday, 15% on Tuesday).

Time periods and overdraft size

2.15 Dividing the forecast period into time periods should coincide as closely as possible with significant cash flow events, to provide management with information about the **high or low points for cash balances**. In other words, as well as predicting the **month end surplus or overdraft**, the maximum overdraft *during* the month should be predicted.

2.16 EXAMPLE: TIMING OF CASH FLOWS

Oak Tree Villa Ltd operates a retail business. Purchases are sold at cost plus $33^1/_3\%$. Or put another way, purchases are 75% of sales.

(a)

	Budgeted sales	Labour cost	Expenses incurred
	£	£	£
January	40,000	3,000	4,000
February	60,000	3,000	6,000
March	160,000	5,000	7,000
April	120,000	4,000	7,000

(b) It is management policy to have sufficient stock in hand at the end of each month to meet sales demand in the next half month.

(c) Creditors for materials and expenses are paid in the month after the purchases are made or the expenses incurred. Labour is paid in full by the end of each month.

(d) Expenses include a monthly depreciation charge of £2,000.

(e) (i) 75% of sales are for cash.
 (ii) 25% of sales are on one month's interest-free credit.

(f) The company will buy equipment for cash costing £18,000 in February and will pay a dividend of £20,000 in March. The opening cash balance at 1 February is £1,000.

Required

(a) A profit and loss account for February and March
(b) A cash budget for February and March

2.17 SOLUTION

(a) PROFIT AND LOSS ACCOUNT

	February		March		Total	
	£	£	£	£	£	£
Sales		60,000		160,000		220,000
Cost of purchases (75%)		45,000		120,000		165,000
Gross profit		15,000		40,000		55,000
Less: labour	3,000		5,000		8,000	
expenses	6,000		7,000		13,000	
		9,000		12,000		21,000
		6,000		28,000		34,000

(b) *Workings*

(i) *Receipts:*

			£
in February	75% of Feb sales (75% × £60,000)		45,000
	+ 25% of Jan sales (25% × £40,000)		10,000
			55,000

			£
in March	75% of Mar sales (75% × £160,000)		120,000
	+25% of Feb sales (25% × £60,000)		15,000
			135,000

(ii)

	Purchases in January		Purchases in February
Purchases:	£		£
For Jan sales (50% of £30,000)	15,000		
For Feb sales (50% of £45,000)	22,500	(50% of £45,000)	22,500
For Mar sales	-	(50% of £120,000)	60,000
	37,500		82,500

These purchases are paid for in February and March.

(iii) *Expenses*: cash expenses in January (£4,000 – £2,000) and February (£6,000 – £2,000) are paid for in February and March respectively. Depreciation is not a cash item.

Part A: Cash management

CASH BUDGET

	February £	March £	Total £
Receipts from sales	55,000	135,000	190,000
Payments			
Trade creditors	37,500	82,500	120,000
Expenses creditors	2,000	4,000	6,000
Labour	3,000	5,000	8,000
Equipment purchase	18,000	-	18,000
Dividend	-	20,000	20,000
Total payments	60,500	111,500	172,000
Receipts less payments	(5,500)	23,500	18,000
Opening cash balance b/f	1,000	(4,500)*	1,000
Closing cash balance c/f	(4,500)*	19,000	19,000

Notes

* The cash balance at the end of February is carried forward as the opening cash balance for March.

1 The profit in February and March does means that there is sufficient cash to operate the business as planned.

2 Steps should be taken either to ensure that an overdraft facility is available for the cash shortage at the end of February, or to defer certain payments so that the overdraft is avoided.

Cash budgets and an opening debtors and creditors

2.18 You might be given a cash budget question in which you are required to analyse an **opening balance sheet** to decide how many outstanding debtors will pay what they owe in the first few months of the cash budget period, and how many outstanding creditors must be paid.

2.19 EXAMPLE: DEBTORS AND CREDITORS

For example, suppose that a balance sheet as at 31 December 20X4 shows that a company has the following debtors and creditors.

Debtors	£150,000
Trade creditors	£ 60,000

You are informed of the following.

(a) Debtors are allowed two months to pay.

(b) 1½ months' credit is taken from trade creditors.

(c) Sales and materials purchases were both made at an even monthly rate throughout 20X4.

Task

Determine in which months of 20X5 the debtors will eventually pay and the creditors will be paid.

2.20 SOLUTION

(a) Since debtors take two months to pay, the £150,000 of debtors in the balance sheet represent credit sales in November and December 20X4, who will pay in January and

February 20X5 respectively. Since sales in 20X4 were at an equal monthly rate, the cash budget should plan for receipts of £75,000 each month in January and February from the debtors in the opening balance sheet.

(b) Similarly, since creditors are paid after 1½ months, the balance sheet creditors will be paid in January and the first half of February 20X5, which means that budgeted payments will be as follows.

	£
In January (purchases in second half of November and first half of December 20X4)	40,000
In February (purchases in second half of December 20X4)	20,000
Total creditors in the balance sheet	60,000

(The balance sheet creditors of £60,000 represent 1½ months' purchases, so that purchases in 20X4 must be £40,000 per month, which is £20,000 per half month.)

2.21 EXAMPLE: A MONTH-BY-MONTH CASH BUDGET IN DETAIL

Now you have some idea as to the underlying principles, let us put these to work. From the following information which relates to George and Zola Ltd, you are required to prepare a month by month cash budget for the second half of 20X5 and to append such brief comments as you consider might be helpful to management.

(a) The company's only product, a calfskin vest, sells at £40 and has a variable cost of £26 made up as follows.

  Material £20   Labour £4   Variable overhead £2

(b) Fixed costs of £6,000 per month are paid on the 28th of each month.

(c) *Quantities sold/to be sold on credit*

May	June	July	Aug	Sept	Oct	Nov	Dec
1,000	1,200	1,400	1,600	1,800	2,000	2,200	2,600

(d) *Production quantities*

May	June	July	Aug	Sept	Oct	Nov	Dec
1,200	1,400	1,600	2,000	2,400	2,600	2,400	2,200

(e) Cash sales at a discount of 5% are expected to average 100 units a month.

(f) Customers are expected to settle their accounts by the end of the second month following sale.

(g) Suppliers of material are paid two months after the material is used in production.

(h) Wages are paid in the same month as they are incurred.

(i) 70% of the variable overhead is paid in the month of production, the remainder in the following month.

(j) Corporation tax of £18,000 is to be paid in October.

(k) A new delivery vehicle was bought in June, the cost of which, £8,000 is to be paid in August. The old vehicle was sold for £600, the buyer undertaking to pay in July.

(l) The company is expected to be £3,000 overdrawn at the bank at 30 June 20X5.

(m) The opening and closing stocks of raw materials, work in progress and finished goods are budgeted to be the same.

Part A: Cash management

2.22 SOLUTION

CASH BUDGET FOR 1 JULY TO 31 DECEMBER 20X5

	July £	Aug £	Sept £	Oct £	Nov £	Dec £	Total £
Receipts							
Credit sales	40,000	48,000	56,000	64,000	72,000	80,000	360,000
Cash sales	3,800	3,800	3,800	3,800	3,800	3,800	22,800
Sale of vehicles	600						600
	44,400	51,800	59,800	67,800	75,800	83,800	383,400
Payments							
Materials	24,000	28,000	32,000	40,000	48,000	52,000	224,000
Labour	6,400	8,000	9,600	10,400	9,600	8,800	52,800
Variable overhead (W1)	3,080	3,760	4,560	5,080	4,920	4,520	25,920
Fixed costs	6,000	6,000	6,000	6,000	6,000	6,000	36,000
Corporation tax				18,000			18,000
Purchase of vehicle		8,000					8,000
	39,480	53,760	52,160	79,480	68,520	71,320	364,720
Excess of receipts over payments	4,920	(1,960)	7,640	(11,680)	7,280	12,480	18,680
Balance b/f	(3,000)	1,920	(40)	7,600	(4,080)	3,200	(3,000)
Balance c/f	1,920	(40)	7,600	(4,080)	3,200	15,680	15,680

Working

Variable overhead

	June £	July £	Aug £	Sept £	Oct £	Nov £	Dec £
Variable overhead production cost	2,800	3,200	4,000	4,800	5,200	4,800	4,400
70% paid in month		2,240	2,800	3,360	3,640	3,360	3,080
30% in following month		840	960	1,200	1,440	1,560	1,440
		3,080	3,760	4,560	5,080	4,920	4,520

Comments

(a) There will be a small overdraft at the end of August but a much larger one at the end of October. It may be possible to delay payments to suppliers for longer than two months or to reduce purchases of materials or reduce the volume of production by running down existing stock levels.

(b) If neither of these courses is possible, the company may need to negotiate overdraft facilities with its bank.

(c) The cash deficit is only temporary and by the end of December there will be a comfortable surplus. The use to which this cash will be put should ideally be planned in advance.

2.23 EXAMPLE: PRODUCTION BUDGET AND MATERIALS PURCHASES

Here is a further example to show how forecasts are built from forecast raw material and finished goods stock levels.

You are assistant accountant for a confectionery manufacturer and you are in the process of preparing budgets for the next few months. The following draft figures are available.

Sales forecast

January	6,000 boxes
February	7,500 boxes
March	8,500 boxes
April	7,000 boxes
May	6,500 boxes

A box has a standard cost of £15 and a standard selling price of £25.

Each case uses 2½ kgs of ingredients and it is policy to have stocks of ingredients at the end of each month to cover 50% of next month's production. There are 5,800 kgs in stock on 1 January.

There are 750 cases of finished goods in stock on 1 January and it is policy to have stocks at the end of each month to cover 10% of the next month's sales.

Tasks

(a) Prepare a production budget (in boxes) for the months of January, February, March and April.

(b) Prepare an ingredients purchase budget (in kgs) for the months of January, February and March.

(c) Calculate the budgeted gross profit for the quarter January to March.

2.24 SOLUTION

(a)

Production budget
Boxes

	January	February	March	April
Sales quantity	6,000	7,500	8,500	7,000
Closing stocks	750	850	700	650
	6,750	8,350	9,200	7,650
Less opening stocks	(750)	(750)	(850)	(700)
Budgeted production	6,000	7,600	8,350	6,950

(b)

Ingredients purchase budget

	January kg	February kg	March kg
Budgeted material usage (Working)	15,000	19,000	20,875
Closing stocks	9,500	10,438	8,688
Less opening stocks	(5,800)	(9,500)	(10,438)
Budgeted ingredients purchases	18,700	19,938	19,125

Working

January = 6,000kg × 2.5 = 15,000 kg
February = 7,600kg × 2.5 = 19,000 kg
March = 8,350kg × 2.5 = 20,875 kg

(c) *Budgeted gross profit for the quarter January - March*

	January £	February £	March £	Total £
Sales (W1)	150,000	187,500	212,500	550,000
Cost of sales (W2)	90,000	112,500	127,500	330,000
Budgeted gross profit	60,000	75,000	85,000	220,000

Part A: Cash management

Workings

1. January 6,000 × £25 = £150,000
   February 7,500 × £25 = £187,500
   March   8,500 × £25 = £212,500

2. January 6,000 × £15 = £90,000
   February 7,500 × £15 = £112,500
   March   8,500 × £15 = £127,500

Activity 2.2

Tom Ward has worked for some years as a sales representative, but has recently been made redundant. He intends to start up in business on his own account, using £15,000 which he currently has invested with a building society. Tom maintains a bank account showing a small credit balance, and he plans to approach his bank for the necessary additional finance. Tom asks you for advice and provides the following additional information.

(a) Arrangements have been made to purchase fixed assets costing £8,000. These will be paid for at the end of September 20X6 and are expected to have a five-year life, at the end of which they will possess a nil residual value.

(b) Stocks costing £5,000 will be acquired on 28 September and subsequent monthly purchases will be at a level sufficient to replace forecast sales for the month.

(c) Forecast monthly sales are £3,000 for October, £6,000 for November and December, and £10,500 from January 20X7 onwards.

(d) Selling price is fixed at the cost of stock plus 50%.

(e) Two months' credit will be allowed to customers but only 1 month's credit will be received from suppliers of stock.

(f) Running expenses, including rent, are estimated at £1,600 per month.

(g) Blair intends to make monthly cash drawings of £1,000.

Required

Prepare a cash budget for the 6 months October 20X6 to March 20X7.

Activity 2.3

You are presented with the following budgeted data for your organisation for the period November 20X2 to June 20X2 has been extracted from functional budgets that have already been prepared.

	Nov X1 £	Dec X1 £	Jan X2 £	Feb X2 £	Mar X2 £	Apr X2 £	May X2 £	June X2 £
Sales	80,000	100,000	110,000	130,000	140,000	150,000	160,000	180,000
Purchases	40,000	60,000	80,000	90,000	110,000	130,000	140,000	150,000
Wages	10,000	12,000	16,000	20,000	24,000	28,000	32,000	36,000
Overheads	10,000	10,000	15,000	15,000	15,000	20,000	20,000	20,000
Dividends		20,000						40,000
Capital expenditure			30,000			40,000		

You are also told the following.

(a) Sales are 40%, cash 60% credit. Credit sales are paid two months after the month of sales.
(b) Purchases are paid the month following purchase.
(c) 75% of wages are paid in the current month and 25% the following month.
(d) Overheads are paid the month after they are incurred.
(e) Dividends are paid three months after they are declared.
(f) Capital expenditure is paid two months after it is incurred.
(g) The opening cash balance is £15,000.

The managing director is pleased with the above figures as they show sales will have increased by more than 100% in the period under review. In order to achieve this he has arranged a bank overdraft with a ceiling of £50,000 to accommodate the increased stock levels and wage bill for overtime worked.

Tasks

(a) Prepare a cash budget for the six month period January to June 20X2.

(b) Comment upon your results in the light of your managing director's comments and offer advice.

(c) If you have access to a computer spreadsheet package and you know how to use it, try setting up the cash budget on it. Then make a copy of the budget and try making changes to the estimates to see their effect on cash flow.

3 CLEARED FUNDS CASH FORECASTS

Cleared funds

3.1 **Float** refers to the amount of money tied up between the time a payment is initiated and **cleared funds** become available in the recipient's bank account for immediate spending.

(a) The existence of float means that there will always be a difference between a company's cash position as stated in the cash book of its accounts system and its cleared funds.

(b) A company needs to know, especially for short-term cash forecasts, what cleared funds will be because this is the amount that the company has available immediately to spend or invest. If cleared funds are negative, it is the amount on which overdraft interest is calculated.

3.2 Knowing what **cleared funds** are likely to be has a direct and immediate relevance to cash management in the **short-term**. If a company expects to have insufficient cleared funds in the next few days to meet a payment obligation, it must either borrow funds to meet the obligation or (if possible) defer the payment until there are cash receipts to cover it.

3.3 A **cleared funds cash forecast** is a short-term cash forecast of the cleared funds available to a company in its bank accounts, or of the funding deficit that must be met by **immediate borrowing**. Cleared funds forecasts should be reviewed and updated regularly, *daily* for companies with large and uncertain cash flows. Uncertainty might be caused by the internal organisation of the recipient.

(a) The recipient might delay the banking of cheques.
(b) Cheques do sometimes get held up by bureaucracy.

Preparing a cleared funds forecast

3.4 There should be relatively few items in a cleared funds forecast, and each forecast might relate to a **particular bank account**. For a division or subsidiary with more than one bank account, a combined forecast for the different accounts should be prepared only if there is a netting or pooling arrangement between the accounts, so that a surplus balance on one account can be transferred immediately to any account with a cash deficit.

3.5 A cleared funds forecast can be prepared by a combination of three methods.

(a) Obtaining information from the company's banks

(b) Forecasting for other receipts and payments that have occurred but have not yet been lodged with a bank (You should be already familiar with bank reconciliations.)

Part A: Cash management

(c) Adapting the cash budget

(i) Analyse the cash budget into suitable time periods
(ii) Identify cash book payments and receipts
(iii) Adjust these for float times

(d) A cleared funds cash forecast could be prepared. Each day, the amount of payments or receipts in the clearance system can be specified so that the forecast shows both cleared funds and clearance float, and unused bank facilities.

Activity 2.4

Kim O'Hara runs an import/export retail business, largely on a cash basis. He likes to negotiate the best possible deals from his suppliers and this generally means a strict adherence to any payment terms so as to benefit from any settlement discounts: he also orders his supplies at the last possible moment, as he is a firm believer in 'just-in-time' philosophy. On the other hand Creighton plc is a large software house, dealing with major clients. Which type of forecast would be most appropriate to each business?

4 CASH FORECASTS BASED ON FINANCIAL STATEMENTS

Balance sheet

4.1 The balance sheet is produced for **management accounting purposes** and so not for external publication or statutory financial reporting. **It is not an estimate of cash inflows and outflows**. A number of sequential forecasts can be produced, for example a forecast of the balance sheet at the end of each year for the next five years.

4.2 A balance sheet based forecast is an estimate of the company's balance sheet at a future date. It is used to identify either the cash surplus or the funding shortfall in the company's balance sheet at the forecast date.

Estimating a future balance sheet

4.3 A balance sheet estimate calls for some prediction of the amount/value of each item in the company's balance sheet, **excluding cash and short-term investments,** as these are what we are trying to predict. A forecast is prepared by taking each item in the balance sheet, and estimating what its value might be at the future date. The assumptions used are critical, and the following guidelines are suggested.

(a) Intangible **fixed assets** (gross book value) and long term investments, if there are any, should be taken at their current value unless there is good reason for another treatment.

(b) Some estimate of **fixed asset purchases** (and disposals) will be required. Revaluations can be ignored as they are not cash flows.

(c) **Current assets**. Balance sheet estimates of stocks and debtors can be based on fairly simple assumptions. The estimated value for stocks and debtors can be made in any of the following ways.

(i) Same as current amounts. This is unlikely if business has boomed.

(ii) Increase by a certain percentage, to allow for growth in business volume. For example, the volume of debtors might be expected to increase by a similar amount.

(iii) Decrease by a certain percentage, to allow for tighter management control over working capital.

(iv) Assume to be a certain percentage of the company's estimated annual turnover for the year.

(v) The firm can assume that the operating cycle will more or less remain the same. In other words, if a firm's debtors take two months to pay, this relationship can be expected to continue. Therefore, if total annual sales are £12m and debtors take two months to pay, debtors at the year end will be $^2/_{12} \times £12m = £2m$. If turnover increases to £18m, and the collection period stays at two months, debtors will amount to $^2/_{12} \times £18m = £3m$. Similar relationships might be plotted for stocks and hence purchases and creditors.

(d) **Current liabilities.** Some itemising of current liabilities will be necessary, because no single set of assumptions can accurately estimate them collectively.

(i) **Trade creditors and accruals** can be estimated in a similar way to current assets, as indicated above.

(ii) Current liabilities include **bank loans** due for repayment within 12 months. These can be identified individually.

(iii) **Bank overdraft facilities** might be in place. It could be appropriate to assume that there will be no overdraft in the forecast balance sheet. Any available overdraft facility can be considered later when the company's overall cash requirements are identified.

(iv) **Taxation.** Any corporation tax payable should be estimated from anticipated profits and based on an estimated percentage of those profits.

(v) **Dividends payable.** Any ordinary dividend payable should be estimated from anticipated profits, and any preference dividend payable can be predicted from the coupon rate of dividend for the company's preference shares.

(vi) **Other creditors** can be included if required and are of significant value.

(e) **Long-term creditors.** Long-term creditors are likely to consist of long-term loans, bond issues, debenture stock and any other long-term finance debt. Unless the company has already arranged further long-term borrowing, this item should include just existing long-term debts, minus debts that will be repaid before the balance sheet date (or debts transferred from long-term to short-term creditors).

(f) **Share capital and reserves.** With the exception of the profit and loss account reserves (retained profits), the estimated balance sheet figures for share capital and other reserves should be the same as their current amount, unless it is expected or known that a new issue of shares will take place before the balance sheet date, the total amount raised (net of issue expenses) should be added to the share capital/other reserves total.

(g) An estimate is required of the change in the company's **retained profits** in the period up to the balance sheet date. This reserve should be calculated as:

(i) The existing value of the profit and loss reserve, **plus**

(ii) Further retained profits anticipated in the period to the balance sheet date (ie post tax profits minus estimated dividends)

4.4 The various estimates should now be brought together into a balance sheet. The figures on each side of the balance sheet will not be equal, and there will be one of the following.

(a) A surplus of share capital and reserves over net assets (total assets minus total creditors). If this occurs, the company will be forecasting a **cash surplus**.

Part A: Cash management

(b) A surplus of net assets over share capital and reserves. If this occurs, the company will be forecasting a **funding deficit**.

4.5 Alpha Limited has an existing balance sheet and an estimated balance sheet in one year's time before the necessary extra funding is taken into account, as follows.

	Existing		Forecast after one year	
	£	£	£	£
Fixed assets		100,000		180,000
Current assets	90,000		100,000	
Short-term creditors	(60,000)		(90,000)	
Net current assets		30,000		10,000
		130,000		190,000
Long-term creditors		(20,000)		(20,000)
Deferred taxation		(10,000)		(10,000)
Total net assets		100,000		160,000
Share capital and reserves				
Ordinary shares capital		50,000		50,000
Other reserves		20,000		20,000
Profit and loss account		30,000		50,000
		100,000		120,000

4.6 The company is expecting to increase its net assets in the next year by £60,000 (£160,000 – £100,000) but expects retained profits for the year to be only £20,000 (£50,000 – £30,000). There is an excess of net assets over share capital and reserves amounting to £40,000 (£160,000 – £120,000), which is a funding deficit. The company must consider ways of obtaining extra cash (eg by borrowing) to cover the deficit. If it cannot, it will need to keep its assets below the forecast amount, or to have higher short-term creditors.

4.7 A revised projected balance sheet can then be prepared by introducing these new sources of funds. This should be checked for realism (eg by ratio analysis) to ensure that the proportion of the balance sheet made up by fixed assets and working capital, etc is sensible.

4.8 **Balance sheet-based forecasts** have **two main uses**:

(a) As longer-term (strategic) estimates, to assess the scale of funding requirements or cash surpluses the company expects over time

(b) As a check on the realism of cash flow-based forecasts (The estimated balance sheet should be **roughly** consistent with the net cash change in the cash budget, after allowing for approximations in the balance sheet forecast assumptions.)

Deriving cash flow from profit and loss account and balance sheet information

4.9 The previous paragraphs concentrated on preparing a forecast balance sheet, with estimated figures for debtors, creditors and stock. Cash requirements might therefore be presented as the 'balancing figure'. However, it is possible to derive a forecast figure for cash flows using both the balance sheet and profit and loss account. In brief, the profit before interest and tax is adjusted first of all for items not involving cash, such as depreciation. This is further adjusted for changes in the levels of working capital (eg debtors and creditors) to arrive at operational cash flows.

4.10 This is examined in the example below, which is based on Activity 1.4 in Chapter 1. For the time being, assume that there is no depreciation to worry about. The task is to get from profit to operational cash flow, by taking into account movements in working capital.

	Profit £	Operational cash flow £
Sales	200,000	200,000
Opening debtors (∴ received in year)		15,000
Closing debtors (outstanding at year end)		(24,000)
Cash in		191,000
Cost of sales	170,000	170,000
Closing stock (purchased, but not used, in year)		21,000
Opening stock (used, but not purchased, in year)		(12,000)
Purchases in year		179,000
Opening creditors (∴ paid in year)		11,000
Closing creditors (outstanding at year end)		(14,000)
Cash out		176,000
Profit/operational cash flow	30,000	15,000

		£	£
Profit			30,000
(Increase)/Decrease in stocks	Opening	12,000	
	Closing	(21,000)	
			(9,000)
(Increase)/Decrease in debtors	Opening	15,000	
	Closing	(24,000)	
			(9,000)
Increase/(Decrease) in creditors	Closing	14,000	
	Opening	(11,000)	
			3,000
Operational cash flow			15,000

4.11 In practice, a business will make many other adjustments. The profit figure includes items which do not involve the movement of cash, such as the annual depreciation charge, which will have to be added back to arrive at a figure for cash.

4.12 Both 'receipts and payments' forecasts and forecasts based on financial statements could be used alongside each other. The cash management section and the financial controller's section should reconcile differences between forecasts on a continuing basis, so that the forecast can be made more accurate as time goes on.

Activity 2.5

Write down an explanation of the difference between a cash flow based forecast and a balance sheet based forecast. Why do some companies use cleared funds forecasts?

5 CONTROL AND CORRECTIVE ACTION

5.1 A forecast is of no use unless actual outturn is compared with the forecast so that corrective action can be taken. An objective of **cash flow control** is to achieve net cash flows or cash balances that satisfy a target or budget that management has set. The cash flow target could be to avoid borrowing, or to keep the amount borrowed within a specified overdraft limit. Targets could also be imposed on a company by a bank.

Part A: Cash management

Uncertainties in forecast cash flows

5.2 Why might a forecast differ from the actual flows?

(a) **Poor forecasting techniques**

(b) Unpredictable **events or developments**, for example:
   (i) Loss of a major customer
   (ii) Insolvency of a major debtor
   (iii) Changes in interest rates
   (iv) Inflation, which may affect various costs and revenues differently

Cash flow control reports

5.3 **Cash flow control reports** should be prepared regularly for managers with responsibility for cash receipts, payments and balances.

(a) In many companies, reports could be restricted to the treasury department or financial controller's department. Reporting can be informal, perhaps a daily check on cleared funds in the company's bank accounts.

(b) Reports can also be distributed more widely, to operational managers as well as to treasurers and financial controllers. Widespread reporting of cash flows will only be useful, however, if operational managers are conscious of a responsibility to control their cash flows as well as their costs and profits.

5.4 Control reports could be prepared for operational cash flows. The frequency, format and structure of a control report can be designed to suit management requirements, but the purpose of the report should be to compare either:

(a) Actual cash flows against a budget or target (as illustrated below), or
(b) A current forecast of cash flows against an original budget or target

5.5 Reports could be discussed at monthly management meetings (or board meetings) and managers asked to explain differences or variances that exceed a certain control limit (perhaps a percentage of the budgeted cash flow figure). In the example below, the managers responsible could be asked to explain the high payments for teaching costs in March (£106,000 or 27% above the budget amount) and advertising (£28,000 or 33% above budget). The financial controller or director might be asked to comment on the company's borrowing limits, and whether these are now expected to be sufficient.

CASH FLOW CONTROL REPORT

Alpha Language Schools: UK Division
Month: March
Currency: Sterling

	Month			Cumulative: year to date		
	Budget £'000	Actual £'000	Difference £'000	Budget £'000	Actual £'000	Difference £'000
Cash receipts						
Tuition	1,100	1,150	50	2,900	2,980	80
Books	70	25	(45)	210	155	(55)
Cassettes	340	355	15	650	692	42
Sale of fixed assets	0	24	24	30	24	(6)
Other income	15	7	(8)	45	44	(1)
	1,525	1,561	36	3,835	3,895	60

2: Forecasting cash flows

		Month			Cumulative: year to date	
	Budget £'000	Actual £'000	Difference £'000	Budget £'000	Actual £'000	Difference £'000
Cash payments						
Staff costs: teaching	390	496	106	1,000	1,270	270
Staff costs: management	250	248	(2)	650	624	(26)
Book purchases	60	32	(28)	155	81	(74)
Materials printing	25	28	3	65	62	(3)
Origination	15	19	4	40	35	(5)
Commissions	60	61	1	155	158	3
Advertising	85	113	28	210	275	65
Marketing expenses	72	69	(3)	185	170	(15)
Travel and entertaining	216	235	19	520	499	(21)
Equipment	60	72	12	150	144	(6)
Establishment	150	146	(4)	450	435	(15)
Office expenses	42	37	(5)	100	96	(4)
Other payments	30	24	(6)	75	72	(3)
	1,455	1,580	125	3,755	3,921	166
Net cash flow	70	(19)	(89)	80	26	(106)
Opening cash balance	22	5	-	12	12	-
Closing cash balance	92	(14)	(89)	92	14	(106)

Of course, the difference in previous periods might have led to a **'revised' forecast**, and it might be this revised forecast that is used for control purposes.

Corrective action

Improving the business

5.6 Cash deficits can arise out of **basic trading factors** underlying the business such as falling sales or increasing costs. Clearly, the way to deal with these items is to take normal business measures, rectifying the fall in sales by marketing activities or, if this cannot be achieved, by cutting costs. Although we have stressed the difference between profits and cash flow, they are two aspects of a business's behaviour, and it is quite possible that falling profits will eventually turn up as operational cash deficits.

Controlling the operating cycle: short-term deficiencies

5.7 Cash deficits can also arise out of the business's management of the operating cycle and from timing differences.

(a) **Short-term borrowing** from the bank is only a short-term measure. It is possible that a bank will convert an overdraft into a long-term loan, or perhaps new overdraft limits can be set up.

(b) Sale of short-term investments could provide liquidity, but not all companies have short-term investments to sell.

(c) **Raising capital** is expensive and should be generally used for long-term investment, not short-term cash management.

(d) The nature and timing of discretionary flows might be changed.

(e) Different sources of finance (such as leasing) might be changed.

(f) Stock levels could also be reduced, to reduce the amount of money that is 'tied up' in their production cost.

(g) The technique of **leading and lagging,** which we mentioned earlier. Effectively this means shortening the operating cycle, by:

   (i) Obtaining money from debtors as soon as possible, in order words reducing the collection period

   (ii) Taking as much trade credit as possible, delaying payment until there is less need for borrowing from the bank

5.8 Let us take a simple example to illustrate 'leading and lagging'. Assume that Gilbert Gosayne Ltd sells Nullas. Each Nulla costs £50 to make and is sold for £100. The bank has refused an overdraft to Gilbert Gosayne. Creditors are normally paid at the end of Month 1; the Nullas are sold on the 15th of Month 2. Payment is received on the first day of Month 3.

(a) Under this system we have the following forecast.

	Inflows £	Outflows £	Balance £
Month 1 (end)	-	50	(50)
Month 2	-	-	(50)
Month 3 (beginning)	100	-	50

In other words the cash cycle means that the firm is in deficit for all of Month 2. As the bank has refused an overdraft, the creditors will not be paid.

(b) If, however, Gilbert Gosayne Ltd persuades its creditors to wait for two weeks until the 15th of Month 2 and offers a settlement discount of £5 to debtors to induce them to pay on the 15th of Month 2, the situation is transformed.

	Inflows £	Outflows £	Balance £
Month 1	-	-	-
Month 2	95	50	45
Month 3	-	-	45

5.9 In practice, it is not that simple. A firm's debtors and creditors might be 'leading and lagging' themselves.

(a) Creditors can object to their customers taking extra credit; and it can also harm their businesses, thus jeopardising their ability to make future supplies. The customer also loses the possibility of taking advantage of trade discounts.

(b) Debtors might refuse to cough up early, despite the inducement of a discount.

5.10 A firm might be in a position to choose which of its creditors should be paid now rather than later. Certain creditors have to be paid early, if they are powerful. The bank is a powerful creditor: it is worth keeping the bank happy even if the firm loses out on a few trade discounts in the process.

5.11 Shortening the operating cycle is helpful in dealing with **short-term** deficiencies and saving interest costs, but it is not necessarily a long-term solution to the business's funding problems. This is because a shorter operating cycle time will reduce the amount of cash that a company needs to invest in its operating activities.

Quality control of forecasts

5.12 When actual results differ from budget, it can be tempting to conclude that plans never work out in practice. However, as planning is a vital management activity, and if actual results differ from the plan, it is important to find out whether the *planning* processes can be improved.

5.13 Accuracy of cash flow forecasts can be enhanced by:

(a) Reviewing actual cash flows against the forecasts, learning from past mistakes, and

(b) Updating rolling forecasts or revised forecasts, where useful, to replace earlier, less reliable forecasts.

5.14 A constant monthly amount for receipts and payments will often indicate either sloppy cash forecasting practice, or a high degree of uncertainty in the forecast, since it is rare for specific receivables and payables to remain unchanged except where there is a formal arrangement.

5.15 As a financial year progresses, the actual cash flows for the past months could show large variances from budget, but a rolling forecast indicates that the original budget for the end-of-year cash balance will still be achieved. This could occur if the rolling forecast has been prepared by adjusting the forecast for the unexpired months of the year, in order to keep the annual budget (on paper at least) for the end-of-year cash position. Where this occurs, suspicion must arise that the rolling forecast has been prepared with little thought.

5.16 Unchanged figures over a number of months of revised forecast submissions are also an indication of a weak forecasting system. It could be that business expectations have not changed; however there are few businesses that do not fluctuate with market conditions. A more likely explanation is that the rolling cash forecast has been prepared by copying the figures from the previous forecast or that a new revised forecast has not been prepared at all.

Key learning points

- **Cash flow forecasts** provide an early warning of liquidity problems and funding needs. **Banks** often expect business customers to provide a cash forecast as a condition of lending.
- There are **two main ways** of preparing a cash forecast.
    - A forecast can be prepared of cash receipts and payments, and net cash flows (cash flow based forecasts).
    - Alternatively, a cash surplus or funding requirement can be prepared by constructing a forecast balance sheet (balance sheet-based forecast), or adjusting other financial statements.
- **Cash flow based forecasts** include **cash budgets**; **cleared funds forecasts for the short term**.
- Cash budgets and forecasts can be used for **control reporting**. Balance sheet based forecasts are used for long-term strategic analysis.
- A **cash budget** is a detailed forecast of cash receipts, payments and balances over a planning period. It is formally adopted as part of the business plan or master budget for the period.
- Cash budgets are prepared by taking **operational budgets** and converting them into forecasts as to when receipts and payments occur. The forecast should indicate the highest and lowest cash balance in a period as well as the balance at the end.
- **Cleared funds** are used for short-term planning. They take clearance delays into account.
- **Cash flow control reports** indicate differences between expected and actual flows, so that corrective action can be taken.

Part A: Cash management

Quick quiz

1. What do cash forecasts estimate?
2. What might be the significance of forecast surpluses?
3. What is a rolling forecast?
4. What is the importance of clearly stating the assumptions in a cash forecast.
5. List the steps in preparing a cash flow budget.
6. How can you estimate when sales receipts will occur?
7. How long do cheques drawn on different banks generally take to clear within England and Wales?
8. What is a float?
9. What is a balance sheet based forecast?
10. What is the purpose of a cash flow control report?
11. Give some examples of poor forecasting.

Answers to quick quiz

1. How much cash is required, when, for how long, and whether it will be available.
2. The surplus could be invested to earn interest.
3. A forecast that is continually updated.
4. It allows the forecast to be tested for reasonableness.
5. Sort out cash receipts from debtors; cash income received; cash payments to suppliers; other cash payments; set out month-by-month cash budget.
6. Make assumptions based on past experience.
7. Three days within England and Wales. Four days for cheques drawn in Scotland and Northern Ireland.
8. The amount of money tied up between the time a payment is initiated and when cleared funds become available.
9. An estimate of the balance sheet of the enterprise at a future date.
10. To help ensure that net cash flows or cash balances satisfy targets set by management.
11. Examples include: monthly figure all set at 1/12 of the annual total; a rolling forecast which does not adjust the end-of-year forecast in the course of the year.

Answers to activities

Answer 2.1

Your list might have included some of the following:

(a) a change in the general economic environment. An economic recession will cause a slump in trade;

(b) a new product, launched by a competitor, which takes business away from a company's traditional and established product lines;

(c) new cost-saving product technology, which forces the company to invest in the new technology to remain competitive;

(d) moves by competitors which have to be countered (for example a price reduction or a sales promotion);

(e) changes in consumer preferences, resulting in a fall in demand;

(f) government action against certain trade practices or against trade with a country that a company has dealings with;

(g) strikes or other industrial action;

(h) natural disasters, such as floods or fire damage, which curtail an organisation's activities.

Answer 2.2

The opening cash balance at 1 October will consist of Tom's initial £15,000 less the £8,000 expended on fixed assets purchased in September, ie the opening balance is £7,000. Cash receipts from credit customers arise two months after the relevant sales.

Payments to suppliers are a little more tricky. We are told that cost of sales is 100/150 × sales. Thus for October cost of sales is 100/15 × £3,000 = £2,000. These goods will be purchased in October but not paid for until November. Similar calculations can be made for later months. The initial stock of £5,000 is purchased in September and consequently paid for in October.

The cash budget can now be constructed.

CASH BUDGET FOR THE SIX MONTHS ENDING 31 MARCH 19X7

	October £	November £	December £	January £	February £	March £
Payments						
Suppliers	5,000	2,000	4,000	4,000	7,000	7,000
Running expenses	1,600	1,600	1,600	1,600	1,600	1,600
Drawings	1,000	1,000	1,000	1,000	1,000	1,000
	7,600	4,600	6,600	6,600	9,600	9,600
Receipts						
Debtors	-	-	3,000	6,000	6,000	10,500
Surplus/(shortfall)	(7,600)	(4,600)	(3,600)	(600)	(3,600)	900
Opening balance	7,000	(600)	(5,200)	(8,800)	(9,400)	(13,000)
Closing balance	(600)	(5,200)	(8,800)	(9,400)	(13,000)	(12,100)

Answer 2.3

(a)

	January £'000	February £'000	March £'000	April £'000	May £'000	June £'000
Sales revenue						
Cash (40%)	44	52	56	60	64	72
Credit (60%, 2 months)	48	60	66	78	84	90
	92	112	122	138	148	162
Purchases	60	80	90	110	130	140
Wages						
75%	12	15	18	21	24	27
25%	3	4	5	6	7	8
Overheads	10	15	15	15	20	20
Dividends			20			
Capital expenditure			30			40
	85	114	178	152	181	235
b/f	15	22	20	(36)	(50)	(83)
Net cash flow	7	(2)	(56)	(14)	(33)	(73)
c/f	22	20	(36)	(50)	(83)	(156)

(b) The overdraft arrangements are quite inadequate to service the cash needs of the business over the six-month period. If the figures are realistic then action should be taken now to avoid difficulties in the near future. The following are possible courses of action.

   (i)   Activities could be curtailed.

   (ii) Other sources of cash could be explored, for example a long-term loan to finance the capital expenditure and a factoring arrangement to provide cash due from debtors more quickly.

   (iii) Efforts to increase the speed of debt collection could be made.

   (iv) Payments to creditors could be delayed.

   (v)   The dividend payments could be postponed (the figures indicate that this is a small company, possibly owner-managed).

Part A: Cash management

(vi) Staff might be persuaded to work at a lower rate in return for, say, an annual bonus or a profit-sharing agreement.

(vii) Extra staff might be taken on to reduce the amount of overtime paid.

(viii) The stockholding policy should be reviewed; it may be possible to meet demand from current production and minimise cash tied up in stocks.

Answer 2.4

Kim O'Hara would be best served by a cleared funds forecast, Creighton plc by a cash book based forecast.

Answer 2.5

Cash flow based forecasts are forecasts of the amount and timing of cash receipts and payments. A balance sheet based forecast is a prediction of the amount of cash that will be needed on a particular date: it is not an estimate of individual inflows and outflows. A cleared-funds forecast is a cash forecast which takes into account the period of time a cash transaction goes through the banking system (ie from making payments from one account to its arrival into the destination account).

Chapter 3 Cash budgeting techniques

Chapter topic list

1. Estimation problems
2. Moving averages and trend analysis
3. Inflation and cash budgeting
4. Computer models and sensitivity analysis

Learning objectives

On completion of this chapter you will be able to:

	Performance criteria	Range statement
• use basic techniques for estimating future trends	15.1	
• understand the use of computer models to assess the sensitivity of elements in the cash budget to change	15.1	

Part A: Cash management

1 ESTIMATION PROBLEMS

Volatility of cash flows

1.1 **Cash flow patterns** vary between businesses and with time and circumstances.

   (a) For some companies, operational cash flows are fairly stable, subject to seasonal variations, with the company regularly generating surplus cash (before capital expenditures).

   (b) Other companies will have much more volatile operational cash flows, particularly if sales income is earned in irregular large amounts rather than in regular smaller amounts.

Uncertainty over time

1.2 One of the problems arising in evaluating forecasts is the **reliability of the data** used. Since the figures are compiled from estimates for the future, there must be considerable uncertainty about the accuracy of the final figures.

1.3 Cash forecasts will inevitably be less accurate in the longer term, because uncertainties grow over time. Business planners can use various operational research techniques to measure the degree of uncertainty in the forecast. These include the simple 'rule of thumb' method of expressing a range of values from worst possible result to best possible result, with the best estimate lying somewhere in between.

1.4 A number of techniques can be used to give cash flow information.

   (a) **Trend analysis** enables a firm to extrapolate into the future on the basis of past data. This assumes that the past is a useful guide to the future. If sales have been rising in the past, it might be reasonable, in some cases, to assume they will continue to do so.

   (b) **Index numbers** are useful in that they enable inflation be taken into account.

2 MOVING AVERAGES AND TREND ANALYSIS

2.1 The past can be used as a guide to the future. A statistical technique by which this is achieved is **time series analysis.** The following are examples of time series.

   (a) Output at a factory each day for the last month
   (b) Monthly sales over the last two years
   (c) Total annual costs for the last ten years
   (d) The Retail Prices Index each month for the last ten years
   (e) The number of people employed by a company each year for the last 20 years

> **KEY TERM**
>
> A **time series** is a series of figures or values recorded over time.
>
> The **trend** is the underlying long-term movement over time in the values of the data recorded.

2.2 There are several **features of a time series** which it may be necessary to identify.

   (a) A trend
   (b) Seasonal variations or fluctuations

3: Cash budgeting techniques

(c) Cycles, or cyclical variations
(d) Non-recurring, random variations (eg caused by unforeseeable circumstances)

The trend

2.3 In the following examples of time series, there are three types of trend.

	Output per labour hour Units	Cost per unit £	Number of employees
20X4	30	1.00	100
20X5	24	1.08	103
20X6	26	1.20	96
20X7	22	1.15	102
20X8	21	1.18	103
20X9	17	1.25	98
	(A)	(B)	(C)

(a) In time series (A) there is a downward trend in the output per labour hour. Output per labour hour did not fall every year, because it went up between 20X5 and 20X6, but the long-term movement is clearly a downward one.

(b) In time series (B) there is an upward trend in the cost per unit. Although unit costs went down in 20X7 from a higher level in 20X6, the basic movement over time is one of rising costs.

(c) In time series (C) there is no clear movement up or down, and the number of employees remained fairly constant around 100. The trend is therefore a static, or level one.

Seasonal and cyclical variations

2.4 **Seasonal variations** are short-term fluctuations in recorded values, due to different circumstances which affect results at different times of the year, on different days of the week, at different times of day, or whatever. Here are some examples.

(a) Sales of ice cream will be higher in summer than in winter, and sales of overcoats will be higher in autumn than in spring.

(b) Shops might expect higher sales shortly before Christmas, or in their winter and summer sales.

(c) Sales might be higher on Friday and Saturday than on Monday.

(d) The telephone network may be heavily used at certain times of the day (such as mid-morning and mid-afternoon) and much less used at other times (such as in the middle of the night).

2.5 '**Seasonal**' is a term which may appear to refer to the seasons of the year, but its meaning in time series analysis is somewhat broader, as the examples given above show.

2.6 In the example below, there would appear to be large seasonal fluctuations in demand, but there is also a basic upward trend. The number of customers served by a company of travel agents over the past four years is shown in the following historigram. (**Historigram** is the name given to a graph of time series.)

Part A: Cash management

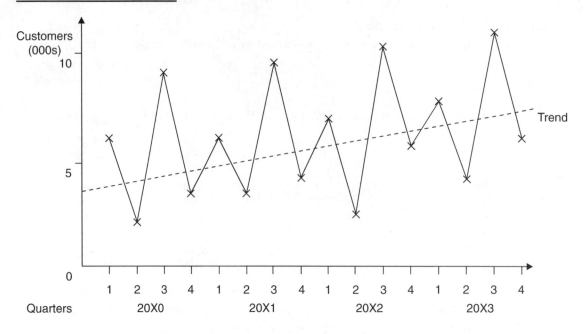

KEY TERM

Cyclical variations are medium-term changes in results caused by circumstances which repeat in cycles.

2.7 In business, cyclical variations are commonly associated with economic cycles, successive booms and slumps in the economy. Economic cycles may last a few years. Cyclical variations are longer term than seasonal variations.

Finding the trend

2.8 The main problem we are concerned with in time series analysis is how to identify the trend and seasonal variations. There are three principal methods of finding a trend and seasonal variations.

(a) **Inspection.** The trend line can be drawn by eye on a graph in such a way that it appears to lie evenly between the recorded points.

(b) **Regression analysis by the least squares method.** This is a statistical technique to calculate the 'line of best fit'.

(c) **Moving averages.** This method attempts to remove seasonal (or cyclical) variations by a process of averaging.

Finding the trend by moving averages

KEY TERM

A **moving average** is an average of the results of a fixed number of periods.

2.9 Since a moving average is an average of several time periods, it is related to the mid-point of the overall period.

2.10 EXAMPLE: MOVING AVERAGES

Year	Sales
	Units
20X0	390
20X1	380
20X2	460
20X3	450
20X4	470
20X5	440
20X6	500

Required

Take a moving average of the annual sales over a period of three years.

2.11 SOLUTION

(a) Average sales in the three year period 20X0 – 20X2 were:

$$\left(\frac{390 + 380 + 460}{3}\right) = \frac{1{,}230}{3} = 410$$

This average relates to the middle year of the period, 20X1.

(b) Similarly, average sales in the three year period 20X1 – 20X3 were:

$$\left(\frac{380 + 460 + 450}{3}\right) = \frac{1{,}290}{3} = 430$$

This average relates to the middle year of the period, 20X2.

(c) The average sales can also be found for the periods 20X2-20X4, 20X3-20X5 and 20X4-20X6, to give the following.

Year	Sales	Moving total of 3 years sales	Moving average of 3 years sales (÷ 3)
20X0	390		
20X1	380	1,230	410
20X2	460	1,290	430
20X3	450	1,380	460
20X4	470	1,360	453
20X5	440	1,410	470
20X6	500		

Note the following points.

(i) The moving average series has five figures relating to the years from 20X1 to 20X5. The original series had seven figures for the years from 20X0 to 20X6.

(ii) There is an upward trend in sales, which is more noticeable from the series of moving averages than from the original series of actual sales each year.

2.12 The above example averaged over a three-year period. In practice, the most appropriate moving average will depend on the circumstances and the nature of the time series. Note the following points.

(a) A moving average which takes an average of the results in many time periods will represent results over a longer term than a moving average of two or three periods.

(b) On the other hand, with a moving average of results in many time periods, the last figure in the series will be out of date by several periods. In our example, the most recent average related to 20X5. With a moving average of five years' results, the final figure in the series would relate to 20X4.

Part A: Cash management

(c) When there is a known cycle over which seasonal variations occur, such as all the days in the week or all the seasons in the year, the most suitable moving average would be one which covers one full cycle.

Moving averages of an even number of results

2.13 In the previous example, moving averages were taken of the results in an **odd** number of time periods, and the average then related to the mid-point of the overall period. If a moving average were taken of results in an **even** number of time periods, the basic technique would be the same, but the mid-point of the overall period would not relate to a single period. For example, suppose an average were taken of the following four results.

Spring	120	
Summer	90	
Autumn	180	average 115
Winter	70	

The average would relate to the **mid-point** of the period, between summer and autumn.

2.14 The trend line average figures need to relate to a particular time period; otherwise, seasonal variations cannot be calculated. To overcome this difficulty, we take a moving average of the moving average. Try the Activity below.

Activity 3.1

Moving averages over an even number of periods

Calculate a moving average trend line of the following results.

Year	Quarter	Volume of sales '000 units
20X5	1	600
	2	840
	3	420
	4	720
20X6	1	640
	2	860
	3	420
	4	740
20X7	1	670
	2	900
	3	430
	4	760

Finding the seasonal variations

2.15 Once a trend has been established, by whatever method, we can find the seasonal variations. The example below shows how this is done.

2.16 EXAMPLE: THE TREND AND SEASONAL VARIATIONS

Output at a factory appears to vary with the day of the week. Output over the last three weeks has been as follows.

3: Cash budgeting techniques

	Week 1 '000 units	Week 2 '000 units	Week 3 '000 units
Monday	80	82	84
Tuesday	104	110	116
Wednesday	94	97	100
Thursday	120	125	130
Friday	62	64	66

With the days numbered from 0 to 14, a trend line has been found using regression analysis. It is y (ie the trend) = 0.42x + 92.7.

Required

Find the seasonal variation for each of the 15 days, and the average seasonal variation for each day of the week.

2.17 SOLUTION

The regression line indicates an upward trend in daily output. Actual results fluctuate up and down according to the day of the week. The difference between the actual result on any one day and the trend figure for that day will be the seasonal variation for the day. The trend figures themselves are found simply by putting the day numbers (0 to 14) as values of x in the equation y = 0.42x + 92.7.

The seasonal variations for the 15 days are as follows.

		Actual	Trend	Seasonal variation
Week 1	Monday	80	92.70	– 12.70
	Tuesday	104	93.12	+ 10.88
	Wednesday	94	93.54	+ 0.46
	Thursday	120	93.96	+ 26.04
	Friday	62	94.38	– 32.38
Week 2	Monday	82	94.80	– 12.80
	Tuesday	110	95.22	+ 14.78
	Wednesday	97	95.64	+ 1.36
	Thursday	125	96.06	+ 28.94
	Friday	64	96.48	– 32.48
Week 3	Monday	84	96.90	– 12.90
	Tuesday	116	97.32	+ 18.68
	Wednesday	100	97.74	+ 2.26
	Thursday	130	98.16	+ 31.84
	Friday	66	98.58	– 32.58

The variation between the actual results on any one particular day and the trend line average is not the same from week to week, but an average of these variations can be taken.

	Monday	Tuesday	Wednesday	Thursday	Friday
Week 1	– 12.70	+ 10.88	+ 0.46	+ 26.04	– 32.38
Week 2	– 12.80	+ 14.78	+ 1.36	+ 28.94	– 32.48
Week 3	– 12.90	+ 18.68	+ 2.26	+ 31.84	– 32.58
Total	– 38.40	+ 44.34	+ 4.08	+ 86.82	– 97.44
Average	– 12.80	+ 14.78	+ 1.36	+ 28.94	– 32.48

Our estimate of the 'seasonal' or daily variation is almost complete, but there is one more important step to take. Variations around the basic trend line should cancel each other out, and add up to 0. At the moment, they do not. We therefore spread the total of the daily variations (–0.2) across the five days (0.2 ÷ 5) so that the final total of the daily variations goes to zero.

Part A: Cash management

	Monday	Tuesday	Wednesday	Thursday	Friday	Total
Estimated daily variation	– 12.80	+ 14.78	+ 1.36	+ 28.94	– 32.48	– 0.2
Adjustment to reduce total variation to 0	+ 0.04	+ 0.04	+ 0.04	+ 0.04	+ 0.04	+ 0.2
Final estimate of daily variation	– 12.76	+ 14.82	+ 1.40	+ 28.98	– 32.44	0.0

These might be rounded up or down as follows.

Monday –13; Tuesday +15; Wednesday +1; Thursday +29; Friday –32; Total 0.

Seasonal variations using the proportional model

2.18 The method of estimating the seasonal variations in the above example was to use the differences between the trend and actual data. This is called the **additive model**. The alternative is to use the proportional model whereby each actual figure is expressed as a **percentage of the trend**. Sometimes this method is called the **multiplicative model**.

2.19 The above example can be reworked on this alternative basis.

		Actual	Trend	Seasonal percentage
Week 1	Monday	80	92.70	86.3
	Tuesday	104	93.12	111.7
	Wednesday	94	93.54	100.5
	Thursday	120	93.96	127.7
	Friday	62	94.38	65.7
Week 2	Monday	82	94.80	86.5
	Tuesday	110	95.22	115.5
	Wednesday	97	95.64	101.4
	Thursday	125	96.06	130.1
	Friday	64	96.48	66.3
Week 3	Monday	84	96.90	86.7
	Tuesday	116	97.32	119.2
	Wednesday	100	97.74	102.3
	Thursday	130	98.16	132.4
	Friday	66	98.58	67.0

2.20 The summary of the seasonal variations expressed in proportional terms is as follows.

	Monday %	Tuesday %	Wednesday %	Thursday %	Friday %
Week 1	86.3	111.7	100.5	127.7	65.7
Week 2	86.5	115.5	101.4	130.1	66.3
Week 3	86.7	119.2	102.3	132.4	67.0
Total	259.5	346.4	304.2	390.2	199.0
Average	86.5	115.5	101.4	130.1	66.3

Instead of summing to zero, as with the absolute approach, these should sum (in this case) to 500 (an average of 100%).

They actually sum to 499.8 so 0.04% has to be added to each one. This is too small to make a difference to figures rounded to one decimal place, so we should add 0.1% to each of two seasonal variations. We could arbitrarily increase Monday's variation to 86.6% and Tuesday's to 115.6%.

3: Cash budgeting techniques

2.21 The proportional model is better than the additive model where the trend is increasing or decreasing over time. In this case, the actual variations will tend to increase (or decrease) so absolute seasonal adjustments will become out of date, unlike percentage adjustments.

Forecasting

2.22 Time series analysis can be used to forecast cash or other transactions, not by removing seasonal data, but by adding it back in.

2.23 Extending a trend line outside the range of known data, in this case forecasting the future from a trend line based on historical data, is known as **extrapolation.** The technique which will be discussed here is that of extrapolating a trend and then adjusting for seasonal variations. Forecasts of future values should be made as follows.

   (a) Calculate a trend line.

   (b) Use the trend line to forecast future trend line values.

   (c) Adjust these values by the average seasonal variation applicable to the future period, to determine the forecast for that period. With the additive model, add (or subtract for negative variations) the variation. With the multiplicative model, multiply the trend value by the variation proportion.

2.24 EXAMPLE: FORECASTING

Sales of product X each quarter for the last three years have been as follows (in thousands of units). Trend values, found by a moving averages method, are shown in brackets.

Year	1st quarter	2nd quarter	3rd quarter	4th quarter
1	18	30	20 (18.75)	6 (19.375)
2	20 (20)	33 (20.5)	22 (21)	8 (21.5)
3	22 (22.125)	35 (22.75)	25	10

Average seasonal variations for quarters 1 to 4 are –0.1, +12.4, +1.1 and –13.4 respectively.

Task

Use the trend line and estimates of seasonal variations to forecast sales in each quarter of year 4.

2.25 SOLUTION

The trend line indicates an increase of about 0.6 per quarter. This can be confirmed by calculating the average quarterly increase in trend line values between the third quarter of year 1 (18.75) and the second quarter of year 3 (22.75). The average rise is:

$$\frac{22.75 - 18.75}{7} = \frac{4}{7} = 0.57, \text{ say } 0.6$$

Taking 0.6 as the quarterly increase in the trend, the forecast of sales for year 4, before seasonal adjustments (the trend line forecast) would be as follows.

Part A: Cash management

Year	Quarter			Trend line
3	*2nd	(actual trend)	22.75, say	22.8
	3rd			23.4
	4th			24.0
4	1st			24.6
	2nd			25.2
	3rd			25.8
	4th			26.4

* last known trend line value.

Seasonal variations should now be incorporated to obtain the final forecast.

	Quarter	Trend line forecast '000 units	Average seasonal variation '000 units	Forecast of actual sales '000 units
Year 4	1st	24.6	−0.1	24.5
	2nd	25.2	+12.4	37.6
	3rd	25.8	+ 1.1	26.9
	4th	26.4	−13.4	13.0

If we had been using the multiplicative model, with an average variation for (for example) quarter 3 of 105.7%, our prediction for the third quarter of year 4 would have been 25.8 × 105.7% = 27.3.

2.26 All forecasts are subject to error, but the likely errors vary from case to case.

(a) The further into the future the forecast is for, the more unreliable it is likely to be.
(b) The less data available on which to base the forecast, the less reliable the forecast.
(c) The pattern of trend and seasonal variations may not continue in the future.
(d) Random variations might upset the pattern of trend and seasonal variation.

Residuals

> **KEY TERM**
>
> A **residual** is the difference between the results which would have been predicted (for a past period for which we already have data) by the trend line adjusted for the average seasonal variation and the actual results.

2.27 The residual is the difference which is *not* explained by the trend line and the seasonal average variation. The residual gives some indication of how much actual results were affected by other factors. Large residuals suggest that any forecast is likely to be unreliable.

2.28 In the example in Paragraph 2.24, the 'prediction' for the third quarter of year 1 would have been 18.75 + 1.1 = 19.85. As the actual value was 20, the residual was only 20 − 19.85 = 0.15. The residual for the fourth quarter of year 2 was 8 − (21.5 − 13.4) = 8 − 8.1 = −0.1.

Trend analysis in cash forecasting

2.29 Trend analysis can be used to predict the overall level of activity of the organisation, and from this can be derived the organisation's cash requirements. Seasonal factors giving rise to peaks or troughs (eg in raw materials or commodity prices) can be introduced to the forecast model over a period.

Trend analysis might also be applied to the firm's cash flows, so that seasonal surpluses or deficits can be identified. For example, a firm might run a surplus in Quarter 3. However, the surplus may be less than normally anticipated for that quarter: if a deficit is expected in Quarter 4, the lower surplus in Quarter 3 indicates a cumulative problem.

Activity 3.2

The quarterly sales of Hopwood Trends Ltd in recent years have been as follows.

Quarter	1	2	3	4
	Units	Units	Units	Units
20X2	200	110	320	240
20X3	214	118	334	260
20X4	220	124	340	278

Tasks

(a) Calculate a moving average of quarterly sales.
(b) Calculate the average seasonal variations.
(c) Use the results of (a) and (b) to predict sales in the third quarter of 20X5.

3 INFLATION AND CASH BUDGETING

The need for index numbers

3.1 If we are making comparisons of costs and revenues over time to see how well an organisational unit is performing, we need to take account of the fact that the unit is operating within an economic environment in which general shifts in costs (ie prices) take place. If a business achieves an increase in sales of 10% in monetary (cash) terms over a year, this result becomes less impressive if we are told that there was general price inflation of 15% over the year. If the business has raised its prices in line with this inflation rate of 15%, then a 10% increase in sales in cash terms indicates a fall in the physical volume of sales. The business is now selling less at the new higher prices.

3.2 When results of a business are being compared over a period of time for internal management purposes, it is up to managers of the business to agree and use an appropriate method of allowing for changing price levels. The usual method is to use a series of index numbers.

KEY TERM

An **index** is a measure, over a period of time, of the average **changes** in the values (prices or quantities) of a group of items.

3.3 An index may be a price index or a quantity index.

(a) A **price index** measures the change in the money value of a group of items over a period of time. Perhaps the most well-known price index in the UK is the **Retail Prices Index** (RPI) which measures changes in the costs of items of expenditure of the average household, and which used to be called the 'cost of living' index. Another example is the FT-SE 100 share index, which measures how share prices in general have performed from one day to the next.

Part A: Cash management

(b) A **quantity index** measures the change in the non-monetary values of a group of items over a period of time. A well-known example is a productivity index, which measures changes in the productivity of various departments or groups of workers.

As we shall see, a suitable **price index** provides a method of allowing for changing price levels when comparing costs or revenues over time.

Index points

3.4 The term '**points**' is used to measure the difference in the index value in one year with the value in another year. For example, it may be said that the cost of living index for a country rose 45 points between 1994 and 2000, reflecting a rise in the relevant index of 100 in 1994 to 145 in 2000.

3.5 Points are used for measuring changes in an index because they provide an easy method of arithmetic. The alternative is to use percentages, because indices are based on percentages, as we shall see.

The base period, or base year

3.6 Index numbers are normally expressed as percentages, taking the value for a **base date** as 100. The choice of a base date or base year is not significant, except that it should normally be 'representative'. In the construction of a price index, the base year preferably should not be one in which there were abnormally high or low prices for any items in the 'basket of goods' making up the index.

3.7 EXAMPLE: CALCULATION OF AN INDEX

Suppose sales for a company over the last five years were as follows.

Year	Sales (£'000)
20X5	35
20X6	42
20X7	40
20X8	45
20X9	50

The managing director decided that he wanted to set up a sales index (ie an index which measures how sales have done from year to year), using 20X5 as the base year. The £35,000 of sales in 20X5 is given the index 100%. What are the indices for the other years?

3.8 SOLUTION

If £35,000 = 100%, then:

20X6 £42,000 = $\frac{42,000}{35,000} \times 100\% = 120\%$

The same calculation can be applied to other figures, and the table showing sales for the last five years can be completed, taking 20X5 as the base year.

Year	Sales (£'000)	Index
20X5	35	100
20X6	42	120
20X7	40	114
20X8	45	129
20X9	50	143

3: Cash budgeting techniques

3.9 In the examples we have seen so far in this chapter, it is not really necessary to calculate an index, because only **one product or item** has been under consideration. Knowing that sales have risen by 20% from £35,000 to £42,000, for instance, is just as informative as knowing that the index has risen 20 points (from 100 to 120). There was no real need to calculate the index.

Indices in practice

3.10 In practice, indices are generally made up of **more than one item**. For example, suppose that the cost of living index is calculated from only three commodities: bread, tea and caviar, and that the prices for 20X1 and 20X5 were as follows.

	20X1	*20X5*
Bread	20p a loaf	40p a loaf
Tea	25p a packet	30p a packet
Caviar	450p an ounce	405p an ounce

3.11 Note that the prices above are given in different units, and there is no indication of the relative importance of each item. In formulating index numbers, these aspects can be overcome by **weighting**. To decide the weighting, we need information about the relative importance of each item. For the purpose of **internal management reporting**, results recorded over a number of periods can be adjusted using an appropriate price index to convert the figures from money terms to 'real' terms.

Activity 3.3

A company wishes to construct a price index for three commodities, A, B and C. The prices in March (the base period) were £2, £3 and £5 respectively and quantities consumed in the same period were 5,000, 6,000 and 3,000 respectively. The prices of the items in April and May were as follows.

	April	May
	£	£
A	2.00	2.20
B	3.24	3.45
C	4.50	5.00

Using the amount spent on an item in March as that item's weighting, construct a price index for April and May.

Guidance notes

1. Begin by calculating a price relative for each item in each month. A price relative is the price of the item in April (or May) as a percentage of its price in March.
2. Calculate the weightings (price in March × quantity consumed in March).
3. For each month, multiply each item's weighting by the price relative and add the result.
4. Calculate the April and May index numbers by dividing the April and May totals by the March total.

Activity 3.4

State how the price indices calculated in Activity 3.3 may be useful in cash forecasting.

Part A: Cash management

The use of index numbers in cash forecasting and budgeting

3.12 What is the use of index numbers in **cash budgeting and forecasting**? The person preparing the cash budget is not particularly interested in prices in 'real terms': instead, it is the exact monetary amount that he or she is interested in. After all, bank overdrafts, for example, are expressed in fixed monetary amounts which do not allow for inflation.

3.13 Index numbers are still useful, however.

(a) Index numbers might be used to predict future cash inflows. For example, if it is assumed that 500,000 units will be sold in three or four months time, an estimate of future monetary prices gives some idea of the amount **in cash terms** that can be expected if a forecast index of prices is applied to estimated sales volumes.

(b) Similarly, with cash outflows, an estimated future price index can suggest the likely size of cash payments.

(c) Their use in forecasting can also suggest a need for increased borrowing limits, which might be fixed in monetary terms.

3.14 Where inflation is very high, the value of financial assets, such as debt, declines. (This is what people mean when they say that £1 in 1999 is only worth 3p, at 1930 prices.)

(a) Companies will try and collect their debts even more quickly, so that the cash can be reinvested.

(b) Delaying payments to creditors reduces the underlying value of the debt.

(c) A company's forecasts become out of date very quickly.

(d) Interest rates might be very high, in the short term, and so a treasurer will invest cash on short-term deposit.

3.15 It needs to be borne in mind that different items, such as capital items, costs of various kinds, and revenues, are likely to be subject to differing rates of inflation, and different indices may therefore be appropriate for different items. As well as the RPI, the UK Office for National Statistics publishes various **producer price indices** to reflect the levels of different types of cost faced by businesses.

Activity 3.5
Explain the general principles and methods involved in the compilation and construction of the UK General Index of Retail Prices (RPI) under the following headings: base year; weights; items included; data collection; calculation.

Activity 3.6

You are assisting with the work on a maintenance department's budget for the next quarter of 20X4. The maintenance department's budget for the current quarter (just ending) is £200,000.

	Quantity used in current quarter	Average price payable per unit	
		Current quarter	Next quarter
	Units	£	£
Material A	9	10	10.20
Material B	13	12	12.50
Material C	8	9	9.00
Material D	20	25	26.00

A base weighted index for the next quarter stands at 103.5, compared to 100 for this quarter, for the price of input quantities.

Tasks

(a) Estimate the budget for the next quarter, assuming that the quantities of each material to be used:

　(i)　remain the same;
　(ii)　increase by 10%.

(b) Give reasons why your budget estimate could be in error.

4 COMPUTER MODELS AND SENSITIVITY ANALYSIS

4.1 **Sensitivity analysis** is a method commonly used in planning, especially by companies using a **spreadsheet model** or other **financial modelling package**. The method may also be used manually - without a computer. Changes are made to estimates of key variables to establish how they could critically affect the outcome of the plan.

4.2 Sensitivity analysis tests the 'responsiveness' of profitability or cash flow to changes in one of the budget variables. For example, it would be possible to test the profit and loss account budget and cash budget for:

(a) An unforeseen 10% rise in material costs
(b) An unforeseen 5% drop in productivity
(c) A shortfall in sales volumes of, say, 10%
(d) A labour strike of, say, one month
(e) A delay of six months in opening a new plant or operation

> **ASSESSMENT ALERT**
>
> Sensitivity analysis is a typical assessment task which you might be expected to carry out for Unit 14.

4.3 **Computer cash forecast models** allow the user to test different assumptions and ask questions about the consequences of different future events or outcomes. Alternative methods of uncertainty analysis include:

(a) Preparing a series of different forecasts, each assuming a different scenario

(b) Preparing cash forecasts as a range of possible outcomes, from most pessimistic through most likely, to most optimistic

(c) Carrying out sensitivity analysis on key items of cash flow (in terms of quantity and timing) to identify the consequences for borrowing/investing

(d) Using probability analysis by assigning probabilities to a range of values for key uncertain cash flow items

4.4 EXAMPLE: SENSITIVITY ANALYSIS

A company setting up a subsidiary prepared a cash budget. As with many start-ups, initial expenditures were expected to be high in comparison with first year revenues. The company's budget year ended on 31 March and the operation was planned to commence on 1 June of the previous year. Selling to customers would not begin until 1 September. Revenue was forecast at £2 million for the period to 31 March.

The initial cash budget, illustrated below along with the revised budget, indicated a maximum deficit of about £750,000–£800,000 in September and October. The main areas of uncertainty were sales revenue, one major item of production cost and marketing costs.

Part A: Cash management

4.5 Lower than anticipated revenues, and excessive production costs, would possibly create a bigger cash deficit than the company could afford. Management believed, however, that controls over marketing expenditure would ensure that such costs should not exceed budget.

4.6 The cash flow model was used for sensitivity analysis. Assumptions were changed. Estimated sales revenue was reduced by 25% and production costs increased by 50%. The output from the revised model indicated a resulting cash deficit of about £1.5 million, **just** within the funding limit the company would allow for the new operation. Management concluded that the budget was acceptable, but that revenue, production costs and marketing costs should be continually reviewed.

Original cash budget	Jun £'000	Jul £'000	Aug £'000	Sept £'000	Oct £'000	Nov £'000	Dec £'000	Total £'000
Sales	0	0	160	210	280	360	490	1,500
Total inflows	0	0	160	210	280	360	490	1,500
Set-up costs	120	20	0	0	0	0	0	140
Production	100	100	100	100	100	100	100	700
Distribution	0	0	20	20	20	20	20	100
Marketing and advertising	0	150	150	75	75	75	75	600
Staff costs	10	20	24	24	24	24	24	150
General overheads	6	14	16	16	16	16	16	100
Accommodation	0	25	0	0	25	0	0	50
Capital equipment	30	0	0	10	0	0	0	40
Total outflows	266	329	310	245	260	235	235	1,880
Net inflow/(outflow)	(266)	(329)	(150)	(35)	20	125	255	(380)
Cumulative cash flow	(266)	(595)	(745)	(780)	(760)	(635)	(380)	(380)

Revised cash budget	Jun £'000	Jul £'000	Aug £'000	Sept £'000	Oct £'000	Nov £'000	Dec £'000	Total £'000
Sales	0	0	120	158	210	270	367	1,125
Total inflows	0	0	120	158	210	270	367	1,125
Set-up costs	120	20	0	0	0	0	0	140
Production	150	150	150	150	150	150	150	1,050
Distribution	0	0	20	20	20	20	20	100
Marktg & advertising	0	150	150	75	75	75	75	600
Staff costs	10	20	24	24	24	24	24	150
General overheads	6	14	16	16	16	16	16	100
Accommodation	0	25	0	0	25	0	0	50
Capital equipment	30	0	0	10	0	0	0	40
Total outflows	316	379	360	295	310	285	285	2,230
Net inflow/(outflow)	(316)	(379)	(240)	(137)	(100)	(15)	82	(1,105)
Cumulative cash flow	(316)	(695)	(935)	(1,072)	(1,172)	(1,187)	(1,105)	(1,105)

3: Cash budgeting techniques

Spreadsheets

> **ASSESSMENT ALERT**
>
> You should be familiar with spreadsheets already. We provide below an example of how a spreadsheet can be used in cash budgeting and forecasting - a possible assessment task for Unit 15.

4.7 EXAMPLE: PREPARING A CASH FLOW PROJECTION

A loan officer of a bank advising a small company wishes to assess the company's cash flow using a spreadsheet model. The cash flow projection is to provide a monthly cash flow analysis over a 5 year period. The following data is relevant.

(a) On 1 January 20X4 the company expects to have £15,000 in the bank. Sales in January are expected to be £25,000, and a growth rate of 1.25% per month in sales is predicted throughout the forecast period.

(b) The company buys stock one month in advance and pays in cash. All sales are on credit. There are no bad debts.

(c) On average, payment is received from customers as follows.

  (i) 60% is one month in arrears
  (ii) 40% is two months in arrears

(d) The cost of sales is 65% of sales value. Overhead costs (cash expenses) are expected to be £6,500 per month, rising by 5% at the start of each new calendar year.

(e) Purchases of capital equipment and payments of tax, interest charges and dividends must also be provided for within the model. The loans officer has advised the company that the interest rate on bank overdrafts is expected to be 1.695% per month.

The loans officer might decide to label the spreadsheet rows and columns as follows.

	A	B	C	D	E	F
1:		20X4				
2:		Jan	Feb	March	April	May
3:		£	£	£	£	£
4:	Sales	—	—	—	—	—
5:	Cash receipts:					
6:	One months in arrears					
7:	Two months in arrears					
8:	Three months in arrears	—	—	—	—	—
9:	Total receipts					
10:						
11:	Cash payments:					
12:	Stock					
13:	Overheads					
14:	Interest					
15:	Tax					
16:	Dividends					
17:	Capital purchases	—	—	—	—	—
18:	Total payments					
19:						
20:	Cash receipts less payments					
21:	Balance b/f	—	—	—	—	—
22:	Balance c/f	—	—	—	—	—

Your task is to construct the formulae necessary.

Part A: Cash management

4.8 SOLUTION

The formulae required can be constructed in a variety of ways. One way would be to insert some 'constant' values into cells of the spreadsheet and then cross-refer each formula to these constants, or absolutes.

Row	Column A	B
23:	Sales growth factor per month	1.0125
24:	Interest rate per month	0.01695
25:	Debts paid within 1 month	0.6
26:	Debts paid within 2 months	0.4
27:	Debts paid within 3 months	0
28:	Bad debts	0
29:	Cost of sales as proportion of sales	0.65

Alternatively, these values could be specified in the formulae in the spreadsheet. The advantage of setting up key data like this separately is that in the event of a change in say, interest rates, only one figure needs to be changed and there is no need for a search through the spreadsheet for relevant formulae.

Examples of constructing formulae for the spreadsheet are as follows.

(a) The formulae for sales in February 20X4, in this example, would be (+B4 * B23), in March 20X1 (+C4 * B23), in April 20X4 (+D4 * B23) etc. Replication of the formula could be used to save input time.

(b) The formula for cash receipts in April 20X4 would be:

E6 = D4 * B25
E7 = C4 * B26
E8 = B4 * B27
E9 = + E6 + E7 + E8

(c) Cash payments for stock would be expressed as the cost of sales in the previous month; for February 20X4, the formula in cell C12 would be:

+ B4 * B29

(d) Total cash payments in May 20X4 would be the sum of cells F12 to F17, ie the formula in cell F18 would be:

@ SUM (F12..F17)

and so on.

Input data would include the opening cash balance on 1 January 20X4, dividend and tax payments, capital purchases, sales in January 20X4, the constant values (in our example in column B, rows 23 to 29) and the other data needed to establish cash receipts and payments in the first month or so of the forecast period (eg receipts in January 20X4 will depend on sales in November and December 20X3, which the simplified model shown here has not provided for).

With this input data, and the spreadsheet formulae, a full cash flow projection for the five year period can be produced and, if required, printed out.

Activity 3.7

Whenever a forecast or budget is made, management should consider asking 'what if' questions, and so carry out a form of sensitivity analysis. Using the example above, how would you take account of the following changed assumptions? Describe what amendments would need to be made to the contents of individual cells.

(a) What if the payment pattern from debtors is:

    1 month in arrears   40%
    2 months in arrears   50%
    3 months in arrears   10%?

(b) What if sales growth is only ½% per month?

Key learning points

- **Cash flow patterns** vary between businesses and with time and circumstances. Management should try and minimise volatility, to avoid over-stretching borrowing requirements.
- A number of **statistical and modelling techniques** can be used to reduce the uncertainty in cash flow forecasting.
- **Time series analysis** is used to analyse seasonal and cyclical patterns and so help predict the future results of the business.
- **Seasonal patterns** change with the time of year. **Cyclical variations** are longer term changes.
- A **moving average** is based on a group of periods, updated over time.
- An **index** is a measure over a period of the average changes in prices of items or a group of items.
- **Sensitivity analysis** tests the results of a forecast to see how sensitive the results are to changes in inputs (eg lower or higher interest rates). **Spreadsheet modelling** is used for this purpose.

Quick quiz

1   Give three examples of time series.
2   What are seasonal variations?
3   How would you make a forecast of future values?
4   What are index numbers?
5   What are some of the practical problems with index numbers?
6   In the context of budgeting, what is sensitivity analysis used for?

Answers to quick quiz

1   Examples might include: the monthly Retail Prices Index over a period of years; daily factory output over a period of a month; total annual costs over a ten-year period.

2   Short-term fluctuations in recorded values due to circumstances which affect the values at different periods, eg at different times of the year.

3   We can extrapolate a trend and then adjust for seasonal variations.

4   A series of numbers showing the relative values of a group of items over a period of time.

5   The index does not itself indicate the relative importance of items covered by it; the weightings given to different items may need to be changed over time.

6   It can be used to test the responsiveness of profitability or cash flow to changes in one of the budget variables.

Answers to activities

Answer 3.1

A moving average of four will be used, since the volume of sales would appear to depend on the season of the year, and each year has four quarterly results.

Part A: Cash management

The moving average of four does not relate to any specific period of time; therefore a second moving average of two will be calculated on the first moving average trend line.

Year	Quarter	Actual volume of sales '000 units (A)	Moving total of 4 quarters' sales '000 units (B)	Moving average of 4 quarters' sales '000 units (B ÷ 4)	Mid-point of 2 moving averages Trend line '000 units (C)
20X5	1	600			
	2	840			
	3	420	2,580	645.0	650.00
	4	720	2,620	655.0	657.50
20X6	1	640	2,640	660.0	660.00
	2	860	2,640	660.0	662.50
	3	420	2,660	665.0	668.75
	4	740	2,690	672.5	677.50
20X7	1	670	2,730	682.5	683.75
	2	900	2,740	685.0	687.50
	3	430	2,760	690.0	
	4	760			

By taking a mid point (a moving average of two) of the original moving averages, we can relate the results to specific quarters (from the third quarter of 20X5 to the second quarter of 20X7).

Answer 3.2

(a)

Year	Quarter	Sales (A)	Moving total of 4 quarters sales	Centred total	Moving average (÷8) (B)	Variation (A – B)
20X2	1	200				
	2	110				
	3	320	870	1,754	219	+101
	4	240	884	1,776	222	+18
20X3	1	214	892	1,798	225	-11
	2	118	906	1,832	229	-111
	3	334	926	1,858	232	+102
	4	260	932	1,870	234	+26
20X4	1	220	938	1,882	235	-15
	2	124	944	1,906	238	-114
	3	340	962			
	4	278				

(b)

Year	Quarter	1	2	3	4	Total
20X2				+101	+18	
20X3		-11	-111	+102	+26	
20X4		-15	-114			
		-26	-225	+203	+44	-4
Unadjusted average		-13.0	-112.5	+101.5	+22.0	-2
Adjustment (4 ÷ 2)		+0.5	+0.5	+0.5	+0.5	+2
Adjusted average seasonal variations		-12.5	-112.0	+102.0	+22.5	0

(c) The average quarterly rise in the trend is (238 – 219)/7 = 2.7 units.

The predicted sales for the third quarter of 20X5 are therefore 238 + (5 × 2.7) + 102 = 353.5, or 354 units to the nearest unit.

Answer 3.3

Price relative for each item in April and May (price in month as a percentage of the base month)

	April	May
A	100 (£2/£2 × 100%)	110 (£2.20/£2)
B	108 (£3.24/£3 × 100%)	115 (£3.45/£2)
C	90 (£4.50/£5 × 100%)	100 (£5/£5 × 100%)

Weightings for each item (price in March × quantity consumed in March)

			Weight
A	£2 × 5,000	= £10,000	10
B	£3 × 6,000	= £18,000	18
C	£5 × 3,000	= £15,000	15

Use 10, 18 and 15 as weights.

Construct price indices

		Price relative × weight		
Period	A	B	C	Total
March	1,000	1,800	1,500	4,300
April	1,000	1,944	1,350	4,294
May	1,100	2,070	1,500	4,670

Price index for April = $\dfrac{4,294}{4,300} \times 100 = 99.8$

Price index for May = $\dfrac{4,670}{4,300} \times 100 = 108.6$

Workings

April:

A The index for April is 1,000, the same as the base month (10 × 100)
B 18 × 108 = 1,944
C 15 × 90 = 1,350

May:

A 10 × 110 = 1,100
B 18 × 115 = 2,070
C 15 × 100 = 1,500

Answer 3.4

These price indices are useful in cash forecasting for the following reasons.

(a) They indicate the potential volatility of expected sales revenue, and hence expected cash inflows.
(b) Seasonal variations in prices can be used in time series analysis to assess long-term revenue trends.

Answer 3.5

(a) *Base year.* Currently the base date for the RPI is January 1987, which was given an index of 100. The index for later months is then given in terms of the January 1987 level. For example the index for November 1999 is 166.7, indicating that prices in November 1999 were on average 66.7% higher than in January 1987.

(b) *Weights.* The weights used in calculating the RPI are designed to reflect the relative importance of the different sorts of expenditure of households.

(c) *Items included.* The items included in the calculation of the index are designed to be a representative selection of goods and services bought in the UK. Items are combined in sections, which in turn are combined in groups.

(d) *Data collection.* The collection of data on prices is carried out for each of the items monthly. Officials visit a sample of shops, geographically spread across the UK, to record the prices actually being charged. Up to 1,000 separate prices could be collected for each item, and the total number of prices collected is likely to be around 150,000.

Part A: Cash management

(e) *Calculation.* The first step to calculate the RPI for a month is to calculate each of the price relatives (being the ratio of the current price for one item to the price at the base date). These price relatives are then weighted using the weights explained in (ii) to give each of the section indices.

The section indices are in turn combined using section weights to give the group indices. The group indices are combined to give the final RPI figure for the month.

Answer 3.6

(a) (i) The index suggests prices will increase by 3.5% and so produces a budget of £200,000 × 1.035 = £207,000.

 (ii) The budget in (i) assumes that quantities consumed remain the same. If quantities increase by 10% the budget will be £207,000 × 110% = £227,700.

(b) The budget estimates could be in error for a number of reasons.

 (i) The estimates of quantities and prices for next quarter could be inaccurate.

 (ii) The current budget (of £200,000) may not be a suitable basis on which to base the next quarter's budget. It may have been incorrectly set or next period's workload may not reflect that of the current period.

 (iii) The maintenance department may have a budget limit imposed on it and may not be allowed to increase its budget.

 (iv) The weightings on which the index is made may go out of date.

Answer 3.7

Using the spreadsheet model, the answers to these questions can be obtained simply and quickly, using the editing facility in the program.

(a) To test the consequences of slower payments by debtors, it would merely be necessary to alter the contents of cells B25, B26 and B27 in our example from 0.6, 0.4 and 0 to 0.4, 0.5 and 0.1 respectively, and then to run the model again.

(b) Similarly, the consequences for cash flow of slower sales growth of only ½% per month can be tested by altering the value of Cell B23 in our example from 1.0125 to 1.005.

Chapter 4   The banking system and the economic context

Chapter topic list

1   The banking system
2   Financial markets
3   Government monetary policy

Learning objectives

On completion of this chapter you will be able to:

	Performance criteria	Range statement
• take account of trends in the economic and financial environment in managing cash balances	15.2.4	
• understand the basic structure of the banking system and the money market in the UK	15.2	
• understand the relationships between financial institutions	15.2	
• demonstrate a basic understanding of government monetary policies	15.2	

Part A: Cash management

1 THE BANKING SYSTEM

Introduction

1.1 The flow of cash in and out of a business has been the subject of earlier chapters, but it is now time to discuss the economic and financial context of these cash flows and some of the institutional arrangements controlling them.

1.2 All businesses have bank accounts. Banks, like other businesses, are profit-making organisations. A bank's policy towards its customers depends on:

(a) Its need to satisfy its own shareholders
(b) Government monetary policy (the level of interest rates and so on)
(c) Its own creditworthiness (ie how cheaply it can borrow money)
(d) The general economic context, which affects the risks of certain industry sectors, for example

1.3 Unfortunately, therefore, bankers have a lot of other things on their mind than the merits of the proposal you have just given them!

Financial intermediation

1.4 Banks borrow money in order to lend it. If you have a deposit account, the bank does not simply sit on this money. It lends it out to receive a return. The bank is what is called a **financial intermediary**, an intermediary between people and businesses who have surplus cash and those who need to borrow cash.

> **KEY TERM**
>
> A **financial intermediary** brings together providers and users of finance, either as broker (an agent handling a transaction on behalf of others) or as principal (eg holding money balances of lenders for lending on to borrowers).

(a) **Bank intermediaries** in the UK include banks such as:
- Barclays, Lloyds, Midland, NatWest, TSB, Royal Bank of Scotland
- Abbey National, Alliance & Leicester, the Halifax, the Woolwich (now banks, formerly building societies)
- Co-operative Bank
- Girobank (owned by Alliance & Leicester)
- 'merchant banks' or 'investment banks'

(b) **Other financial intermediaries** include:
- Building societies
- Finance houses
- Insurance companies
- Unit trust companies
- Investment trust companies

1.5 The cost of borrowing money is the interest (or dividend) that a depositor or an investor expects to receive. Financial intermediaries make their profit by obtaining funds from lenders at one rate of interest and re-lending to borrowers at a higher rate. The difference

4: The banking system and the economic context

represents gross profit, out of which the financial intermediary must pay for its own operating expenses and make a net profit.

1.6 The importance of **financial intermediation** is that it is easier for savings to be loaned to borrowers through an intermediary than directly.

(a) For example, some large companies borrow millions of pounds at a time. There are few **individuals** with that sort of money to lend, and it would be a long complex and expensive matter for a firm to canvass potential savers. The bank does this job, by **aggregating** individual savings.

(b) In theory, banks should be better at assessing credit risk (the risk that the borrower will default on the loan) than individuals. With financial intermediation, an individual's savings are also not tied directly to the fate of one borrower: in other words, financial intermediation involves **reduction and pooling of risks.** If the borrower defaults on the loan, this should not affect savers directly at all: the cost will be charged to the shareholders of the bank, not depositors. Financial intermediaries are subject to strict supervision. This is not necessarily foolproof, as the cases of the Barings and BCCI bank collapses demonstrate.

(c) Many lenders or depositors want a reasonable degree of liquidity, while borrowers may need loans, for example in order to buy a house or build a factory, over a very long period. By dealing with a large number of customers over a long period, a financial intermediary can provide long-term funds to borrowers while operating facilities to meet lenders' or depositors' needs for liquidity. This process of facilitating short-term and long-term needs is known as **maturity transformation**.

Activity 4.1
Identify and explain briefly the advantages of financial intermediation.

Banks in the UK

1.7 A useful way of analysing banks in the UK is to divide them into two categories.

> **KEY TERMS**
>
> (a) **Primary banks** are the banks which operate the payments mechanism (ie the money transmission service in the economy). These are often referred to as the commercial banks, retail banks, or clearing banks.
>
> (b) **Secondary banks** consist of merchant banks, other British banks, foreign banks in the UK, and consortium banks. They do not themselves carry out cheque clearing, nor are they members of the Committee of London Clearing Banks, although one of the retail (clearing) banks may clear cheques on their behalf.

1.8 **Retail banking** is the banking activity of the traditional 'high street' bank, dealing with relatively small deposits and small loans to customers. Retail services are also now conducted over the telephone or the Internet by many banks. Retail banks have extensive branch networks and the bulk of their business is in sterling. They:

(a) Provide a payments mechanism
(b) Provide a place where people store wealth

Part A: Cash management

(c) Lend money on overdraft or by loan
(d) Offer a variety of services

1.9 **Wholesale banking** involves small numbers of customers with larger deposits or requiring larger loans. Because large sums are involved, customers expect the banks to trim their profit margins and offer a cheaper, more competitive service (eg by offering higher rates of interest to depositors or charging lower rates to borrowers). Wholesale banking is essentially the **merchant banking** area of operations and, in the UK, wholesale banking is conducted principally in London. The clearing banks also carry out wholesale banking operations, but again, mainly in London.

Assets and liabilities of banks

1.10 A bank needs to maintain **liquidity** (the extent to which its assets are cash or can be converted easily to cash) and **profitability**. A bank has a balance sheet, as does any other company, but obviously its assets and liabilities are mainly made up of different types of money. Liquidity is necessary should customers withdraw money from the banking system as a whole or transfer amounts within it.

1.11 A bank's **liabilities** can include the following.

(a) There are two types of **sterling deposits**.

(i) **Sight deposits,** or **current accounts,** which arise from the banks' function of providing a mechanism for transmitting money. Your normal bank account is the main form of sight deposit. You can withdraw money when you like, but you are unlikely to receive much interest. The holding of non-interest bearing or low interest current account funds benefits the banks. They offer little interest, but can lend the money profitably to borrowers.

(ii) **Time deposits** (or term deposits) bear interest, but cannot be drawn on by cheque. Normally they can be withdrawn at once with only a modest loss of interest, although the term 'time deposit' means that depositors should give notice of withdrawal of funds (say, seven days) or that depositors agree not to withdraw their funds until the end of a certain period of time.

(b) **Other currency deposits** are deposits held by customers of UK banks in US dollars or other currencies.

1.12 The **assets** of the retail banks represent the uses to which the banks put the money deposited with them. The banks make their profit by investing in assets which earn a higher rate of interest than the banks pay to their depositors.

(a) **Notes and coin** are required as till money to meet demands for cash withdrawals by depositors. These do not earn any interest at all.

(b) **Balances with the Bank of England** consist of:

(i) **'Cash ratio' deposits.** The Bank of England requires all banks to keep a certain percentage of their deposits in their Bank of England account. This is not for the purpose of control, but it provides the Bank with a source of working capital.

(ii) **Operational deposits.** The banks all need funds to meet their obligations, principally debts which arise out of their clearing operations.

(c) **Bills** are effectively 'IOUs'. These may consist of the following.

(i) **Treasury bills** are three-month loans. They are issued by the Bank of England on behalf of the government to obtain money as short-term working capital.

(ii) **Local authority bills** are in a similar fashion bills issued by various local authorities to raise short-term working capital.

(iii) **Commercial bills of exchange** are either trade bills (a promise by one firm to pay another a stated sum of money on a certain date in the future) or bank bills. A bank bill is a commercial bill which has been guaranteed or accepted by a recognised bank.

(iv) **Eligible bills** are bills which the Bank of England will purchase for cash in the money markets. They are commercial bills that have been guaranteed by a reputable financial institution.

(d) **Market loans** refer to short-term loans to the money markets or to other banks (the **inter-bank market**). Market loans differ from advances in that:

(i) Market loans are loans made through existing markets such as the discount market and inter-bank market (see below), whereas

(ii) Advances are loans made direct to customers

(e) **Advances** are loans direct to customers, and overdrafts. As you might well expect, the bulk of sterling advances are to firms and individuals in the UK private sector.

(f) **Investments** are securities (eg gilts and shares). The most important type of security held by clearing banks is British Government securities. Most of these securities can be bought and sold on the Stock Exchange.

Activity 4.2

In the balance sheet of a retail bank, which one of the following items do you think would constitute the largest asset?

(a) Customers' overdrafts and bank loans
(b) Customers' deposits
(c) Land and buildings

Income and expenses of a bank

1.13 Much of the bank's profit will come from the difference between interest received (**income** to the bank) and interest paid (an **expense** for the bank). The higher the interest it can charge, the better the profit; and the lower the rates it pays for funds, the better the profit too.

1.14 **Other sources of income** for banks include:

(a) Charges on current accounts
(b) Commissions and fees on other services such as insurance, personal pensions
(c) Activities on the foreign exchange markets
(d) Mortgage lending

1.15 **Other expenses** facing banks consist of:

(a) Staff wages/salaries
(b) Maintenance of premises and equipment
(c) Other running costs of branches and Head Office
(d) Advertising
(e) Bad debts

Part A: Cash management

1.16 The cost of the branch network is significant, and banks have been looking at ways to enhance earnings. This is especially true since banks have been facing competition from building societies.

(a) Throughout the 1970s, the banks turned more and more to the wholesale money markets for their deposits, since it certainly seemed that obtaining money this way was cheaper than running expensive branch networks.

(b) The banks are reducing the branch network and the number of employees, by computerisation.

(c) The banks are involved in mortgage lending.

(d) With a strong and growing **customer base** there is a ready market for selling a range of financial services which will provide more interest, fee income, and commissions for the bank in the future.

The central bank

> **KEY TERM**
>
> A **central bank** is an institution which typically has the roles of controlling the monetary system of a country, acting as banker to the banks, and acting as a lender of last resort. Most are established as public bodies, but the degree of independence varies between countries.

1.17 The functions of the central bank vary from one country to another. Below, we use the UK as our reference point.

1.18 The **Bank of England** ('the Bank') is a public corporation and is the central bank of the UK. The Bank of England has the following functions.

(a) It acts as banker to the central government.
(b) It is responsible for issuing bank notes in the UK.
(c) It deals with government borrowing.
(d) It intervenes in the foreign exchange markets.
(e) It is (currently) the supervisor of the banking system.
(f) It is a banker to the commercial banks.
(g) It is the lender of last resort to the banking system.
(h) It acts as advisor to the government on monetary economic policy.
(i) It acts as agent for the government in carrying out its monetary policies.
(j) It participates in international economic institutions, discussions and arrange-ments.

1.19 **The Bank of England is a banker**. The Bank's customers are the **government** and **other banks** in the financial system, and in particular the clearing banks and discount houses. Every commercial bank has a bank account with the Bank of England. Banks use these deposits to settle debts between each other, and to pay amounts due to the government, and when the government makes payments to the banks, there will be a transfer of funds from the government's account with the Bank to the bank's accounts with the Bank. A feature of the Bank's role as a banker is therefore:

(a) Daily transfers of funds between the deposits of the banks as inter-bank debts are settled

(b) Daily transfers of funds between the government's public deposits and the bankers' deposits

1.20 The Bank of England is the central authority in England and Wales for the **issue of banknotes**.

1.21 **The Bank manages the National Debt**. The Bank of England issues government securities to raise funds on behalf of the government, and is active in buying and selling government (and other) securities. The Bank also administers the repayment of government debt. Long-term government debt is referred to collectively as gilt-edged securities or gilts. Short-term government debt takes the form of Treasury bills.

1.22 **The Bank manages the Exchange Equalisation Account**. This account represents the deposits of the nation's gold and foreign currency reserves. It is used to stabilise the *exchange rate* of sterling against other currencies. When the government considers that sterling's value is:

(a) Too **high**, the Bank can step in to sell sterling in exchange for foreign currencies, and so encourage dealers to lower the price of sterling

(b) Too **low**, the Bank can step in to buy sterling by selling some of its foreign currency reserves, causing the price of sterling to stabilise or to increase in value

The Bank of England's foreign exchange reserves are limited, and this imposes constraints on its ability to influence exchange rates.

1.23 **The Bank is a lender of last resort**. The Bank will provide funds for banks that are short of cash. The consequences of a bank's failure of liquidity are very severe.

1.24 **The Bank supervises the banking system**. The Bank has this responsibility under the 1987 Banking Act. It must try to ensure that individual banks retain sufficient liquidity and do not undertake ventures that are too risky. Banks are required to disclose information to the Bank of England. They must also follow Bank guidelines on their lending operations and must maintain sufficient capital to support their activities. In 1997, the new Labour Government announced that this supervisory role would be transferred to the Financial Services Authority in the future.

1.25 **The Bank of England is involved with monetary policy**. (The Bank and the Treasury make up what are called the **monetary authorities**.) There are three main areas where the Bank is involved in monetary policy.

(a) **Interest rate policy**. Since mid-1997, the Bank of England has had the role of setting short-term interest rates at the level it thinks appropriate in order to meet the Government's target for inflation.

(b) **Funding policy**. If the government needs to borrow to finance its spending, borrowing from the banking system increases the money supply. The Bank will usually be required to fund as much of the PSBR as it can in the least inflationary way, and this means selling gilt-edged stock to the general public and to non-bank financial intermediaries, rather than to the banks.

(c) **Control of bank lending**. Since banks create new money when they create new deposits, the Bank of England has for many years tried to restrict bank lending to levels considered desirable in view of economic conditions. At the moment, the main weapon is interest rates.

Part A: Cash management

(d) **Exchange rate policy**. The strength of the pound is important when considering monetary conditions. The Bank of England is responsible for carrying out government policy with regard to the exchange rate, selling pounds if sterling is 'too strong' and buying pounds if sterling is considered to be too weak.

Other banks

1.26 We will now go on to look at the other banks which exist in the financial system.

Merchant banks

1.27 The **merchant banks** (or **investment banks**), provide a range of specialist services for customers, mainly in the industrial and commercial sector, including the following.

(a) **Accepting bills of exchange** on behalf of commercial customers.

(b) **Activities in the money market**. Merchant banks are particularly active in the money market dealing in very large (wholesale) loans and deposits, in both sterling and foreign currency.

(c) **Large-scale term lending**. Merchant banks can provide finance to UK, overseas and multinational companies particularly for long-term needs.

(d) **Activities in the bullion (precious metal) markets**. Merchant banks deal in the gold and silver market particularly, either on their own behalf or on behalf of their clients.

(e) **Assisting in new issues of company shares**. When a company is issuing shares, in other words inviting the public and other financial institutions to apply for shares, it is usual for the company to enlist the support of a merchant bank.

(f) **Managing investments in stock and shares for clients**. This is called **portfolio management**. For example, if a company or private individual has a large sum of money to invest (usually over £100,000) a merchant bank may be able to provide suitable investments and monitor the return on these investments.

(g) **Advice on corporate financial matters**. This includes general advice provided by merchant banks on the management of businesses and more specifically on company mergers and takeovers.

(h) **Leasing**. If a firm needs an expensive piece of equipment it may not be able to find the money to buy it outright. Leasing involves a company such as a merchant bank purchasing the equipment itself and then renting or hiring it to the company which needs it.

Foreign banks

1.28 Since the early 1960s the number of foreign banks operating in the City of London has increased dramatically. There are now around 600 such banks. At least fifty of these are American and around thirty are Japanese.

International banks

1.29 Just as there are foreign banks in Britain, there are also British banks abroad. Most of the 'big four' retail banks has an international banking subsidiary. There are also British banks whose main operations are concerned with overseas banking such as Standard Chartered Bank and Grindlays Bank. These are sometimes termed **British overseas banks**. Their main services are concerned with finance for international trade and providing banking services for UK importers and exporters.

Building societies

1.30 **Building societies** are not subject to the 1987 Banking Act. They are regulated by the Building Societies Act 1986, and their supervisory body is the Building Societies Commission, not the Bank of England. However, they are important deposit-taking institutions and compete with clearing banks and other financial institutions to obtain deposits from customers.

(a) Building societies offer a wide range of savings schemes to attract deposits, aimed mainly at the personal sector. Some are for fixed terms, but most provide for withdrawal on demand, possibly with some interest penalty. Some offer current account services similar to banks.

(b) Most building society assets take the form of mortgages - ie loans to borrowers for house purchase, over periods of up to 25 years. However, since house-owners move to a new house every 7 years or so on average, when they pay off their existing mortgage (and then probably take out a new mortgage) the actual duration of most mortgage loans is less than 25 years, although new loans to the same person, of course, replace the old ones.

Activity 4.3
Explain briefly the principal functions of a central bank.

---

2 FINANCIAL MARKETS

2.1 We have now looked at the banking institutions in the UK, and at building societies. Let's turn now to the financial markets in which the banks carry out some of their operations, and in particular at the money markets.

The money markets

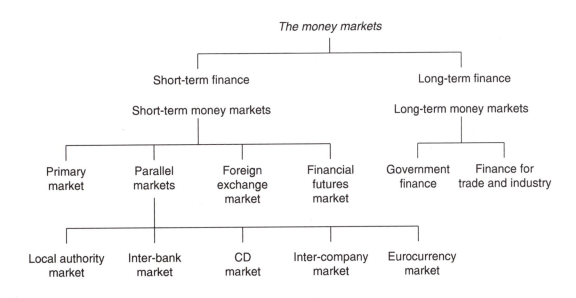

Part A: Cash management

> **KEY TERM**
>
> The **money markets** are markets just like any other with buyers, sellers and traders. The commodity traded in these markets is, however, very specific - it is money, which is lent and borrowed in wholesale amounts.

2.2 We have seen how financial intermediaries act as go-betweens for lenders and borrowers of money. In addition, the financial intermediaries themselves may also be lenders or depositors of money at particular times. The money markets provide financial institutions with a means of covering deficits (shortages of money) and also providing profitable ways of lending surplus funds especially in the short term. The money markets or wholesale markets exist mainly for lending and borrowing between financial institutions, in 'wholesale' amounts.

2.3 The markets are operated today via complex dealing communications technology within the financial institutions involved. Very little 'face to face' dealing takes place.

2.4 The traders or participants in the money markets are:

(a) Financial intermediaries, (mainly banks)
(b) The government, essentially through the Bank of England
(c) The local authorities, who also need to raise capital
(d) Brokers, jobbers, market makers and other 'go-betweens' in the markets
(e) Firms and individuals

What are the main money market financial instruments?

2.5 The main financial instruments in the money markets are as follows.

(a) **Deposits**. These are simple deposits of money in bank accounts (both current and deposit accounts) and deposits with other financial intermediaries. In the inter-bank money market, for example, banks lend to other banks by placing money on deposit (overnight, at call, for 7 days, or 3 months, etc).

(b) **Bills**. Bills are short-term financial assets which can be converted into cash at very short notice, by selling them in the discount market.

(c) **Commercial paper**. This represents short-term IOUs issued by large companies which can be held until maturity or sold to others

(d) **Certificates of deposit (CDs)**. These are available to customers who deposit £50,000 or more for fixed terms. Should the customer wish to obtain cash before the term is up, the CD can be sold on the CD market.

The short-term money markets

2.6 The main wholesale markets are:

(a) The **primary market**;

(b) The **parallel markets**, which include:

(i) The local authority market
(ii) The interbank market
(iii) The certificates of deposit market
(iv) The inter-company market

4: The banking system and the economic context

(v) The commercial paper markets
(vi) The eurocurrency markets

2.7 The distinction between the markets is not clear-cut and there are reasons in fact for regarding the money markets as unified. All of the money markets deal in short-term lending and borrowing.

The primary market

2.8 The **primary money market** consists of approved banks and securities firms.

(a) The primary market is a money market in which the banks can place surplus funds in a very liquid form. They can draw on these funds to make settlements with other banks or the government when their operational deposits get too low.

(b) Because of transactions between the government and the banks' customers, there may be large movements of funds between the government and the banks - ie large transfers of funds between public deposits and bankers' deposits at the Bank of England. When the banking system as a whole runs short of cash (or has surplus cash) because of these funds transfers, the Bank of England can:

(i) Provide more cash by buying bills and other short-term financial instruments (from the institutions), or

(ii) Withdraw surplus cash by selling Treasury bills (etc)

in the primary market.

(c) The primary market is therefore a go-between, and is used by the Bank of England to smooth out the fluctuations in cash shortages and cash surplus arising from transactions between government and the private sector. The Bank of England, by operating in this market, also has the opportunity to set short-term interest rates that will usually by adopted throughout the money markets. (Institutions called the '**discount houses**' used to have a special role in this market, but they no longer enjoy a privileged status.)

Other markets

2.9 **Local authority markets.** Local authorities have a special wholesale market in which they can borrow short term funds. Local authority short term borrowing takes two forms.

(a) **Local authority bonds** have a maturity of around one year, and so although they are short-dated stock, they are not as liquid for investors as other investments.

(b) **Local authority bills** are short-term debt in the same way that Treasury bills are short-term government debt.

2.10 The **inter-bank market** is an important market in unsecured loans between banks. A large proportion of the dealing is for very short term funds (overnight money) although some loans are for longer periods up to one year. The inter-bank market is used by banks for three purposes.

(a) It can be used to smooth out fluctuations in receipts and payments by the bank.

(b) A well-established bank can use the market to borrow funds in its own name and lend the funds to a less well-established bank at a higher rate of interest.

(c) It may be used to sound out the market for the likely future trends in rates.

Part A: Cash management

The interest rate charged in the largest inter-bank market is the **London Inter-Bank Offered Rate (LIBOR)** and this is used by individual banks to determine their own base rates, and so the rate of interest at which they will lend to their own customers.

2.11 **Certificates of deposit market**. Certificates of deposit (CDs) are explained in a later chapter of this text.

2.12 **Inter-company market**. In the market, companies with surplus funds lend direct (through a broker) to companies which need to borrow money. The size of this market is very small in comparison to the local authority market, the inter-bank market and the CD market. Direct lending between companies in this market is a form of **disintermediation** as no financial intermediary is used.

KEY TERM

Disintermediation refers to the bypassing of financial intermediaries in order to arrange lending and borrowing directly from the ultimate parties to the transaction.

2.13 The **commercial paper market**. Commercial paper is an IOU issued by a company. It is issued when a company wants to raise short term money. It is not for a specific debt. 'Medium term notes' (MTNs) are similar to commercial paper except that they have a maturity of over one up to and including five years.

2.14 **Eurocurrency markets**. A **eurocurrency** is a deposit of funds with a bank outside the currency's country of origin. A deposit of US dollars with a bank in London, or a deposit of Japanese Yen with a bank in Paris, is a eurocurrency deposit. A eurocurrency loan is a loan of eurocurrency by the bank with which the money has been deposited. The main feature of a eurocurrency loan is therefore that it is money that is deposited with and lent by a bank *outside* the currency's country of origin. London is an important eurocurrency market centre.

ASSESSMENT ALERT

Do not make the mistake which many students make of assuming that the 'euro-' prefix means that a European currency or bank must be involved in a 'eurocurrency' transaction. The term 'eurocurrency' has nothing to do with the European single currency, the 'euro', either.

Other financial markets

2.15 Of other financial markets, one of the most important is the stock market regulated by the London Stock Exchange. This is a capital market where firms and the government obtain *long-term* finance.

(a) **Shares**. This is where shares in companies can be bought and sold. Banks may own shares, and many banks run subsidiaries who buy and sell shares on their own behalf and that of their clients.

(i) Companies can raise *long*-term finance from the stock market, by issuing shares to investors, in return for money.

(ii) Investors can sell shares or buy them.

(b) **Government bonds**. A bond offers a fixed rate of interest. The face value of the bond is repaid at a specified date. In the UK, government bonds are referred to as gilt-edged securities, or **gilts**. We have already mentioned Treasury bills which are used for short-term working capital for the government. Gilts generally denote long-term government borrowing.

2.16 The **foreign exchange market** is, by its very nature, a 'global' market. Like many of the other short-term markets, the foreign exchange market is based on communications technology. Very little 'face-to-face' trading ever takes place.

2.17 The **financial futures market** is one of the most complex of all the short-term markets and is also one of the most recent. It was introduced in London in 1982 and it is centred in the London International Financial Futures and Options Exchange (LIFFE). The idea behind financial futures is that a deal for a loan or deposit of money to take place sometime in the future can be made now. In other words, an interest rate for finance in the future can be set many months before that finance is actually needed, just as in the commodity market dealers might buy oil for delivery in three months time. Outside London, one of the other main centres for financial futures is Chicago.

3 GOVERNMENT MONETARY POLICY

The quantity of money

3.1 The amount of money in an economy is measured in a number of ways, too technical to describe here. These measurements are called monetary aggregates and range, in order of complexity, from the 'narrow' definition M0 (comprising mainly notes and coin) to the 'broader' definition M4 (in the UK). Let us briefly consider the broad money supply measure M4. An *increase* in M4, in other words an increase in the money supply, can come about as a result of any of the following.

(a) **Government prints/mints more notes and coins**.

(b) **Government spends more than it raises in taxes and other income**. Payments *to* the government reduce the money supply and payments *from* the government increase the money supply. So if the government is a net spender, the payments by the government will increase M4.

(c) **Banks and building societies lend more money**. Every loan creates a deposit, so if the banking system lends more to firms and individuals, the money supply will rise.

(d) **Money from abroad entering the accounts of UK residents**. This happens, for example, when a UK firm sells goods abroad and is paid in sterling, or when it borrows sterling abroad and brings it back into the UK. Bank/building society deposits will be affected by the flow of money between ourselves and other countries. If other countries are paying more to us then we are paying to them the likely result is an increase in bank/building society deposits in this country.

Note. **The sale of government debt**. When the government sells debt instruments, such as government stock or **Treasury bills**, to private sector firms and individuals, it *reduces* the money supply M4. The more it sells, the more it reduces M4 as it *receives* money from the sales.

Government monetary policy

3.2 The government of a country intervenes in its economy for a number of reasons. The UK Government has objectives for price stability, economic growth, and employment, which a government can influence in two ways.

Part A: Cash management

(a) **Fiscal policy** is concerned with government spending and taxation.
(b) **Monetary policy** is described in more detail below.

Monetary policy

3.3 **Monetary policies** are policies implemented by the Treasury and the Bank of England (referred to jointly as the monetary authorities) and are aimed at influencing the **quantity of money**, the **price of money** (interest rates) and the **availability of credit** in the economy. Its importance, some economists have argued, is that too much money in the economic system causes inflation.

The availability of credit in the economy

3.4 Bank lending and hence the amount of money people and businesses can borrow, can be controlled by **reserve requirements (ratios)**; **other direct controls**; and **interest rate policy**.

3.5 **Reserve requirements**. These require that a certain proportion of a bank's assets are held in reserve, and are not used for lending. One type of reserve requirement might be a **compulsory minimum cash reserve ratio** (ratio of cash to total assets). In the absence of compulsion, however, banks might apply their own voluntary reserve requirements, perhaps under the influence and supervision of the Bank of England. The Bank keeps a close watch on the capital adequacy and liquidity of banks. There are international guidelines for the amount of capital a bank must have (for example, to cover possible bad debts).

3.6 **Other direct controls** may be quantitative or qualitative.

(a) **Quantitative**. The government might put 'lending ceilings' on the clearing banks which restrict the growth of the banks' lending (assets). For example, banks might be forbidden to increase their lending by more than 5% per annum. Such controls have not featured in UK monetary policy for many years. With the global financial market, and London's importance in it, they are probably moribund.

(b) **Qualitative** controls are used to alter the *type* of lending by banks. For example, the government (via the Bank) can *ask* the banks to limit their lending to the personal sector, or lend more to industry or lend less to a particular type of firm, such as property companies, and more to manufacturing businesses. This is sometimes referred to as **moral suasion**. *Compulsory* controls, however, would be hard to enforce.

(c) **Prudential control** refers to the supervision of banks and other financial institutions by the authorities to ensure that they have an adequate capital structure, liquidity and/or foreign exchange exposure. Prudential controls are not used directly to control the money supply but they might have some *indirect* influence and so it is useful to mention them here. As mentioned earlier, the role of supervising banks in the UK is due to move from the Bank of England to the Securities and Investments Board in the future.

(d) **Open market operations in gilts**. When the government wishes to reduce bank lending, it can issue attractive gilts; these are purchased by individuals and financial institutions who pay for them by cheques drawn on their banks. The result of this is a reduction in bank deposits and a reduction in the banks' ability to lend as their cash base is reduced, when cash is transferred from the banks to the Bank of England.

(e) **Open market operations in bills.** This has been the main thrust of government policy to control bank lending over past years. By its operations in the bill market the Bank of England tries to achieve the interest rate of its choice as opposed to **imposing a minimum lending rate**.

   (i) Selling Treasury bills (or other financial instruments) for cash takes cash out of the system.

   (ii) Buying Treasury bills for cash puts cash into the system. By refusing to buy at a certain price, the Bank of England can effectively influence interest rates.

Activity 4.4
Write notes on why a government might seek to control the growth of bank lending.

Interest rate policy: the price of money

3.7 **Interest rate policy** is designed to control the growth in *demand* for loans rather than the *supply* of bank lending. Looked at simply, the interest rate is the price of money and so increasing this price should reduce the demand for money. As we saw earlier, the interest rate control process involves operations conducted by the Bank of England in the primary money market.

3.8 The success of interest rate policy depends on the interest elasticity of demand for loans. In other words, raising interest rates should reduce the demand for borrowing by making it more expensive both for individuals and for companies. Paying 20% on a loan is much less attractive than paying 5%. However, you might not be in a position to choose. If higher rates do not deter borrowers, then lending will not be controlled and money supply growth will not be restrained. Many individuals are more concerned with the monthly repayment than with the interest rate.

3.9 By reducing the demand for borrowing, higher interest rates will have a dampening effect on consumer demand. Consumers will buy less on credit, and the knock-on effect for many companies is that less of their products will be purchased. Companies may therefore find themselves squeezed on both sides: a rise in interest rates will increase costs on any variable rate finance which the company has, and may reduce revenues from sales. The effect may be particularly felt in markets for high value items (such as furniture and cars) which are often bought on credit.

3.10 Higher interest rates can also have a significant effect on the housing market because potential housebuyers may be deterred from buying a house on mortgage finance. Then, businesses closely connected with house purchase, such as estate agents and home improvements companies, may be particularly affected.

The importance of the PSBR/PSDR

3.11 An excess of public sector spending over revenue - a **Public Sector Borrowing Requirement (PSBR)** - feeds directly into increases in the money supply. The bigger the PSBR, the bigger the increase in the money supply. This has important implications for the control of the growth of the money supply.

  (a) If the government wishes to control the money supply it will wish to keep the size of the PSBR within a certain limit.

Part A: Cash management

(b) When the government has to borrow - when the PSBR is positive - it is better to finance the PSBR by borrowing from the *non-bank* private sector (the public, insurance companies etc), by means of National Savings and issue of gilts, to avoid increasing the money supply to the banks.

3.12 A **PSDR (public sector debt repayment)** - occurring when public sector revenue is greater than public sector expenditure - has a negative effect on money supply growth. In the late 1980s, when there were significant surpluses, debt in the hands of the overseas sector was almost eliminated and the holdings of banks and the private sector were reduced, indicating a 'tight' monetary policy. As the finances of government have changed in recent years however, the problem of what to do with a public sector surplus is not one that concerns us today.

Activity 4.5

Suppose that interest rates fall significantly and unexpectedly. Identify the effects on a carpet retailing company which has a large overdraft.

Key learning points

- **Financial intermediaries** exist to smooth the flow of funds from surplus sectors of the economy to deficit sectors.
- **Primary (retail) banks** are banks that operate the payments mechanism and are usually called commercial banks or clearing banks. **Secondary banks** deal mostly with wholesale business in the secondary money markets not in the high street.
- The balance sheet of a bank consists of its liabilities (mostly **deposits** of one sort or another) and its assets (mostly **loans** to customers of one sort or another). Banks must make sure that their assets are sufficiently **liquid** to meet their depositors' needs, but not so liquid that their profits suffer.
- Banks make a **profit** by lending at a higher rate of interest that the rate they pay for deposits. Net profit will also take account of overheads and running expenses such as wage costs, advertising and bad debts. Other forms of income such as fees and commissions are increasingly important sources of income for banks.
- The **central bank** (the Bank of England in the UK) has various roles and is particularly important for the government's monetary policy.
- The **money markets**, or wholesale markets, consist of a **primary market**, which the Bank of England uses to regulate interest rates, and **secondary markets**.
- The secondary markets include the **local authority**, the **interbank** market, the **CD** market, the **intercompany** market, the **commercial paper** markets and the **eurocurrency** market). They deal principally with the short-term finance of banks, governments, and large commercial organisations.
- **Money** can be defined in different 'narrow' or 'broad' senses, depending on what financial assets are considered to be money.
- **Fiscal policy** deals with taxation, government spending and government borrowing.
- **Monetary policy** deals with the supply of money, the price of money (interest) and the availibility of credit (to make borrowing harder or easier). The UK government prefers to regulate the price of money, through **interest rates**, rather than **quantitative or qualitative controls** over amounts that can be lent.

Quick quiz

1 Name four types of financial intermediary.

2 For whom does the Bank of England operate as banker?

3   What is the Exchange Equalisation Account?

4   Identify the main wholesale money markets.

5   Is (a) a deposit of US dollars with a Japanese bank; and (b) a deposit of pounds sterling with a bank in the USA, a 'eurocurrency' deposit?

6   How do you think might a company obtain long-term finance?

7   Monetary policy is mainly concerned with government spending and taxation: true or false?

8   If interest rates have risen, what, in effect, is the change in monetary policy?

Answers to quick quiz

1   Any four of: retail banks; merchant banks; building societies; finance houses; insurance companies; pension funds; unit trust companies; investment trust companies. Other examples could also be given.

2   The government, and other banks.

    The Bank of England also operates some (but very few) accounts for individuals.

3   It shows the government's reserves of gold and foreign currency.

4   The primary market; the local authority; the interbank bank; the certificates of deposit market; the inter-company market; the commercial paper markets; the eurocurrency markets.

5   Yes - both are deposits of funds with banks outside the country's currency of origin. (The 'euro' prefix, remember, does not mean that a European country or currency must be involved.)

6   It might obtain a long-term loan, for example through a merchant bank, or it might issue new shares on the stock market. (Sources of finance will be covered more fully later in this text.)

7   False. The description given is of fiscal policy.

8   Monetary policy has been tightened: money is more expensive.

Answers to activities

Answer 4.1

Financial intermediation links lenders of money with potential borrowers. A lender does not need to find an individual borrower, but can deposit his money with a bank, building society, investment trust or other financial intermediary instead. The intermediary can 'package' the amounts lent by savers into the amounts which borrowers require. For example, numerous building society accounts containing deposits of relatively small sums finance the smaller number of relatively large sums which mortgage borrowers require.

The intermediation process pools the risks of lending money to borrowers among the various lenders who deposit money with the intermediary. Unit trust companies reduce risk by spreading investments across a variety of stocks and shares, enabling a small investor to take advantage of portfolio diversification effects normally only easily available to the larger investor.

The financial intermediary provides 'maturity transformation', bridging the gap between the desire of many lenders for liquidity and the need of most borrowers for loans over longer periods.

Answer 4.2

The answer is (a). Item (b) is not an asset of the bank - it is a liability (a sum of money owed by the bank to its customers). It might be tempting to choose item (c), if you think about the large number of High Street sites owned by the retail banks, but in fact the value of this asset is dwarfed by the financial assets of the banks.

Part A: Cash management

Answer 4.3

All developed countries have a central bank. In the UK the central bank is the Bank of England and although it has certain special functions, its major activities are the same as any other central bank.

(a) The Bank acts as *banker to the government*. This embraces various activities including the handling of receipts, such as tax revenues, paid to the government and releasing funds to meet the spending commitments of the different government departments.

(b) The Bank *implements the government's monetary policy*: by manipulating or influencing the liquidity position of the banks and hence their ability to make loans, and (since 1997) by setting short-term interest rates at a level designed to meet the government's inflation target.

(c) The Bank functions as the *lender of last resort* to the banking system by making loans to the banking system when it is short of liquidity.

(d) The Bank has responsibility for *converting* foreign exchange receipts are converted into sterling and *vice versa*.

(e) In England and Wales, the Bank is the *sole note-issuing authority*.

(f) The Bank of England is also *banker to the monetary system*. All banks and licensed deposit takers are required to hold operational deposits at the Bank and these are effectively used as current accounts.

(g) The Bank exercises a *supervisory role* aimed at ensuring the stability of the financial system. In this capacity it draws up regulations on banks' liquidity reserves, and has strict guidelines on which organisations can refer to themselves as banks. The UK Government proposed (in 1997) that this supervisory role should be transferred to the new Financial Services Authority.

Answer 4.4

The greater part of the money supply consists of bank and building society deposits. Levels of deposits will be determined in part by the level of bank and building society lending. (Through the operation of the 'credit multiplier', the banking system is able to 'create' credit. Funds lent by a bank effectively become the bank deposits of others. Each loan creates new deposits which can be used by the banking system to create further loans. The process can create new deposits several times larger than the original funds advanced.)

This ability of banks to 'create' credit affects the overall money supply. Growth in the money supply may be undesirable because it may lead to inflation. Bank borrowing by individuals is often used to finance current consumption out of future income, and excessive bank lending may fuel aggregate demand leading to inflationary pressures and to increased imports. For such reasons, a government may seek to reduce growth in levels of bank lending.

If the government finances a budget deficit by sales of gilts to the banking sector, it may try to offset the impact of monetary growth by curbs on credit.

Political views about different forms of economic policy intervention can also be important. Some governments may be unwilling to impose controls, preferring market forces to take their course. One method of seeking to subdue bank lending is to conduct policies which keep the cost of credit - the interest rate - relatively high. Such a policy seeks to inhibit the demand for credit by the operation of the market forces in the lending sector, although the policy often involves careful government intervention through the management of interest rates. Other methods include imposing reserve asset ratios on banks, requirements on banks to lodge special deposits at the Bank of England, and 'lending ceilings' on banks.

The means by which the UK government sought to curb credit in the late 1980s was by raising interest rates: this policy makes credit more expensive and should therefore reduce demand for it. From 1997, short-term interest rates are set by the Monetary Policy Committee of the Bank of England. The authorities could carry out open market operations in such a way as to absorb excess liquidity and thus reduce the balances held by the public.

Answer 4.5

The cost of overdraft interest will fall. Carpets are often brought on credit, and so people may buy more carpets on the cheaper credit available. Lower interest rates mean cheaper mortgages and so people will be encouraged to move to larger houses and more first time buyers will enter the market. More house sales mean that more people will want to replace carpets. The company's sales should hopefully increase.

Chapter 5 Dealing with banks

Chapter topic list

1   Why do banks exist?
2   The banker/customer relationship
3   Services offered by banks: money transmission

Learning objectives

On completion of this chapter you will be able to:

	Performance criteria	Range statement
• understand the legal relationship between bank and customer	15.2	
• know about money transmission and other services offered by banks	15.1	

Part A: Cash management

1 WHY DO BANKS EXIST?

1.1 In the previous chapter, we identified the role of banks as **financial intermediaries** in the **economy** as a whole. From the point of view of a business or individual who uses the services of a bank, the uses of a **bank** are: to **provide a safe place where money can be deposited**; to **provide short-term finance**; to **provide other financial services**.

1.2 The **Banking Act 1987** sets out the characteristics which would be used by the Bank of England in deciding whether an institution should be allowed to use the title 'bank'. Such an institution must be substantial in size, with capital of £5 million or more. The Act stipulates that use of the word 'bank' is confined to institutions with at least £5 million paid-up capital. Although other **authorised institutions** with at least £1 million paid-up capital may provide financial services and accept deposits, they are forbidden to use the word 'bank' in their title. Unauthorised institutions may not take deposits.

KEY TERM

The judge in the *United Dominions Trust* case stated that a **banker** is a person (or persons) who will:

(a) Credit money and cheques collected on a customer's behalf to their account

(b) Debit the customer's account by paying all cheques and orders drawn on the account by the customer, and

(c) Keep accounts such as current accounts which can be used to make credits or debits on the customer's behalf.

Note. In law, a *person* can be an individual human being, of course, but also a limited company, which for certain purposes, is a 'person' in the eyes of the law.

What is a customer?

1.3 It is important to know if a person is a **customer** because banks owe many legal duties to customers and can be sued if they do not carry out these duties adequately. The term **'customer'** is not defined in the banking legislation. However, case law (ie the law arrived at through judicial decisions in the court) has established the following.

KEY TERM

A person becomes a **customer** in respect of cheque transactions as soon as the bank opens an account for him in his name. In any other situation, for example when investment advice is given, a person becomes a customer as soon as the bank accepts his instructions and undertakes to provide a service.

Activity 5.1

You have a rich friend who lends money to some of her friends and acquaintances at a low rate of interest. They repay her in monthly instalments. Is she running a bank?

2 THE BANKER/CUSTOMER RELATIONSHIP

2.1 The relationship between bank and customer arises from a legal **contract** between them which it is necessary to understand. (Contract law is discussed in Chapter 8, in the context of trade credit.) There are four main types of **contractual relationship** which may exist between bank and customer: **debtor/creditor**; **principal/agent**; **bailor/bailee**; and **mortgagor/mortgagee**. In addition there is a **fiduciary relationship**. Each of these types of relationship is described further below.

Debtor/creditor relationship

2.2 If Bill owes money to Ben then Bill is a **debtor** of Ben and Ben is said to be Bill's **creditor**. The same terms apply to the relationships between bank and customer.

2.3 The customer deposits his money with the bank. These funds are placed in the customer's account and can be withdrawn at any time. It follows that in this case **the bank is the debtor** (for the money owed to the customer) and the **customer is a creditor**. However, there are circumstances where this relationship can be reversed. If, for example, a customer account is overdrawn, then the customer owes money to the bank. In this case, the bank is the creditor and the customer is the debtor.

2.4 The *Joachimson v Swiss Bank Corporation (1921)* case laid down the essential terms of this area of the bank/customer relationship.

  (a) The bank undertakes to receive money, cheques etc for its customer's account.

  (b) The bank borrows the proceeds and undertakes to repay them.

  (c) The bank will not cease to do business with the customer except upon reasonable notice.

  (d) The bank is not liable to pay until the customer demands payment from the bank.

  (e) The customer undertakes to exercise reasonable care in executing his written orders so as not to mislead the bank or to facilitate forgery.

Bailor/bailee relationship

2.5 Banks have safes or strong rooms and will usually be willing to offer a **safe deposit service** to customers. In law the arrangement is called a **bailment**. There is a bailment whenever one person (the **bailor**) delivers personal property to another person (the **bailee**) on the basis described above. On accepting a customer's property, the bank has two obligations.

  (a) To take 'reasonable' care to safeguard it against damage or loss (In case of loss or damage, the burden of proof rests on the bailee.)

  (b) To re-deliver it only to the customer or some person authorised by the customer

Principal/agent relationship

2.6 In many transactions one person (the **agent**) acts for another (the **principal**) usually, for the purpose of making a contract between the principal and a third party. For example an estate agent negotiates a house sale for the owner and an employment agency finds a new or temporary employee for an employer.

Part A: Cash management

2.7 The bank may act as **agent** for its customers, as in the examples below.

(a) A customer who receives payment of a debt by a crossed cheque must have a bank account and employs his bank as agent to present the cheque for payment and credit the proceeds to his account.

(b) Where the bank arranges insurance such as household contents insurance, the bank is acting as an insurance broker and is the agent of its customer.

2.8 The bank may have to employ **other agents** such as stockbrokers, solicitors and other types of specialist qualified to handle particular transactions.

Mortgagor/mortgagee relationship

2.9 This relationship can come into being when the bank asks a customer to secure a loan by a charge or mortgage over assets such as property: the customer is the **mortgagor**, granting the mortgage to the bank, while the bank is the **mortgagee**, accepting the mortgage from the customer. This means that if the customer does not repay the loan, the bank can sell the asset and use the proceeds to pay off or reduce the outstanding loan.

Fiduciary relationship

2.10 If one of the parties in a relationship based on trust can be said to be in an influential position then that person could exert **undue influence** to make the other party enter into a contract which he otherwise might not. The law therefore expects the 'superior' party in the relationship to act in **good faith**. It is said to be a **fiduciary relationship** (or **special relationship**). The law expects banks to act with **utmost good faith**, particularly where the bank is advising the customer.

Activity 5.2

What legal relationship exist between banker and customer in each of the following cases?

(a) A customer asks the bank to keep his jewellery in safe deposit.
(b) A customer pays a cheque in for the credit of her account. The cheque is drawn on another bank.
(c) A customer asks the bank for financial advice.

The bank's rights

2.11 Banks' rights in relation to customers accrue on the basis of accepted legal or moral justice. These are as follows.

(a) **Charges and commissions.** The bank may charge its customers bank charges and commissions (eg on travellers' cheques) over and above interest on advances, provided these are 'reasonable'.

(b) **Use of customers' money.** The bank can use the customer's money in any way which is legally and morally acceptable. However, the customer's money must be available for withdrawal in line with the terms of his deposit. For example, with a current account money must be able to be withdrawn on demand.

(c) **Overdrawn balances.** The bank has a right to be repaid overdrawn balances on demand, except where the terms of the overdraft require a period of notice.

(d) **Customers drawing cheques.** The customer owes a duty of care to the bank when drawing cheques to ensure fraud is not facilitated.

(e) **Lien over securities.** A lien is a right to retain possession of another's property providing discharge of a debt. For example, where a customer has an account which is already overdrawn and has deposited cheques for collection, these could be used to clear a debt owed to the bank. The principle would not apply to items held in safe custody, such as jewellery.

(f) **Indemnification.** To **indemnify** means to secure against possible loss or damage. In the context of the business of banking, indemnification refers to a bank being secured against possible loss when acting on a customer's behalf.

The bank's duties

2.12 The definition of a **duty** is a task or action which a person is bound to perform for moral or legal reasons. A bank has a number of duties which are as follows.

(a) **Honour customers' cheques.** The bank has a duty to honour (pay) a customer's cheques as long as:

   (i) The cheques are correctly made out and properly drawn

   (ii) The customer has sufficient funds in his account or payment of the cheque would not exceed an agreed overdraft limit, and

   (iii) There is no legal reason why the cheques should not be paid

(b) **Receipt of customers' funds.** The bank has a duty to credit cash or cheques paid to a customer's account.

(c) **Repayment on demand.** The bank must repay a customer's funds on demand provided that:

   (i) There is a **written** request from the customer, in the form of a cheque or as otherwise agreed

   (ii) The transaction takes place during the bank's opening hours, and

   (iii) The transaction takes place either at the customer's home branch or at another agreed branch or bank

(d) **Comply with customers' instructions.** The bank must comply with instructions from a customer to pay funds through a direct debit mandate or standing order, provided that the customer has sufficient funds in the account.

(e) **Provide a statement.** A bank must provide a statement showing transactions on a customer's account in a 'reasonable time'. The bank must also provide details of the balance on the account on request. However, there is no duty for the customer to ensure that he keeps records of the account and he is not bound to check the statements he gets from the bank.

   (i) This puts the onus on the bank to ensure that transactions are correctly applied to a customer's account because there are circumstances under which any amounts **credited in error** to a customer's account may not be recoverable.

   (ii) What if a bank inadvertently **debits** money from a customer's account? The danger here for the banks is that, if the customer draws cheques on the strength of his true balance, the actual balance following the error may be insufficient to pay these cheques. Under such circumstances, the bank could be liable for compensation for damage caused to a customer's standing as a result of not paying cheques correctly drawn.

Part A: Cash management

(f) **Confidentiality.** A bank should keep in confidence what it knows about a customer's affairs. There are four recognised exceptions where a bank may disclose information about its customer's affairs.

   (i) **Where the bank is required by law to disclose.**

   (ii) **Where there is a public duty to disclose:** for example, if the bank is aware that the customer's transactions are damaging to the national interest (such as trading with the enemy in time of war).

   (iii) **Where the interest of the bank requires disclosure:** for example, when the bank sues a customer to recover what he owes.

   (iv) **Where the customer has given express or implied consent:** for example, by inviting a third party to apply to the bank for a 'banker's reference'.

   The 1992 **Code of Banking Practice** suggests that banks should be required to obtain the customer's express consent before passing 'white' credit information (about customers who are not in default) to credit agencies, although it sees no problem with passing information about customers to other parts of a banking group (such as insurance or credit card subsidiaries) and considers that it is in the bank's interest to give details of customers in default to credit reference agencies ('black' credit information).

(g) **Advice of forgery.** A bank must advise a customer if it becomes apparent that cheques bearing a forgery of the customer's signature are being drawn on his account.

(h) **Care and skill.** Banks are expected to use care and skill in their actions. This is not purely for professional reasons. It also ensures that the banks are afforded certain legal protections.

(i) **Closure of accounts.** Bankers have a duty to provide reasonable notice to a customer when the bank wishes to close the account, say, because of misuse by the customer. Such a period of notice is required to allow a customer to make other financial arrangements.

Customer's duties

2.13 The customer has two main **duties**.

   (a) The customer must exercise care in drawing cheques, so that fraud is not facilitated. For example, customers should not issue blank cheques, write them out in pencil etc. Arguably, this might extend to taking care of debit cards, PINs (personal identification numbers) and so on.

   (b) The customer must tell the bank of any known forgeries.

2.14 A customer has **no** duty to check his or her bank statements for any incorrect entries.

Activity 5.3

For the purpose of a presentation to colleagues, list the rights and duties of a bank in its relationship with its customers.

5: Dealing with banks

Maintaining a good relationship with the bank

2.15 The Treasury department of a firm should maintain appropriate relationships with the firm's bank (or banks, if the firm maintains more than one bank account). The main reason is that many businesses, especially in the UK, rely on **overdraft finance** for their short-term needs. As money is the lifeline of a business, the danger of this lifeline being cut off should not be underestimated. Maintaining a good relationship involves the following.

(a) Maintaining the value of any security which is pledged to secure a loan

(b) Informing the bank as to the progress of the business, especially its demands for cash (Forecasts of expected future cash flow are often required for credit to be advanced.)

(c) Only using the overdraft for appropriate financial needs and within authorised limits

Activity 5.4

Your managing director is concerned about the circumstances in which a bank may legitimately disclose information about a customer's affairs. Explain this matter to her.

3 SERVICES OFFERED BY BANKS: MONEY TRANSMISSION

3.1 To earn a profit, banks offer a variety of services to their customers.

(a) **Savings accounts** (Investing surplus cash is discussed in Chapter 7.)
(b) **Lending** (Business loans and overdrafts will be discussed in Chapter 6.)
(c) **Funds transfer** (See below)
(d) **Other services**, including safe custody, insurance and financial advice

Cheques and guaranteeing them

3.2 Cheques are one of the most significant means by which a business's customers will pay their debts, and by which a business will pay its suppliers.

ASSESSMENT ALERT

You will already have learned about cheques but a few reminders are in order here.

KEY TERMS

A **cheque** is a written instruction to a bank authorising and requiring the bank to make a payment to a third party or to the customer himself. A legal definition of a cheque would be:

'an unconditional order in writing addressed by a person to a bank, signed by the person giving it requiring the bank to pay on demand a sum certain in money to or to the order of a specified person or to bearer.'

(a) The **collecting bank** collects the proceeds of the cheque on behalf of its customers (the payee or endorsee).

(b) The **paying bank** pays the cheque from its customer's account (the drawer of the cheque).

Part A: Cash management

Dates

3.3 If an **undated cheque** is presented to a bank for payment, it is entitled to refuse payment on the grounds that its authority to pay is uncertain by reason of the omission. The cheque could properly be returned unpaid.

3.4 A cheque may also be **ante-dated** (bear a date earlier than the date of issue) or be **post-dated** (bear a future date which has not arrived when the cheque is presented for payment). In either case the cheque is valid. But the following additional rules may apply.

(a) **Stale cheques:** the banks consider that the customer's authority to pay his cheque expires after six months from the date of issue. The bank would return it marked 'stale cheque' or 'out of date' so that the drawer may either confirm his authority to pay it or (as is more usual practice) issue a fresh cheque bearing a current date.

(b) **Post-dated cheques:** if the cheque is post-dated and presented for payment before the date inserted on it, the bank may (and should) refuse to pay it until the date arrives. If the bank, usually by oversight, does pay before the due date, the customer is often unable to deny the bank's right to debit his account since the payment usually discharges a debt which the customer owes to the payee. Credit controllers should be wary of customers sending post-dated cheques.

Crossings

3.5 A **general crossing** is usually designated by two vertical lines on the face of the cheque (usually pre-printed on the cheques when issued by the bank to customers). A general crossing instructs the paying bank to make payment **only to another bank**.

3.6 A **special crossing** is the name of the collecting bank (and often its branch address) written across the cheque. This is an instruction to the paying bank to make payment **only to the bank designated by the special crossing** (or to its London agent which must be another bank).

3.7 A general or special crossing may be combined with either or both of the 'not negotiable' or 'a/c payee' crossings. The words **not negotiable** may be written between the lines of the crossing, primarily for protection against theft. The 'not negotiable' crossing on a cheque does not prevent its transfer. It merely ensures that the transferee has no better rights than his transferor had.

3.8 The **account payee** crossing is an instruction to the collecting bank to collect payment **only** for the original payee. A collecting bank would be at fault if it ignored that instruction. The Cheques Act 1992 requires collecting banks to treat cheques crossed in this way as non-transferable.

Bars to payment of cheques

3.9 (a) **Legal bars to payment** of a customer cheque include: the customer's subsequent death; the customer's bankruptcy; and court orders against the customer.

(b) A customer is entitled to **stop payment** of a cheque by giving instructions, confirmed in writing, to the bank given before the cheque is paid, **unless by using his cheque guarantee card** in issuing the cheque, the customer committed his bank to honour the cheque.

Sufficiency of funds

3.10 A bank has **no** obligation to honour a customer's cheque unless the customer has a credit balance or an agreed overdraft which suffices to provide funds for the payment of the cheque. However cheques issued under the **cheque guarantee scheme** must be honoured even if the customer has an unauthorised overdraft.

3.11 The **reason for refusing payment** may be such that the customer cannot complain of prejudice by disclosure. **Examples** are: 'words and figures differ'; 're-present on due date' (on a post-dated cheque); 'drawer deceased'. The problem usually arises when the bank indicates that there are insufficient funds available to the customer to meet the cheque. It is defamatory to state that a person has issued a cheque, which he knows will be dishonoured, if there were or should have been sufficient funds in the account. The bank could be sued for libel.

Cheque guarantee scheme

3.12 A cheque guarantee card creates a contract by which the bank, through the customer as its agent, undertakes to pay the holder of the cheque the lesser of its value or a fixed amount (£50, £100 or £250, as shown on the cheque card). A cheque guarantee card is not itself a method of payment: it is a **guarantee that a cheque will be** paid.

Debit cards

3.13 **Debit cards** are designed for customers who like paying by plastic card but do not want credit. Many customers now hold multi-function plastic cards which act as ATM, debit and cheque guarantee card in one, so that they can be used to withdraw money from a current account in three ways: cash, payment by debit card to a third party accepting such cards, or payment by cheque, supported by the guarantee card.

3.14 Debit cards are designed to be used in EFTPOS systems (**Electronic Funds Transfer at Point of Sale**) which, as the name suggests, can initiate an immediate transfer of funds from the customer's account to that of the person providing him with goods or services. In practice, in the UK, debit card transactions are not exclusively processed in EFTPOS systems. There are two main brands, Switch and Delta.

Credit cards

3.15 **Credit cards** provide credit to cardholders. A credit card holder uses the card to purchase goods or services within a total credit limit. A monthly statement will be issued to the cardholder by the card company. The cardholder must pay at least a certain minimum amount. Interest is charged on unpaid amounts. (They are not the same as **charge cards**, such as American Express, whose balance must be paid in full every month.)

3.16 Credit cards also provide a means of payment (ie money transmission). Traders who sell goods or services to customers with a bank's credit card are reimbursed by the card company, which takes a commission. It is therefore the banking organisations that give the credit, and not the traders. The trader forwards his Visa or Mastercard sales vouchers to a **merchant acquirer** who processes the transaction in return for a **merchant service charge** from the retailer (averaging about 1.8% of the sales value). The merchant acquirer has to pay about 1% of the sales value to the credit card issuer, which bears the cost of fraud.

Part A: Cash management

Banker's draft

3.17 This is a method of payment which is available on request (and on payment of a fee) to customers who need to eliminate the risk of a cheque being 'bounced'. The **banker's draft** is effectively a cheque drawn on the bank by itself, payable to a person specified by the customer. (Sometimes it might be called a bank cheque.) An alternative to a banker's draft is the **building society cheque:** although unlikely to be dishonoured, since it is a cheque drawn on a building society, there have been cases of fraudulent use of stolen building society cheques. Credit controllers might require payment by banker's draft from some customers. Banker's drafts are also commonly used in the purchase of property.

Standing orders

3.18 **Standing (or banker's) orders** are a means of making a series of payments at a known date to a known recipient. The bank asks the customer to fill in a standard form giving the recipient's bank account details (or the customer uses the recipient's pre-printed form) and the bank then automatically makes the payments as directed until the customer directs it to stop or until the final date stated on the instructions. The **customer** is in complete control of payments. When the amount payable changes, the customer has to inform the bank in writing of the new amount.

3.19 Standing orders are now mainly processed via BACS (see below). Manual orders are used for complicated transactions or where the bank wants to be sure that funds are available to cover the transaction before it is debited to the customer's account. A **credit transfer voucher** then has to be completed and cleared as normal to make the payment and a debit applied manually to the customer's account.

Direct debits

3.20 **Direct debits** are similar to standing orders in that they allow the customer to make regular payments automatically. However, as well as authorising the bank to make the payment, the customer gives his bank details to the **creditor** (eg local authority, insurance company, hire purchase company) which then tells the bank how much to debit to the customer's account.

3.21 **Examples of payments frequently made by direct debit**

- Mortgage and other loan repayments
- Insurance and personal pension premiums
- Minimum amounts due to credit card issuers
- Subscriptions to large clubs and associations
- Utilities (gas, electricity, telephone)
- Equipment rental and maintenance

All of these payments are likely to vary (for example, because of changes in interest rates or the basic rate of tax), and so the alternative would often be to pay by cheque or cash rather than standing order. This is less convenient and more expensive for all parties.

3.22 Many **firms receiving regular payments** from customers prefer to collect by direct debit. A large organisation with hundreds of thousands of similar amounts to collect will spend less on administration if it initiates (and can therefore identify) all the credits to its account. It can also easily (and quickly) spot which amounts have not been received (because the debit was refused by the bank). Direct debits, like automated standing orders, are mostly processed by BACS (see below). The debit to the customer's account is made simultaneously with the credit to the originator's account (unlike cheque clearing). The refusal of a direct debit is known more quickly than the dishonouring of a cheque.

3.23 When the amount to be collected changes, the change is made centrally without delay. The creditor knows the timing of its receipts, enhancing its cash management.

3.24 **Safeguards** are to be built into the system to protect the public.

(a) All changes in amount and collection dates must be notified to the payers 14 days in advance.

(b) The customer can cancel the direct debit by notifying the bank.

(c) The bank makes an immediate refund of any incorrect debit notified by customers, thus taking on the chore of getting a refund from the creditor.

(d) Only approved organisations can operate a direct debit scheme and they must be sponsored by their banks.

(e) The originator must provide an indemnity to its sponsoring bank so that the banks are guaranteed a refund of incorrect debits which they have refunded to their customers.

BACS

3.25 **Bankers' Automated Clearing Services** (BACS) is a company owned by the high street banks which operates the electronic transfer of funds between accounts within the banking system. When a business uses BACS, it sends information (which will be input into the books of the business) to BACS for processing. Many different business use BACS; even small businesses can do so because their bank will help to organise the information for BACS. The most important advantage of the BACS system is that it operates with very reduced amounts of paperwork. To give examples, BACS is widely used for monthly salaries paid by an employer into employees' bank accounts, for standing order payments and for payments to suppliers.

Clearing House Automated Payments System (CHAPS)

3.26 The **Clearing House Automated Payments System** is a computerised system to enable **same-day** clearing, guaranteed if instructions are received before 2pm. There are several settlement banks, each with its own 'gateway' computer into the CHAPS system. Each bank transmits and receives payment instructions through its gateway computer. Messages, once accepted by CHAPS, are **irrevocable. Payment is certain.** The settlement banks can sell access to their CHAPS computer as a service to other banks (foreign banks) and corporate customers in any part of the country (provided that a telecommunication data link is set up). CHAPS could therefore be used by corporate treasurers with an office computer terminal, but the company must have high value (£5,000 plus) receipts and payments, and must want instantaneous clearing of transferred funds.

Activity 5.5

Outline the main services offered by banks to the small or medium-sized business.

Part A: Cash management

Key learning points

- The principal **legal relationships** which may exist between bank and customer are debtor/creditor, principal/agent, bailor/bailee and mortgagor/mortgagee. Under certain circumstances, there may be a special (or fiduciary) relationship between bank and customer, where the bank is in a position to exert 'undue influence' on the customer. The law requires banks to act 'in the utmost good faith' in such circumstances.

- A bank's **rights** are:
  o to charge reasonable commissions on services and interest on advances;
  o to use its customers' money in a way acceptable to the bank;
  o to be repaid on demand for overdrawn balances;
  o to expect customers to take reasonable care in drawing cheques;
  o to have a lien over cheques deposited to discharge a debt owed to the bank;
  o to be indemnified by the customer.

- A bank's **duties** are:
  o to honour a customer's cheques properly drawn;
  o to credit cash or collected cheques paid into a customer's account;
  o to repay a customer's funds on demand;
  o to comply with a customer's payment instructions by order or mandate;
  o to provide a statement of account to the customer;
  o to maintain confidentiality about a customer's affairs;
  o to advise a customer of any forgery affecting his account;
  o to exercise care and skill in carrying out its duties;
  o to provide reasonable notice upon closure of account.

- Banks provide a number of **clearing and money transmission services**, and are increasingly using IT.

- **Direct debits** are useful for companies which sell goods on credit, as they can collect amounts directly from customers' accounts.

Quick quiz

1 Banks act as a link between borrowers and savers. What is this role called?

2 What is a bailment?

3 A bank's loan to a customer is secured by a charge on the customer's house. Who is the mortgagor and who is the mortgagee?

4 What is a fiduciary relationship?

5 List: three rights and three duties of a banker.

6 What is the difference between a standing order and a direct debit?

7 What safeguards are given to customers with regard to direct debits?

Answers to quick quiz

1 Financial intermediation.

2 An arrangement in which one person (the bailor) delivers personal property to another person the *bailee*) as, for example, with a bank's safe deposit service.

3 The customer is the mortgagor and the bank is the mortagee.

4 A relationship based on trust in which the superior party must act in good faith.

5 Examples of rights include to levy reasonable charges and commissions; to use customer's money in a legal and morally acceptable way; to be repaid overdrawn balances on demand. Examples of duties include to honour customer's cheques; to receive customers' funds; to comply with customers' instructions; to provide statements in a reasonable time.

6   With a standing order, the customer authorises the bank to make a series of payments. With a direct debit, the creditor is authorised to tell the bank how much to debit to the customer's account.

7   Charges and payment dates must be notified to the payer 14 days in advance; the customer can cancel the direct debit at any time; the bank may refund amounts incorrectly debited directly to the customer; only approved organisations can operate a direct debit scheme.

Answers to activities

Answer 5.1

Look at all the factors involved in defining a bank given at the beginning of the chapter to help you decide.

Answer 5.2

(a)   Bailor (customer)/bailee.

(b)   Debtor/creditor (we don't know the account balance so we can't say which way round) and principal (customer)/agent.

(c)   Fiduciary relationship. The customer has the right to expect the bank to act in the utmost good faith in giving its advice.

Answer 5.3

(a)   Banks' *rights* accrue on the basis of accepted legal or moral justice. These can be summarised as:

   (i)   Making charges or commissions
   (ii)   Using customers' money
   (iii) Demanding repayment of overdrawn balances
   (iv)   Expecting a duty of care from customers to ensure that fraud is not facilitated
   (v)   Possessing lien (the right to retain the possession of someone else's property in discharge of a debt) over securities, and
   (vi)   expecting indemnification

(b)   The definition of a *duty* is a task or action which a person is bound to perform for moral or legal reasons. A bank has a number of duties which can be summarised under nine main headings.

   (i)   To honour customers' cheques
   (ii)   To receive customers' funds
   (iii) To make repayments on demand
   (iv)   To comply with customers' instructions
   (v)   To provide a statement
   (vi)   To keep information confidential
   (vii) To advise of forgery
   (viii) To maintain due care and skill
   (ix)   To give notice of closure of accounts

Answer 5.4

There are four recognised exceptions where a bank may disclose information about its customer's affairs.

(a)   *Where the bank is required by law to disclose.*

(b)   *Where there is a public duty to disclose.*

(c)   *Where the interest of the bank requires disclosure:* for example, when the bank sues a customer to recover what he owes.

(d)   *Where the customer has given express or implied consent:* for example, by inviting a third party to apply to the bank for a 'banker's reference' or when a business customer sends an employee to collect a bank statement. [The *Code of Banking Practice* suggests that banks should be required to obtain the customer's express consent before passing 'white' credit information (about customers who are not in default) to credit agencies, although it considers that it is in the bank's interest to give details of customers in default to credit reference agencies ('black' credit information), provided that 28 days

Part A: Cash management

notice of such action has been given to the customer. Under the Code, information will only be passed to associated or interconnected members of a banking group (such as insurance or credit card subsidiaries) at the customer's specific request. Note that banks are very careful with the wording of credit references to avoid legal action for negligence.]

Answer 5.5

Bank customers can be broadly divided into personal customers and business customers. Within this broad division are several sub-groups: for example in the business sector there are small businesses and large corporates.

Business customers can operate a high interest instant access account with rates linked to money market rates and with the interest paid gross. If they have surplus funds for 3 months or more they may want certificates of deposit (CDs) which they can turn into cash if they need to at a later date.

Money transmission services. Customers want to be able to pay money in, move their money around, withdraw money and make payments.

Efficient money transmission is very important to businesses and they will make use of all the regular payment services plus one or two specific products. A firm may use the BACS facilities to make large payments such as wages and salaries. Firms will make more extensive use of CHAPS and those retail businesses accepting credit cards will need the merchant services provided by the bank to facilitate payments.

The third group of products used is lending products, including overdrafts, budget accounts, loans, mortgages and credit cards.

Businesses naturally need finance and this may be provided through commercial loans, overdrafts and mortgages. The merchant banking division would be able to offer leasing and hire purchase too.

Firms involved in foreign trade would be interested in foreign services. Payments can be made overseas using SWIFT, currencies exchanged, finance provided in foreign currency, and bills of exchange discounted, collected or negotiated.

Chapter 6 Raising finance

Chapter topic list

1　Budgeting for borrowings
2　Banks' criteria for lending
3　Overdrafts
4　Medium and long-term loans
5　Leasing as a source of finance
6　Other forms of finance

Learning objectives

On completion of this chapter you will be able to:

	Performance criteria	Range statement
• understand bank overdrafts and loans and their terms and conditions	15.2	
• arrange overdraft and loan facilties in anticipation of requirements and on the most favourable terms available	15.2.1	
• observe the organisation's financial regulations and security procedures in respect of raising finances	15.2.4	

Part A: Cash management

1 BUDGETING FOR BORROWINGS

1.1 Although we have discussed in general terms the nature of the cash budget in earlier chapters, we need to examine in more detail the sources of finance for the business. A cash flow forecast, as we have seen, is an essential aid to maintaining **liquidity**. As far as borrowing is concerned, there are three aspects to the maintenance of liquidity.

(a) The firm needs enough money to function operationally, pay salaries, creditors and so on. Of course, eventually it will receive funds from debtors, but the length of the cash cycle can mean reliance on **overdraft finance** at times.

(b) The firm also needs to minimise the **risk** that some of its sources of finance will be removed from it.

(c) The firm also needs to provide against the **contingency** of any sudden movements in cash. Contingency measures can take the form of special arrangements with the bank, insurance policies and so on. A fire at the firm's premises for example is a contingency that must be insured against.

1.2 Some of these needs are more pressing than others.

(a) **Working capital**. Working capital is often financed by overdraft - this is a result of lagged payments and receipts as discussed earlier and the willingness of businesses to offer credit.

(b) **Long-term finance** is used for major investments. Capital expenditure is easier to put off than, say, wages in a crisis, but a long-term failure to invest can damage the business and reduce its capacity.

(c) Thirdly, the borrowing might be required to finance assets **overseas**, in which case the **currency** of the borrowing might be important.

KEY TERMS

Bank borrowing can be obtained in the following ways.

(a) **Overdraft facility**. A company, through its current account, can borrow money on a short-term basis up to a certain amount. Overdrafts are repayable on demand.

(b) **Term loan**. The customer borrows a fixed amount and pays it back with interest over a period or at the end of it.

(c) **Committed facility**. The bank undertakes to make a stipulated amount available to a borrower, on demand.

(d) A **revolving facility** is a facility that is renewed after a set period. Once the customer has repaid the amount, the customer can borrow again.

(e) **Uncommitted facility**. The bank, if it feels like it, can lend the borrower a specified sum. The only purpose of this is that all the paperwork has been done up front. The bank has no obligation to lend.

(f) **Banker's acceptance facilities**. This relates to bills of exchange, which are discussed in Chapter 7.

2 BANKS' CRITERIA FOR LENDING

2.1 Before we look at the types of lending on offer from banks, we first consider the principles of good lending (called the **canons of lending**) which guide a bank's decision about whether or not to lend money. This will enable you to present the right case in support of the request for money. The bank wishes to ensure that the borrower will be able to make the scheduled repayments, in full and within the required period of time.

2.2 If the bank makes a loan which is not repaid, a bank's profits suffer in a number of ways.

(a) The expected interest from the loan is not earned.
(b) The amount advanced and not recoverable is written off as a bad debt.
(c) The costs of administering the account are much increased.
(d) There are legal costs in chasing the debt.

Lending criteria

2.3 A bank's decision whether or not to lend will be based on the following factors. The mnemonic is **CAMPARI**.

Character of the customer
Ability to borrow and repay
Margin of profit
Purpose of the borrowing
Amount of the borrowing
Repayment terms
Insurance against the possibility of non-payment.

Character of the borrower

2.4 The **character of the borrower** can be established and judged.

(a) The borrower's **past record** with the bank is examined.
(b) **Personal interviews** are mainly used for business lending.
(c) Personal lending is more often **credit scored** (by computer).
(d) In the case of a company, the bank may look at **key ratios** which indicate the company's performance. We look at **ratio analysis** in Chapter 9.

Ability to borrow and repay

2.5 The bank will look at a business customer's **financial performance** as an indication of **future trends**. Hopefully the loan will be invested in such a way as to generate profit.

2.6 Re-investment of retained profits is a sign of the owner's faith in the business. (In other words, the owner does not take out all profits as dividends or drawings.) Revaluations (eg of buildings) would be viewed cautiously.

Bankers will look at financial statements for signs of: low/declining profitability; increased dependence on borrowing; overtrading; inadequate control over working capital; sudden provisions; delays.

See Chapter 9 for ratios that a bank can make use of, such as **gearing** and **interest cover**. Although a bank will use published accounts and management accounts, it will not lend **solely** on that basis: the viability of the loan itself will also be assessed.

Part A: Cash management

2.7 The bank should check whether the company has the **legal capacity** to borrow. A company might be prohibited by its Articles of Association (the legal instrument setting it up) from certain types of borrowing.

Margin of profit

2.8 Remember, banks want to lend money to make money! It is therefore important to consider the rate of interest at which they are prepared to lend.

   (a) **Fixed rates**: the lending policies of most banks stipulate different rates for different purposes to customers.

   (b) **Discretionary rates**: the bank will decide on the return which it requires from the lending. A loan for a risky venture (such as a new business) will typically be offered at a higher rate of interest, so as to compensate the bank for the risk it takes that the lending will not be repaid, than a loan perceived to be of low risk.

Purpose of the borrowing

2.9 The customer must specify the **purpose of the borrowing**. (Bankers do not lend money unless they know what it is going to be used for, other than with overdrafts.) Loans for certain purposes will normally not be granted at all. Some will be granted only on certain conditions.

   (a) **Illegal loans**. A loan which is for an illegal purpose, such as drug smuggling, obviously must be refused.

   (b) **Lending to finance working capital**. Lending money (usually on overdraft) to finance some of the working capital of a business is quite normal, but when the intended purpose of an advance is to finance a big increase in stock-holding or debtors, the bank will consider the liquidity of the business, and whether the customer will need more and more financial assistance from the bank as time goes on.

   (c) **Loans for new business ventures**. A loan to set up a new business venture should be viewed in the context that all new ventures are risky; while many do succeed a considerable number of them fail to make profits and survive.

Amount of the borrowing

2.10 The lending proposition must state exactly **how much** the customer wants to borrow. This might seem self-evident, but there are two important points to consider.

   (a) The banker will check that the customer is not asking for too much, or more than is needed for the particular purpose. This is especially important with requests for an overdraft facility. Clearly this consideration is linked in with the customer's wealth and ability to repay.

   (b) The banker checks that the customer has not asked for *less* than he or she really needs. Otherwise the bank may later have to lend more, purely to safeguard the original advance.

2.11 The bank's lending policy will indicate limits on the amount of certain loans; and the amount which must be paid 'up front' by the customer.

6: Raising finance

Repayment terms

2.12 The likelihood that the advance will be repaid is the most important requirement for a loan. A bank should not lend money to a person or business who has not got the resources to repay it with interest, even if it also has **security** for the loan. Security for the loan gives the lender the right to take certain assets if the borrower defaults. Security is only a **safety net**, to be called upon only in the event of an unfortunate and unexpected inability to repay.

2.13 The timescale for repayment is very important. Overdrafts are technically repayable **on demand** (though it is rare for a bank to insist on this without first having discussed a different timescale). Other loans might be payable in instalments, especially loans to acquire assets.

Insurance against the possibility of non-payment

2.14 If a bank *needs* to take **insurance** against the possibility that the loan will not be repaid (in the form of security, such as title deeds or a life policy) then the loan should not be made - as stated above, **security** is only a safety net. That said, many customers might take out payment protection insurance, for peace of mind. Such insurance can be very profitable for the lender!

Security for lending

2.15 The **security for a loan** should have the following characteristics.

(a) **Easy to take**. The bank will want to have, or to obtain easily, title to the secured property so that it may be sold and the loan repaid.

(b) **Easy to value**. The security should have an identifiable value which:

(i) Is stable or increasing, and
(ii) Fully covers the lending plus a margin

You can see this most clearly when banks and building societies refuse to lend more than, say, 95% of the value of a house. It has (at the time of lending) a margin of safety of 5% (which incidentally comprises the customer's stake in the purchase) and can expect this margin to increase if house prices rise. However in periods of falling house prices, such security is less certain.

(c) **Easy to realise**. The ideal security is one which can readily be sold and converted to cash. Banks prefer readily realisable security for the following reasons.

(i) The administrative costs are thereby kept to a minimum.

(ii) There is less danger of deterioration (say, of premises) between the time of default and that of realisation.

(iii) A quick pay-off reduces the length of time over which interest accrues on the unpaid advance.

2.16 **Security** may take the form of either a **fixed charge** or a **floating charge**.

(a) **Fixed charge**. Security would be related to a specific asset or group of assets, typically land and buildings. The company would be unable to dispose of the asset without providing a substitute asset for security, or without the lender's consent.

(b) **Floating charge**. With a floating charge on certain assets of the company (for example stocks and debtors), the lender's security in the event of a default of payment is whatever assets of the appropriate class the company then owns (provided that another

Part A: Cash management

lender does not have a prior charge on the assets). The company would be able, however, to dispose of its assets as it chose until a default took place. In the event of default, the lender would probably appoint a receiver to run the company rather than lay claim to a particular asset.

Personal guarantees

2.17 It is a principle of accounting practice that a business is a separate entity from the person who owns it for accounting purposes. It is also a principle of company law that in most cases the liability of shareholders for the debts of a company is limited to the capital they contributed. The debts of a business clearly include bank loans and overdrafts. However, in practice, it is often the case that, in its search for security, the bank will ensure that a business loan is supported by a **personal guarantee**. Such requirements are mainly a concern of smaller or medium sized businesses, largely run by their owners.

2.18 For example, Mr Badger is Managing Director of Setts Ltd. Setts Ltd has an overdraft arrangement with the bank, but Mr Badger has to give a personal guarantee of the overdraft. This means that if Setts Ltd fails to pay its debt *to the bank*, the bank can call in the guarantee, and Mr Badger will have to pay the debt out of his own resources.

Activity 6.1

Grog Ltd is a wholesaler, selling alcoholic beverages to shopkeepers for resale to the general public. Grog Ltd has a large warehouse at Ponders End, North London. Its cash cycle is such that most of the time it makes a cash surplus but recently a number of thefts and unexplained account movements have reduced the size of the surplus. The managing director, Lil Drop, has recently decided that she wants to move house. Rather than take out a mortgage, she suggests to the bank that the company borrows money, on overdraft, to buy her a house. She will personally guarantee the loan, although at the moment her only asset she can pledge as security is a port wine making firm in Portugal, which she inherited from a great aunt: other members of the family are suing her for a share.

What chance do you think Grog Ltd has of obtaining the loan?

Activity 6.2

Hymer Bigshott is the wealthy director of a major public company, which has business accounts at other branches of a bank at which you are employed. He does not have a personal account with your bank, but he approaches the bank with a banking proposition.

He has been reliably informed about an investment which promises to yield a very good return in the next few years, and he has the opportunity now to purchase £15,000 of shares, with tax advantages to himself.

He asks the bank for a personal loan of £15,000, the full amount of the investment cost. He would like to repay the loan as follows:

(a) Interest payments only until the end of the term of the loan
(b) Capital repayment in full at the end of the term

He would like the term of the loan to be 5 years. He would make the interest payments out of his regular income, and would repay the capital by selling off the shares after 5 years.

He will offer no security, other than the shares themselves. He also asks for a favourable rate of interest, only 2½% above the bank's base rate.

Explain what answer the bank will give to his proposition.

3 OVERDRAFTS

3.1 Where payments from a current account exceed income to the account for a temporary period, the bank finances the deficit by means of an **overdraft**. It is very much a form of **short-term lending**, available to both personal and business customers.

3.2 Factors associated with an overdraft are as follows.

(a) **Amount**. The debit amount should not exceed a certain limit agreed between the bank and the borrower, usually with reference to known income.

(b) **Margin**. Interest is charged on the amount overdrawn, usually as a margin over base rate. Interest is calculated on the daily amount overdrawn and is charged to the account quarterly. A fee may also be levied where the bank has agreed a large facility with the customer, even where this facility is not fully used.

(c) **Purpose**. Overdrafts are usually required to cover short-term deficits: for instance, many people run short at the end of each month before their salaries are paid in.

(d) **Repayment**. Overdrafts are technically repayable on demand and it is usual in the facility letter to make this plain to the customer.

(e) **Security**. Depending on the size of the facility open to the customer, security may be required by the bank.

(f) **Benefits**. The customer has a flexible means of short term borrowing; the bank has to accept the fluctuation in the account.

3.3 By providing an overdraft facility to a customer, the bank is committing itself to provide an overdraft to the customer whenever the customer wants it, up to the agreed limit. The bank will earn interest on the lending, but only to the extent that the customer uses the facility and goes into overdraft. If the customer does not go into overdraft, the bank cannot charge interest.

3.4 The bank will generally charge a **commitment fee** when a customer is granted an overdraft facility or an increase in his overdraft facility. This is a fee for granting an overdraft facility and agreeing to provide the customer with funds if and whenever he needs them.

Overdrafts and the operating cycle

3.5 Many businesses require their bank to provide financial assistance for normal trading over the **operating cycle**. To some extent, a business can - and should - put up finance to cover the needs of the operating cycle - ie the need to invest in stocks and debtors; and to some extent, trade creditors will provide financial support by granting credit. However, a bank might also provide financial support by allowing the business an overdraft facility.

3.6 For example, suppose that a business has the following operating cycle.

	£	£
Stocks and debtors		10,000
Bank overdraft	1,000	
Creditors	3,000	
		4,000
Working capital		6,000

It now buys stocks costing £2,500 for cash, using its overdraft. Working capital remains the same, £6,000, although the bank's financial stake has risen from £1,000 to £3,500.

Part A: Cash management

	£	£
Stocks and debtors		12,500
Bank overdraft	3,500	
Creditors	3,000	
	6,500	
Working capital		6,000

A bank overdraft provides support for normal trading finance. In this example, finance for normal trading rises from £(10,000 − 3,000) = £7,000 to £(12,500 − 3,000) = £9,500 and the bank's contribution rises from £1,000 out of £7,000 to £3,500 out of £9,500.

3.7 A feature of bank lending to support normal trading finance is that the amount of the overdraft required at any time will depend on the **cash flows of the business** - the timing of receipts and payments, seasonal variations in trade patterns and so on. An overdraft will increase in size if the customer writes more cheques, but will reduce in size when money is paid into the account. There should be times when there will be no overdraft at all, and the account is in credit for a while. In other words, the customer's account may well *swing* from overdraft into credit, back again into overdraft and again into credit, and so on. The account would then be a **swinging account**. The purpose of the overdraft is to bridge the gap between cash payments and cash receipts, which means that it must by its very nature be short-term in character.

3.8 When a business customer has an overdraft facility, and the account is always in overdraft, then it has a **solid core** (or **hard core**) instead of swing. For example, suppose that the account of Blunderbuss Ltd has the following record for the previous year.

Quarter to	*Average balance* £	*Range* £	£	*Debit turnover* £
31 March 19X5	40,000 debit	70,000 debit	- 20,000 debit	600,000
30 June 19X5	50,000 debit	80,000 debit	- 25,000 debit	500,000
30 September 19X5	75,000 debit	105,000 debit	- 50,000 debit	700,000
31 December 19X5	80,000 debit	110,000 debit	- 60,000 debit	550,000

These figures show that the account has been permanently in overdraft, and the hard core of the overdraft has been rising steeply over the course of the year (from a minimum overdraft of £20,000 in the first quarter to one of £60,000 in the fourth quarter).

3.9 If the hard core element of the overdraft appears to be becoming a long-term feature of the business, the bank might wish, after discussions with the customer, to convert the hard core of the overdraft into a medium-term loan, thus giving formal recognition to its more permanent nature. Otherwise annual reductions in the hard core of an overdraft would normally be a requirement of the bank.

The purpose of an advance for day-to-day trading

3.10 The purpose of a bank overdraft for normal day-to-day trading is to help with the financing of current assets. However, there are a number of different reasons why a business might need an overdraft facility. Only **some** of these reasons will be sound and acceptable to a bank.

3.11 Borrowing by a business will do one of two things:

(a) Increase the assets of the business, or
(b) Decrease its liabilities

6: Raising finance

Increasing business assets

3.12 If borrowing is to increase the business assets, a bank will first check whether the purpose is to acquire more **fixed assets** or more **current assets**. A customer might ask for an overdraft facility to help with day to day trading finance, when the *real* cause of his shortage of liquidity is really a decision to purchase a new fixed asset. There is nothing wrong with asking a bank for financial assistance with the purchase of fixed assets. But borrowing to purchase a fixed asset reduces the liquidity of the business, and might even make it illiquid.

Activity 6.3

The directors of Wrong Wreason Ltd have asked their bank for a £50,000 overdraft which they say will be used for normal trading operations. They present two balance sheets, one indicating the firm's position before the loan and one after. What do you think the bank's response will be?

WRONG WREASON LIMITED - BALANCE SHEET (BEFORE)

	£	£
Fixed assets		200,000
Current assets	120,000	
Current liabilities: trade creditors	60,000	
Working capital		60,000
		260,000
Share capital and reserves		260,000

WRONG WREASON LIMITED - BALANCE SHEET (AFTER)

	£	£	£
Fixed assets (200,000 + 50,000)			250,000
Current assets		120,000	
Current liabilities: bank overdraft	50,000		
trade creditors	60,000		
		110,000	
Working capital			10,000
			260,000
Share capital and reserves			260,000

3.13 An overdraft facility for **day-to-day trading** should therefore be:

(a) Either to increase total current assets
(b) Or to reduce other current liabilities

Increasing total current assets

3.14 A request for an overdraft facility to increase total current assets can be pinpointed more exactly, to a wish by the company:

(a) To increase its stock levels
(b) To increase its overall debtors
(c) To increase its overall sales turnover

3.15 The underlying guide to a bank's attitude to lending (in addition to avoiding risk) is whether the finance will be temporary (and 'swinging') or longer term. There might be a number of reasons for a business **increasing its stock levels** without increasing its total sales.

Part A: Cash management

(a) The business might have received a large, firm order from a customer, and must produce goods to order before the customer will pay for them. The need for finance is only **temporary**, and a bank overdraft would be suitable.

(b) The business might wish to build up stocks in anticipation of a seasonal peak demand. Again the business will need **temporary** finance to support the cost of the stocks, and again, an overdraft would be a suitable form of finance.

(c) The business might want to make a **speculative** purchase of stocks - for example to take advantage of an opportunity to purchase a consignment of raw materials at a favourable price. Provided that the 'speculative' nature of the stock build-up is not unacceptably risky, and provided that the build-up is **temporary**, an overdraft would again be a suitable form of finance.

(d) The business might be building up its stock levels **permanently**, without increasing its sales turnover. In such a situation, there would be a danger that some stocks are becoming **slow-moving or unsaleable** through deteriorating quality or obsolescence. A build-up of stock also implies a need for a review of finance facilities, and an overdraft may *not* be suitable.

3.16 Reasons for a business wanting to **increase its total debtors** without increasing its sales turnover might be:

(a) A loss of efficiency in the credit control, invoicing and debt collection procedures of the business, or

(b) The inability of existing customers to pay without being allowed more credit

In both cases, the bank will be cautious about agreeing to an increased overdraft facility. Delays in invoicing should be eliminated by the business; however, if more credit must be allowed to maintain sales, a bank might agree to an overdraft facility for this purpose.

3.17 When a business **increases its sales turnover**, it will almost certainly have to increase its investment in stocks and debtors. It will probably be able to obtain more credit from trade creditors, but the balance of the extra finance required will have to be provided out of extra proprietors' capital or other lending. A danger with business expansion is **overtrading**, and a bank will be wary of requests to support ambitious expansion schemes.

Using an overdraft to reduce other current liabilities

3.18 A bank might be asked to provide an overdraft facility to enable a business to pay its tax bills, or to reduce its volume of trade creditors. The payment of tax might be VAT (generally every quarter) or year end corporation tax. An overdraft facility to help a business to pay tax when it falls due is a 'legitimate' and acceptable purpose for an overdraft, although the bank might wish to know why the business had not set funds aside to pay the tax. A bank should be able to expect that the overdraft would soon be paid off out of profits from future trading.

3.19 An extension to an overdraft in order to pay trade creditors must be for the purpose of **reducing the overall average volume of trade creditors**, which in turn implies a significant change in the trade credit position of the business, all other things being equal. Why might such a reduction in total trade creditors be required?

(a) **To take advantage of attractive purchase discounts offered by suppliers for early settlement of debts.** This should be an acceptable purpose for an extra overdraft to a bank, because taking the discount would reduce the costs and so increase the profits of the business.

(b) **To pay creditors who are pressing for payment**. A bank will deal cautiously with such a request. It might be because the creditor is desperate for money. If the business **customer** is getting into difficulties, and is falling behind with paying his debts, a banker would take the view that agreeing to an increased overdraft would simply mean taking over debts that might one day never be paid, and so may not agree to such a proposition.

4 MEDIUM AND LONG-TERM LOANS

4.1 Interest payments on a loan are based on the full amount borrowed. The loan is repayable not later than the date agreed in the loan agreement; or at an earlier date if the borrower breaks a 'loan covenant'.

The uses of loans

4.2 The main advantage of lending on a loan account for the bank is that it makes monitoring and control of the advance much easier. The bank can see immediately when the customer is falling behind with his repayments, or struggling to make the payments. With overdraft lending, a customer's difficulties might be obscured for some time by the variety of transactions on his current account.

4.3 There are certain features about medium-term lending on loan account that make it different from lending on overdraft.

(a) The customer knows what he will be expected to pay back at regular intervals and the bank can also predict its future income with more certainty (depending on whether the interest rate is fixed or floating).

(b) Once the loan is agreed, the term of the loan must be adhered to, provided that the customer does not fall behind with his repayments. It is not repayable on demand by the bank.

(c) Because the bank will be committing its funds to a customer for a number of years, it may wish to insist on building certain written safeguards into the loan agreement, to prevent the customer from becoming over-extended with his borrowing during the course of the loan.

The term of the loan

4.4 The term of the loan will depend on four factors.

(a) The term of the loan, which should not exceed the **useful life of the asset** to be purchased, because the customer will presumably expect to repay the loan whilst he is still enjoying the use of the asset and any profits it might be earning.

(b) The **internal guidelines** of the individual bank.

(c) Government **regulations**, if any, on the maximum term for certain types of lending.

(d) **Negotiations** between customer and banker, which involve the opinion of the customer about what term of loan he would like, and the banker's judgement about what term he would be willing to offer.

Part A: Cash management

Loan repayment profiles

4.5 Loans can be repaid in three ways.

(a) **Bullet**. With a bullet repayment loan, the borrower does not repay any of the loan principal until the end of the loan period. The principal is then repaid in full. For example, if a five-year loan of £100,000 has a bullet repayment profile, the loan principal outstanding will be the full £100,000 to the end of the loan period.

(b) **Balloon**. With a balloon repayment loan, some of the loan principal is repaid during the term of the loan. At maturity, however, there is still a substantial proportion of loan principal outstanding, which is then repaid.

(c) **Amortising**. With an amortising loan, the loan principal is repaid gradually over the term of the loan. Loan repayments at regular intervals (usually every month, quarter or six months) consist of interest and a repayment of some of the principal. With the final loan payment, the principal outstanding falls to zero. Mortgage repayment loans operate on this principle.

Loan interest

4.6 The interest on a loan will either be paid back in fixed instalments with the capital as above; or calculated at the set rate at the end of the balance period so that the bulk of the interest is paid early on (as in a repayment mortgage) or equally throughout the loan.

4.7 The interest rate on a loan can be:

(a) **Fixed** throughout the period of the loan, or

(b) **Variable**, depending on interest rates obtainable in the money markets. Variable rates are usually arranged as a specified number of percentage points above either base rate or the **London Inter-Bank Offered Rate (LIBOR)**. For example, a variable rate loan may be offered at 3% above the 3 month LIBOR, subject to quarterly reviews.

4.8 In addition to the interest payable, a firm might have to pay an **arrangement fee** to the bank, for considering the loan application and so on; **legal costs**; **commitment fees** (for the bank agreeing to provide the money on demand).

Activity 6.4

Why do you think banks often charge higher rates of interest on overdrafts than on loans?

Loan covenants

4.10 Taking out a loan often entails certain obligations for the borrower over and above repaying the loan on demand. These obligations are called covenants.

(a) **Positive covenants** require a borrower to do something, for example: to provide the bank with its annual financial statements; to submit certificates signed by a director that the company is keeping to the loan agreement; to provide management accounts.

(b) **Negative or restrictive covenants** are promises by a borrower not to do something, eg the company pledges not to borrow more money until the current loan is repaid; or the company promises not to take over another company during the period of the loan.

(c) **Quantitative covenants** set limitations on the borrower's financial position. For example, the company might agree that its total borrowings shall not exceed 100% of shareholders' funds.

5 LEASING AS A SOURCE OF FINANCE

The nature of leasing

5.1 Rather than buying an asset outright, using either available cash resources or borrowed funds, a business may lease an asset. **Leasing** has become a popular source of finance in the UK. Leasing can be defined as a contract between lessor and lessee for hire of a specific asset selected from a manufacturer or vendor of such assets by the lessee. The lessor retains ownership of the asset. The lessee has possession and use of the asset on payment of specified rentals over a period.

5.2 Many lessors are financial intermediaries such as banks and insurance companies. The range of assets leased is wide, including office equipment and computers, cars and commercial vehicles, aircraft, ships and buildings.

Types of leasing

5.3 **Operating leases** are rental agreements between a lessor and a lessee whereby:

(a) The lessor supplies the equipment to the lessee

(b) The lessor is responsible for servicing and maintaining the leased equipment

(c) The period of the lease is fairly short, less than the expected economic life of the asset, so that at the end of one lease agreement, the lessor can either:

  (i) Lease the same equipment to someone else, and obtain a good rent for it, or
  (ii) Sell the equipment second-hand

5.4 **Finance leases** are lease agreements between the user of the leased asset (the lessee) and a provider of finance (the lessor) for most or all of the asset's expected useful life. Suppose that a company decides to obtain a company car and finance the acquisition by means of a finance lease. A car dealer will supply the car. A finance house will agree to act as lessor in a finance leasing arrangement, and so will purchase the car from the dealer and lease it to the company. The company will take possession of the car from the car dealer, and make regular payments (monthly, quarterly, six monthly or annually) to the finance house under the terms of the lease.

5.5 There are other important characteristics of a finance lease.

(a) The lessee is responsible for the upkeep, servicing and maintenance of the asset. The lessor is not involved in this at all.

(b) The lease has a primary period, which covers all or most of the useful economic life of the asset. At the end of this primary period, the lessor would not be able to lease the asset to someone else, because the asset would be worn out. The lessor must therefore ensure that the lease payments during the primary period pay for the full cost of the asset as well as providing the lessor with a suitable return on his investment.

(c) It is usual at the end of the primary period to allow the lessee to continue to lease the asset for an indefinite secondary period, in return for a very low nominal rent, sometimes called a 'peppercorn rent'. Alternatively, the lessee might be allowed to sell the asset on a lessor's behalf (since the lessor is the owner) and to keep most of the sale proceeds, paying only a small percentage (perhaps 10%) to the lessor.

5.6 Under some schemes, a lessor leases equipment to the lessee for most of the equipment's life, and at the end of the lease period sells the equipment himself, with none of the sale proceeds going to the lessee.

5.7 Returning to the example of the car lease, the primary period of the lease might be three years, with an agreement by the lessee to make three annual payments of £6,000 each. The lessee will be responsible for repairs and servicing, road tax, insurance and garaging. At the end of the primary period of the lease, the lessee might be given the option either to continue leasing the car at a nominal rent (perhaps £250 a year) or to sell the car and pay the lessor 10% of the proceeds.

5.8 A further type of leasing arrangement is **sale and leaseback**, an arrangement which is similar to mortgaging. A business which already owns an asset, for example a building or an item of equipment, agrees to sell the asset to a financial institution and to lease it back on terms specified in the agreement. The business has the benefit of the funds from the sale while retaining use of the asset, in return for regular payments to the financial institution.

Attractions of leasing

5.9 The following are attractions of finance or operating leases to the supplier of equipment, the **lessee** and the **lessor**.

(a) The supplier of the equipment is paid in full at the beginning. The equipment is sold to the lessor, and apart from obligations under guarantees or warranties, the supplier has no further financial concern about the asset.

(b) The lessor invests finance by purchasing assets from suppliers and makes a return out of the lease payments from the lessee. Provided that a lessor can find lessees willing to pay the amounts he wants to make his return, the lessor can make good profits. He will also get capital allowances on his purchase of the equipment.

(c) Leasing might be attractive to the lessee:

(i) if the lessee does not have enough cash to pay for the asset, and would have difficulty obtaining a bank loan to buy it, and so has to rent it in one way or another if he is to have the use of it at all; or

(ii) if finance leasing is cheaper than a bank loan. The cost of payments under a loan might exceed the cost of a lease.

The lessee may find the tax relief available advantageous.

5.10 **Operating leases** have these further advantages.

(a) The leased equipment does not have to be shown in the lessee's published balance sheet, and so the lessee's balance sheet shows no increase in its gearing ratio.

(b) The equipment is leased for a shorter period than its expected useful life. In the case of high-technology equipment, if the equipment becomes out of date before the end of its expected life, the lessee does not have to keep on using it, and it is the lessor who must bear the risk of having to sell obsolete equipment secondhand.

Hire purchase

5.11 Another form of credit finance with which leasing can be contrasted is **hire purchase**, which is a form of instalment credit. There are two basic forms of instalment credit, whereby an individual or business purchases goods on credit and pays for them by instalments.

    (a) **Lender credit** occurs when the buyer borrows money and uses the money to purchase goods outright.

    (b) **Vendor credit** occurs when the buyer obtains goods on credit and agrees to pay the vendor by instalments. Hire purchase is an example of vendor credit.

Hire purchase is similar to leasing, with the exception that ownership of the goods passes to the hire purchase customer on payment of the final credit instalment, whereas a lessee never becomes the owner of the goods. Hire purchase typically involves a finance house.

    (a) The supplier sells the goods to the finance house.
    (b) The supplier delivers the goods to the customer who will eventually purchase them.
    (c) The hire purchase arrangement exists between the finance house and the customer.

5.12 The finance house will nearly always insist that the hirer should pay a deposit towards the purchase price, perhaps as low as 10%, or as high as 33%. The size of the deposit will depend on the finance company's policy and its assessment of the hirer. This is in contrast to a finance lease, where the lessee might not be required to make any large initial payment.

5.13 Goods bought by businesses on hire purchase include company vehicles, plant and machinery, office equipment and farming machinery. Hire purchase arrangements for fleets of motor cars are quite common, and most car manufacturers have a link with a leading finance house so as to offer hire purchase credit whenever a car is bought.

5.14 When a company acquires a capital asset under a hire purchase agreement, it will eventually obtain full legal title to the asset. The HP payments consist partly of 'capital' payments towards the purchase of the asset, and partly of interest charges.

5.15 For example, if a company buys a car costing £10,000 under an HP agreement, the car supplier might provide HP finance over a three year period at an interest cost of 10%, and the HP payments might be, say, as follows.

	Capital element £	Interest element £	Total HP payment £
Year 0: down payment	2,540	0	2,540
Year 1	2,254	746	3,000
Year 2	2,479	521	3,000
Year 3	2,727	273	3,000
Total	10,000	1,540	11,540

5.16 The tax position on a hire purchase arrangement is as follows.

    (a) The buyer obtains whatever capital allowances are available, based on the capital element of the cost. Capital allowances on the full capital element of the cost can be used from the time the asset is acquired.

    (b) In addition, interest payments within the HP payments are an allowable expense against tax, spread over the term of the HP agreement.

    (c) Capital payments within the HP payments, however, are not allowable against tax.

Part A: Cash management

6 OTHER FORMS OF FINANCE

Syndicated loans

6.1 Large companies may use several banks to provide funds for borrowing.

   (a) A **syndicated loan** is a term loan to a group of borrowers from a group of banks. Each bank lends a certain proportion of the loan. A syndicated loan is arranged by a **lead bank**. There are a number of variants on syndication, to cover borrowing in foreign currencies and borrowing involving different financial instruments, but these are outside the scope of this Unit.

   (b) With **bilateral loans** the company negotiates with each bank individually.

Issuing securities

6.2 A security is a financial instrument such as shares or loan stocks, which a company may issue and which can be traded. Investors holding such **loan stocks** are creditors, who are entitled to interest. They are like IOUs which can be sold.

> **KEY TERMS**
>
> A **debentures** is, legally speaking, a written acknowledgement of a debt incurred by a company, though the term is generally used to describe loans that are secured on the company's assets.
>
> **Unsecured loan stock** are loans with no greater security than the company's ordinary creditors. However, conditions attached to the loan often place some restrictions upon the company's future borrowing powers.
>
> **Convertible loan stock** is loan stock which is convertible into ordinary shares.

6.3 Most loan stock is **redeemable** (ie will be repaid) at some future date but there are a few perpetual or irredeemable debentures in issue. The rate of interest is normally fixed, although a few companies have issued variable (or floating) rate stocks, with interest normally linked to movements in a well known market interest rate such as the 3-month London Inter-Bank Offered Rate (**LIBOR**).

Equities

6.4 **Equity capital** is sought for long-term investment by issuing shares. For the **company**, equity is the least risky form of finance, whereas for the investor it offers the highest return for the highest risk. The return to shareholders (dividends) is, in theory, at the discretion of the directors who can vary the dividend if they so choose.

Trade creditors

6.5 Rather than rely on the bank overdraft as a source of working capital, companies frequently use **trade creditors** as a source of short-term borrowing. The use of trade creditors as short-term borrowings has advantages from the borrower's point of view.

   (a) Many suppliers offer 60-day terms, with the possibility of a settlement discount for early payment.

6: Raising finance

(b) Whereas a firm has relationships with only a few banks, it has relationships with many suppliers, few of whom have the sort of clout that the bank has.

(c) Trade creditors have an interest in the commercial relationship.

6.6 That said, later in this Interactive Text, we look at the measures that creditors can take to enforce payment.

Not-for profit organisations

6.7 A **not-for-profit organisation**, such as a **charity,** may be able to call upon the following forms of external funding: government grants (eg job creation grants; development funding); charitable donations; bank loans.

Key learning points

- Companies often have to rely on **bank finance**, but it is important that the right type of finance is obtained.
- **Overdrafts** are subject to an agreed limit, and are repayable on demand. The customer has a flexible means of short term borrowing.
- An overdraft is best considered as support for normal working capital. A customer's account can be expected to swing between surplus and overdraft. Banks will look cautiously at overdrafts which are used in effect to purchase fixed assets, by leaving current assets of a company unchanged. An overdraft might be used to reduce trade creditors: the bank will want to know why.
- A **term loan** is drawn in full at the beginning of the loan period and repaid at a specified time or in defined instalments.
    - Term loans are offered with a variety of repayment schedules (eg bullet, balloon, amortising)
    - Often, the interest and capital repayments are predetermined.
    - The term of the loan will be determined by the useful life of the asset purchased, the guidelines of the bank, and the results of any negotiations.
- Other sources of finance (medium-term) include **hire purchase**, **finance leases** and **operating leases**.
- **Other types of lending** by banks include discounted bills, documentary credits and factoring.

Quick quiz

1. What is a term loan?
2. What factors will influence a banks' decision to lend?
3. What is a commitment fee?
4. What is meant by the term 'swinging account'?
5. How is the loan principal repaid in the case of a bullet repayment loan?
6. What is meant by an amortising loan?
7. With a finance lease, who is responsible for upkeep of the asset - the lessor or the lessee?
8. What is the difference between hire purchase (HP) and leasing?
9. What is a debenture?

Answers to quick quiz

1. A loan for a fixed amount for a specified period.

2. The character of the customer; ability to borrow and repay; margin of profit; purpose of the borrowing; amount; repayment terms; insurance against possible repayment.

3. A fee charged by a bank to increase an overdraft facility.

119

Part A: Cash management

4   An account which 'swings' between an overdraft and a credit balance from time to time.

5   At the end of the loan period.

6   A loan where the principal is repaid gradually over the term of the loan.

7   The lessee.

8   With HP, ownership of goods passes when the final instalment is paid; a lessee never becomes the owner of the goods.

9   A written acknowledgement of a debt incurred by a company, generally a loan that is secured on the company's assets.

Answers to activities

Answer 6.1

The banker will pour himself a glass of CAMPARI, as it were, and say no. Lil Grog can pledge no security, and the purpose of the loan is not for business reasons. Furthermore, Grog Ltd's ability to repay looks increasingly in doubt.

Answer 6.2

On the face of it, nearly everything is wrong with this banking proposition from the bank's viewpoint.

(a) The purpose of the advance is speculative.
(b) The borrower would be putting in no capital at all, and so the entire risk would be the bank's.
(c) The repayment terms - no capital repayment until the end of the term - are far from ideal!
(d) The 5 year term of the loan is rather long for personal lending (although not unacceptably long).
(e) There is no security.
(f) The interest rate offered is poor.

It is hard to see any case at all for agreeing to the advance. Yet this example is based on an actual situation in practice, where the banker agreed to the customer's proposition. His overriding considerations were the character and the connection of the borrower. The customer appeared to have considerable personal integrity, business experience and financial acumen; and a refusal to lend to the director of a major national company which had various accounts with the bank seemed to be inviting unnecessary bad will for the bank.

Answer 6.3

Although the directors might believe that they are asking the bank to help with financing their current assets, they are really asking for assistance with the purchase of a fixed asset, because the bank lending would leave the total current assets of the company unchanged, but will increase the current liabilities. Consequently, bank borrowing on overdraft to buy a fixed asset would reduce the working capital of Wrong Wreason Limited from £60,000 to £10,000. In contrast, borrowing £50,000 to finance extra current assets would have increased current assets from £120,000 to £170,000, and with current liabilities going from £60,000 to £110,000, total working capital would have remained unchanged at £60,000 and liquidity would arguably still be adequate.

Answer 6.4

A loan is for a fixed amount, repayable in a certain period. A customer's demand for overdraft credit is much more volatile; the bank has to keep the facility open, even though it is not being used all the time.

Chapter 7 Investing money

Chapter topic list

1. Budgeting for surpluses
2. Cash investments: bank and building society accounts
3. Marketable securities: prices and interest rates
4. Government securities
5. Local authority and other public sector stocks
6. Certificates of deposit
7. Bills of exchange
8. Other commercial stocks
9. Making investments

Learning objectives

On completion of this chapter you will be able to:

	Performance criteria	Range statement
• arrange the investment of surplus funds in marketable securities within defined financial authorisation limits	15.2.2	
• observe the organisation's financial regulations and security procedures in respect of the investment of funds	15.2.3	
• maintain adequate levels of liquidity in line with cash forecasts	15.2.5	
• know about types of marketable security, terms and conditions, and risks		15.2.1
• understand the management of risk and exposure	15.2	
• understand that in public sector organisations there are statutory and other regulations relating to the management of cash balances	15.2	

Part A: Cash management

1 BUDGETING FOR SURPLUSES

1.1 The previous chapter dealt with borrowing. However, many companies have temporary cash surpluses which they need to manage so as to earn a return. **Banks** provide one avenue for investment, but larger firms can invest in other forms of financial instrument in the money markets. Generally speaking, the greater the return offered, the riskier the investment.

1.2 A business's management of cash should be conducted with **liquidity**, **safety** and **profitability** as the three considerations in mind. Clearly a company which runs persistent cash surpluses has little problem with liquidity: it should be able to pay its debts as they fall due. Moreover the firm's expenses are lower as it does not have to pay overdraft charges. However, the other factors identified still apply. Cash is an asset of a business; if it is to be invested, and it must be invested profitably, the investment must be secure.

What should be done with a cash surplus?

1.3 In asking what a business should do with a cash surplus, we should ask why a business needs cash.

(a) Firstly, a business needs cash to meet its **regular commitments** of paying its creditors, its employees' wages, its taxes, its annual dividends to shareholders and so on. This reason for holding cash is what the economist J M Keynes called the **transactions motive**.

(b) Keynes identified the **precautionary motive** as a second motive for holding cash. This means that there is a need to maintain a 'buffer' of cash for **unforeseen contingencies**. In the context of a business, this buffer may be provided by an **overdraft facility**, which has the advantage that it will cost nothing until it is actually used.

1.4 Keynes identified a third motive for holding cash - the **speculative motive**. However, most businesses do not hold surplus cash as a speculative asset (eg in the hope that interest rates will rise).

1.5 The **cash management policy** of a business will reflect its **strategic position**. Thus, if a company is planning future major **fixed asset purchases**, or if it is planning to **acquire another business**, it will consider whether any cash surplus should be retained and invested in marketable securities until it is needed. Using surplus cash to make such future investments will reduce the extent to which it may need to borrow. If a company has no plans to grow or to invest, then surplus cash not required for transactions or precautionary purposes should be returned to shareholders.

1.6 Surplus cash may be returned to shareholders by:

(a) Increasing the usual level of the **annual dividends** which are paid

(b) Making a one-off **special dividend payment**. For example, National Power plc made such a payment to its shareholders in 1996, and BT plc made one during 1997

(c) Using the money to **buy back its own shares** from some of its shareholders. This will reduce the total number of shares in issue, and should therefore raise the level of earnings per share, assuming that the company can earn more on its ordinary activities than it would from investing its cash. Repurchase of a company's own shares, sometimes called a **share buy-back**, has become increasingly common, with for example many of the privatised regional electricity companies returning funds to their shareholders in this way in recent years.

7: Investing money

How much cash will a business require for transactions and precautionary purposes?

1.7 We noted earlier that a number of mathematical **cash management models** have been developed to try to establish a basis to the idea of an **optimal cash balance**, taking into account such variables as the interest rate a business might earn on surplus cash, the costs of making a transaction, and the variability of cash balances. Although many larger companies use such models in practice, for the medium-sized or smaller business, deciding how to manage cash balances is more often a matter left to the judgement and skill of the financial manager, in the light of the cashflow forecast. Once an 'optimal' cash balance is established, the remainder of a surplus should be invested in marketable securities.

ASSESSMENT ALERT

In a Unit 14 assessment, you could be asked to communicate cash management policies to managers in the organisation.

Activity 7.1

Thinking back to what we covered earlier in this Study Text, state what attributes an asset must possess in order to be considered liquid.

Liquidity

1.8 We need to consider what we mean by surplus. Take the following example.

1.9 **EXAMPLE: LIQUIDITY**

(a) Drif Ltd receives money every month from cash sales and from debtors for credit sales of £1,000. It makes payments, in the normal course of events of £800 a month. In January, the company uses an overdraft facility to buy a car for £4,000.

	Jan £	Feb £	March £
Brought forward	-	(3,800)	(3,600)
Receipts	1,000	1,000	1,000
Payments	(800)	(800)	(800)
Car	(4,000)	0	0
Overdrawn balance	(3,800)	(3,600)	(3,400)

The company has been left with a persistent overdraft, even though, in operating terms it makes a monthly surplus of £200.

(b) Guide Ltd on the other hand has monthly cash receipts of £1,200 and monthly cash payments of £1,050. The company sets up a special loan account: it borrows £5,000 to buy a car. This it pays off at the rate of £80 a month.

	Jan £	Feb £	March £
Brought forward	-	70	140
Receipts	1,200	1,200	1,200
Payments	(1,050)	(1,050)	(1,050)
Loan repayment	(80)	(80)	(80)
Operating surplus	70	140	210

Part A: Cash management

1.10 Which do you consider has the healthier finances? Clearly Drif Ltd produces an operating surplus (before the motor purchase) of £200 (£1,000 – £800) a month, which is more than Guide (£150, ie £1,200 – £1,050). Furthermore Guide Ltd has a much higher net debt, the loan for the car being £5,000 as opposed to £4,000.

1.11 Yet, in effect the financing arrangements each has chosen has turned the tables. Drif Ltd is relying on normal overdraft finance which will be **repayable on demand**. Its normal **operating surplus** of receipts from sales and debtors over payments to purchasers and creditors has been completely swamped by the long-term financing of a car.

1.12 On the other hand, Guide Ltd, by arranging a separate term loan, which is more secure from Guide Ltd's point of view, is able to run an **operating surplus** of £70 a month. It has effectively separated an operating surplus arising out of month to month business expenses from its cash requirements for capital investment (in the car), a **financial inflow**.

1.13 This goes to show the following.

(a) A 'surplus' can sometimes be created by the way in which financial information is presented.

(b) It is often necessary to distinguish different kinds of cash transaction (eg capital payments).

(c) Different types of debt have different risks for the company attached to them.

1.14 Cash surpluses may arise from **seasonal factors**, so that surpluses generated in good months are used to cover shortfalls later. In this case, the management of the business needs to ensure that the surpluses are big enough to cover the later deficits. The mere existence of a surplus in one or two months in a row is no guarantee of liquidity in the long term.

Safety

1.15 Considerations of **safety** are also important. Cash surpluses are rarely hoarded on the company's premises, where they can be stolen: but what should be done with them, in the short term?

(a) They are assets of the company, and do need to be looked after as well as any other asset.

(b) In time of inflation, money effectively falls in value.

(c) Any surplus must be kept secure: as depositors in the collapsed Bank of Credit and Commerce International must be painfully aware, some banks are not as secure as others. Some investments are riskier than others.

Profitability

1.16 We can approach this aspect by means of the Activity below.

Activity 7.2

Compare the following two situations. Steve and Andy are both in the car repair business. Both own equipment worth £4,000 and both owe £200 to creditors. Steve, however, has accumulated £1,000 in cash which is deposited in a non interest bearing current account at his bank. Andy has £100 in petty cash.

7: Investing money

	Steve £	Andy £
Fixed assets	4,000	4,000
Cash at bank	1,000	100
Creditors	(200)	(200)
Net assets	4,800	3,900
Profit for the year	1,200	1,200

Which would you say is the more profitable?

1.17 There is the other question about cash surpluses: what do you do with them, to make a profit? They are business assets like any other.

(a) In the long term, a company with an ever increasing cash balance can:

(i) Invest it in new business opportunities for profit
(ii) Return it to owners/shareholders by way of increased drawings/dividends

(b) In the short term, surplus funds need to be invested so that they can earn a return when they are not being used for any other purpose.

(i) A return can be earned perhaps by an earlier payment of business debts. The return is the 'interest' saved.

(ii) Otherwise, there is a variety of deposit accounts and financial instruments which can be used to earn a return on the cash surpluses until they are needed. These are discussed in the next section of this chapter.

Guidelines for investing

1.18 Any business will normally have a number of guidelines as to how the funds are invested. A firm will try and maximise the return for an **acceptable** level of risk. What is acceptable depends on the preferences of the firm in question.

1.19 Generally speaking, a higher **return** involves a higher **risk**. A risk of an investment is its propensity to fluctuate in value. Assume you have £100.

(a) **Shares**. The price of shares on the stock market can 'go down as well as up'. For example, on Day 1 you might have paid £100 for shares which on Day 2 had fallen in value to £90, whereas on Day 3 their value might have increased to £120.

(b) **Deposit**. The amount of money you deposit in your bank account will not change, ie £100 will still be £100, and there will be an amount of accrued interest.

1.20 To maintain liquidity it is often company policy that the surplus funds should be invested in financial instruments which are easily converted into cash; in effect, enough of the surplus funds should be invested to maintain liquidity.

1.21 There have been a number of reported incidents where a firm's corporate treasury department took too many risks with the firm's funds, investing them in risky financial instruments to gain a profit. These went sour, and firms have been left with high losses, arising solely out of treasury operations, with little relevance to the firm's main business.

1.22 Guidelines can cover issues such as the following.

(a) Surplus funds can only be invested in specified types of investment (eg no equity shares).

Part A: Cash management

(b) All investments must be convertible into cash within a set number of days.

(c) Investments should be ranked: surplus funds to be invested in higher risk instruments when only a sufficiency has been invested in lower risk items (so that there is always a cushion of safety).

(d) If a firm invests in certain financial instruments, a credit rating should be obtained. Credit rating agencies, discussed in a later chapter, issue gradings according to risk.

Legal restrictions on investments

1.23 The type of investments an organisation can make is restricted by law in certain special cases:

(a) Where public (ie taxpayers') money is invested by a **public sector** (central or local government) institution

(b) Where the money is invested by a company on behalf of personal investors in cases such as **pension schemes**

(c) In the case of **trusts** (as determined by the Trustee Investment Act)

1.24 A fairly recent example was the participation of Hammersmith and Fulham Council in an interest rate swap arrangement. A court ruled that this was *ultra vires:* outside the powers of the Council.

Activity 7.3

The treasurer of B plc has forecast that, over the next year, the company will generate cash flows in excess of its requirements.

List *four* possible reasons for such a surplus, and explain the circumstances under which the board of directors might decide to keep the excess in liquid form.

2 CASH INVESTMENTS: BANK AND BUILDING SOCIETY ACCOUNTS

2.1 Before looking at different forms of cash investment, let us be clear on the point about comparing rates of interest.

(a) If interest on an account is paid more frequently than annually, the annual return is higher than available from an account paying interest at the same rate at the end of each year. This is because some interest can be earned in the year on the interest which is paid before the end of the year.

(b) A comparison can be made between such accounts by calculating the **compound annual rate of interest** (CAR).

KEY TERM

If x% interest is paid n times per year, then the **compound annual rate of interest** is given by the following.

$$\text{CAR} = \left(\left(1 + \frac{x}{n}\right)^n - 1\right) \times 100$$

For example, account A offers 5.3% gross payable annually, while Account B offers 5.25% gross, payable quarterly. The CAR for B is:

$$\left(\left(1+\frac{0.0525}{4}\right)^4 - 1\right) \times 100$$
$$= 5.35\%$$

[handwritten annotations: £10 × 12% ; 11.20 ; or £10 × 1% × 12 months 11.26% ; ∴ $\left(1+\frac{0.12}{12}\right)^{12} - 1 \times 100 = 13.80\%$]

This is higher than the annual return on Account A.

2.2 Interest rates on cash investments may or may not vary, depending on the terms of the account.

High street bank deposits

2.3 All of the retail 'High Street' banks offer a wide range of different types of interest earning account, the variety having increased in recent years in competition with the building societies. The main clearers and many building societies also pay interest on some types of current account. Some of these may be of limited relevance to large corporations, but for sole traders and small businesses, high street bank offerings are important. Apart from current accounts, various alternative facilities are offered to depositors by the clearing banks.

2.4 For someone who wishes to invest a small sum for a short period, **deposit account** facilities are available from the banks. However, the interest rate is relatively low, and many of these accounts are now being discontinued.

2.5 **High interest deposit accounts and high interest cheque accounts**. If you have a larger amount of money to invest (typically a minimum of £500), you can place the money in a high interest account. Access is usually still immediate, but the rate of interest offered will be higher.

2.6 **Option deposits** are for predetermined periods of time ranging from 2 to 7 years with minimum deposits of (say) £2,500. The interest rates, which may be linked to base rates, reflect the longer term nature of the arrangement and the corresponding lack of withdrawal facilities before the expiry of the agreed term. For businesses, these might be of limited relevance.

2.7 **Other facilities**. All banks can offer special facilities for larger amounts. For example, with amounts of, say, over £50,000 it is usually possible to get fixed rate quotes for **money market deposits** for varying intervals from seven days up to eighteen months or longer. For still larger amounts it is possible to arrange for the money to be deposited with the bank's finance company at better rates than that available for normal deposits. In general, however, seven days remains the minimum unless the funds deposited are over £100,000 in which case overnight rates can be obtained. It is normal to find that rates increase with the term of the deposit.

Activity 7.4

Write notes on why a commercial bank might operate with various different rates of interest.

Part A: Cash management

Finance company deposits

2.8 All of the larger finance companies will accept cash deposits for varying periods from 7 days upwards. Most of them insist on a minimum deposit of (say) £10,000 but they do pay a higher rate of interest than for basic bank deposits. Finance companies are involved in lending of above average risk.

Activity 7.5

It was stated above that lending by finance companies is of above average risk. What sort of return would you expect by depositing money with a finance company?

The Banking Act 1987

2.9 The Banking Act 1987 created a single set of criteria for authorisation and a supervisory regime applicable to all banks and other deposit-taking bodies, collectively known as **authorised institutions**. These institutions must pass tests concerned with their solvency and the competence of their management. Authorised institutions subscribe to the **deposit protection scheme**, under which depositors are protected from the collapse of their institution up to the extent of 90% of the first £20,000 of their deposits. Needless to say, this affects small depositors and sole traders particularly.

Building societies deposits

2.10 The Building Societies Act 1986 allowed building societies to compete with banks over a much wider range of activities than they used to, and increasingly the societies are offering cheque or credit card facilities. Like the banks, the building societies have developed a wide range of different investment facilities, which are mainly for non-corporate investors.

3 MARKETABLE SECURITIES: PRICES AND INTEREST RATES

3.1 In the cash investments discussed in the previous section, the investor's initial capital is secure. He cannot get back less than he put in. Another common feature is that such investments are not marketable. Indeed, in many cases, the rules relating to the investment specifically prohibit transfer to another person except in closely defined circumstances, such as death. None of these conditions apply with **marketable securities**, such as gilts, bills and certificates of deposit. Such securities are bought and sold, and they earn interest. What determines their price?

Prices of fixed interest stocks

3.2 The price of marketable securities is affected by the following.

(a) The **interest rate** on a stock is normally fixed at the outset, but it may become more or less attractive when compared with the interest rates in the money markets as a whole. Let us take an example. Suppose that investors in the market expect a return of 6.47%.

(i) $2^1/_2$% Consolidated Stock was issued in 1883, paying £2.50 interest for every £100 of the stock's nominal value. However, the increased return means that:

$$\frac{£2.50}{\text{Price of £100 nominal}} = 6.47\% \therefore \text{the expected price is } £2.50/0.0647 = £38.64$$

Where general interest rates rise, the price of stocks will fall.

(ii) Where general interest rates fall, the price of stocks will rise. For example, if the market required a return of 6.47%, the price of £100 nominal of a non-redeemable 8% stock would be:

$$\frac{£8}{Price} = 6.47\% \therefore \text{the expected price is } £123.65.$$

Both these examples ignore two other features affecting prices of stocks.

(b) The **risk** associated with the payment of interest and the **eventual repayment of capital**. British Government securities are considered virtually risk free but other fixed interest stocks may not be.

(c) The **length of time to redemption** (or maturity, ie when the nominal sum will be repaid). Suppose the following market values were quoted on 25 March 1999:

9% Exchequer Stock 2002 £113.8029
9% Treasury Stock 2012 £142.6311

The two stocks have the same 'coupon' rates and are in other respects similar except for the redemption dates. (The fact that one is called 'Exchequer' stock and the other 'Treasury' stock is irrelevant: both are British Government stocks.) The first stock is due to be redeemed in 2002, whereas the second will not be redeemed until the years 2012. In both cases, as with all government securities except those that are index-linked, the stocks will be redeemed at their nominal value of £100. The closer a stock gets to its redemption date the closer will the price approach £100. This is known as the **pull to maturity**.

Yields on fixed interest stocks

3.3 The paragraphs below concentrate on gilts but the principles involved apply equally to any other fixed interest stocks including, for example, company debentures.

Interest yield

3.4 The yield for a particular gilt is an expression for the return on the stock if it was bought at the price ruling and held for one year.

> **KEY TERM**
>
> The **interest yield** (also known as the flat yield or running yield) is the interest or coupon rate expressed as a percentage of the market price.

Activity 7.6

On 19 March 1999 the market price of 9% Treasury Stock 2008 is £134.1742. What is the interest yield?

3.5 The interest yield in practice is influenced by two other factors.

(a) **Accrued interest.** The interest on 10% Treasury Stock 2003, is paid in two equal instalments on 8 March and 8 September each year. Thus, if an investor were to sell his stock on 1 June 1999, in the absence of any other rules he would be forgoing a considerable amount of interest which will be received on 8 September 1999 by the purchaser. **The price paid by the purchaser must reflect this amount of accrued interest**, and this type of calculation is tested in Activity 7.7 below.

(b) **Cum div (int)** and **Ex div (int)**. For administrative reasons, issuers of securities (eg the government) must close their books some time before the due date for the payment of interest or dividends so that they can prepare and send out the necessary interest or dividend warrants in time for them to reach the registered owner of the security before the due dates.

(i) Any person who buys stocks or shares **ex div** or **ex int** will not receive the next interest or dividend payment. This will be sent to the former owner. Government stocks normally go ex div about five weeks before the interest payment date. During that period the stock is quoted 'ex div'.

(ii) The purchaser of a stock **cum div** will receive the next interest or dividend payment.

Redemption yields

3.6 The interest yield takes no account of the fact that most Government stocks are redeemable (ie that their face value will be repaid) nor of the proximity of the redemption date although we have seen how the pull to maturity can affect the price. A more realistic measure of the overall return available from a stock is the **gross redemption yield**. This takes account of both the **interest payable until redemption** and the **redemption value**.

3.7 Yields are determined by market prices which in turn reflect the demand for particular stocks. Thus, if a yield is relatively low it can be concluded that the price is relatively high and that the demand for the stock is also relatively high. Conversely, a high yield means that a stock is relatively unpopular.

3.8 The major factors affecting choice are these.

(a) Whether the investor is looking for income or capital appreciation.

(b) The investor's tax position.

(c) The investor's attitude to the risk inherent in gilts resulting from changes in interest rates. It is important to remember that although the eventual repayment of a gilt is not in doubt, the market price may fluctuate widely between the date of purchase and the eventual redemption.

(d) Other aspects of the investor's business. The banks and building societies tend traditionally to concentrate on holding short-dated stocks (redeemable soon) whilst the insurance companies and pension funds which have long-term liabilities often match these with long-dated gilts (redeemable further in the future).

4 GOVERNMENT SECURITIES

KEY TERM

The term **gilts** is short for 'gilt-edged securities' and refers to marketable British Government securities. These stocks, although small in number (around 100), dominate the fixed interest market.

7: Investing money

4.1 The *Financial Times* classifies gilts as follows.

(a) Shorts - lives up to five years.

(b) Mediums - lives from five to fifteen years.

(c) Longs - lives of more than fifteen years.

(d) Undated stocks. Issued many years ago these are sometimes known as irredeemable or one-way option stocks. These include *War Loan 3½ %*, *Conversion Loan 3½ %*, *Consolidated Stock 2½ %*. Each has certain other peculiarities.

(e) Index-linked stocks.

By 'life' is meant the number of years before the issuer repays the principal amount. There is a slight complication in that the Stock Exchange defines shorts as being gilts due to be redeemed within *seven* years (rather than five) and mediums as being seven to fifteen years, but as long as you are familiar with both sets of definitions, you won't be caught out.

Fixed interest gilts

4.2 Most gilts are fixed interest, and their prices and yields follow the principles outlined in the previous Section. There are some other types of gilt, outlined below.

Index-linked stocks

4.3 There are various **index-linked Treasury stocks** in issue. The first such stock, 2% Treasury Stock 1996, was issued in March 1981.

4.4 Both the interest and the eventual redemption value are linked to inflation. The half yearly interest payment is calculated on the basis of the value of the Retail Prices Index eight months before the interest payment date. Thus if a 2% index-linked stock was issued 8 months after the index had stood at 100 and the index stood at 150 eight months before a particular interest payment date, then the interest payable would be:

$$\text{Interest payable} = \frac{1}{2} \times \frac{150}{100} \times 2\% = 1.5\%$$

The ½ is needed as the **interest is payable half-yearly**. The redemption value is similarly indexed.

4.5 From the above, it should be apparent that these gilts offer a guaranteed real return equal to the coupon rate. Many investment fund managers would have considered such a return highly satisfactory over the last fifteen years.

Convertible gilts

4.6 There are a small number of **convertible gilts**. These stocks are redeemable on the date shown or, at the holder's option, convertible into a new longer dated stock. Convertible stocks have gross redemption yields lower than those of similar unconvertible stocks with the same redemption date. The difference arises because of the terms of conversion which, so as to be attractive to investors, offer an enhanced yield from the new stock.

Gilt prices in the Financial Times

4.7 **Gilt prices** are to be found in the *Financial Times*. For all categories other than index-linked gilts, the information is presented as follows.

Part A: Cash management

Monday edition

Notes	Price (£)	Wk% +/-	Amount £m	Interest due	Last xd
Treas 10pc 2003	121.0801	0.4	2,506	Mr 8 Se 8	22.2

Tuesday to Saturday editions

	Yield				52 week	
Notes	Int	Red	Price (£)	+ or −	High	Low
Treas 10pc 2003	8.27	4.72	120.9273	+0.0600	123.52	115.44

4.8 The first (Monday) example (from Monday 22 March 1999) above shows that 10% Treasury Stock 2003 was quoted at £121.0801 at the close of business on the previous Friday, a change of +0.4% in the week. £2,506 million of the stock was in issue, and interest is due on 8 March and 8 September. The stock last went **ex-dividend** on 22 February. In other words, if you bought the stock after 22 February 1999, you will not receive the interest due on 8 March 1999. This interest will be paid to whoever held the stock up to 22 February.

4.9 The second (Tuesday to Saturday) example shows that the current price of the same stock was £120.9273 at the close of business on the previous day, which is £0.06 higher than the price on the day before. The highest quoted price in the 52 weeks to date is £123.52; the lowest is £115.44. The gross interest yield and the gross redemption yield are given in the first two columns.

Index-linked gilts

4.10 For **index-linked gilts**, it is not possible to calculate exact yields because, of course, the rate of inflation in the future is not known. As a rough guide to the yield of index-linked gilts, the *Financial Times* shows the prospective real redemption yield based on projected inflation at rates of 10% and 5%. The RPI base used for indexing (ie eight months prior to issue) is also shown, in brackets next to the title of the gilt.

Purchase, sale and issue of gilts

4.11 Gilt-edged stocks may be purchased or sold through the following media.

(a) Through a stockbroker, who deals on the stock exchange and who will receive commission

(b) Through a registered agent (normally a bank, solicitor or accountant) who will, in turn, act through a stockbroker. Both the agent and the broker will charge commission

(c) Through larger post offices acting as agents for the Bonds and Stock Office

Activity 7.7

Suppose that a client wishes to purchase 13¾% Treasury Stock 2000-03 with a nominal value of £5,000. The transaction is executed by a stockbroker, who charges commission of 0.8%, in March 2000 at a price of £111.5064. Accrued interest is 56 days. What will be the total cost?

4.12 Gilts can be dealt in any amount down to 1p. It is therefore quite possible to buy, say, £13,456.83 worth of a particular stock. This facility is often useful to investors who wish to round up an existing holding to some convenient figure. Similarly, it is quite possible to spend an exact amount on a particular stock. For example, an investor might ring up his stockbroker and ask him to buy £5,000 worth of the 13¾% Treasury Stock 2000-03 on the day referred to in the Activity above. The broker would then buy stock with a nominal value of:

$$£5,000 \times \frac{£100}{£111.5064} = £4,484.05$$

Activity 7.8

Your Managing Director tells you that he has read of how the British Government has issued a number of index-linked stocks. Explain to him the reasons why these stocks have been issued and the extent to which they are likely to be attractive to potential investors.

5 LOCAL AUTHORITY AND OTHER PUBLIC SECTOR STOCKS

5.1 We have already mentioned that it is possible for investors to deposit their money with local authorities. In addition to these investments there are a very large number of marketable local authority securities. Stocks may be issued by any size of authority from County Councils to Borough Councils.

5.2 Some of the **local authority stocks** are issued with long lives (eg 13½% Leeds 2006) and there are several one way option stocks and even a handful of genuinely irredeemable stocks. These stocks may, in most respects, be considered as being very similar to British Government Stocks. The main differences are as follows.

(a) The security of a local authority is not considered quite as good as that of the central government.

(b) The market in most of the stocks is much thinner (ie there are not many transactions) than for gilts, since the amounts involved are smaller and the stocks tend to be held by just a few institutions.

As a result of the points listed above, the yield on local authority stocks tends to be rather higher than on gilts.

5.3 Fewer than ten local authority stocks are listed in the *Financial Times*. This is only a fraction of the total number quoted on The Stock Exchange. Details of the others can be obtained from the Stock Exchange Daily Official List or from a stockbroker.

5.4 In addition to the longer term loan stocks, many local authorities issue bonds which are redeemable after one or two years. These are commonly known as **yearlings**.

Public board loans

5.5 There are a number of loans from other 'public' bodies from the UK and overseas such as the Agricultural Mortgage Corporation, the Port Authorities and organisations such as Investors in Industry. As with local government stocks, only a small proportion of those quoted on The Stock Exchange is listed in the *Financial Times*. The security of these bodies is not considered as good as either central or local government and consequently the return expected should be slightly higher.

6 CERTIFICATES OF DEPOSIT

> **KEY TERM**
>
> A **certificate of deposit (CD)** is a negotiable instrument in bearer form. In other words, it is a certificate which can be bought and sold. Title belongs to the holder and ownership is transferred by physical delivery from buyer to seller.

6.1 **Certificates of deposit (CDs)** are issued by an institution (bank or building society), certifying that a specified sum has been deposited with the issuing institution, to be repaid on a specific date. The term may be as short as seven days, or as long as five years. Most are for a term of six months. The minimum nominal amount is usually £50,000, or its foreign currency equivalent.

6.2 Since CDs are negotiable, if the holder of a CD cannot wait until the end of the term of the deposit and wants cash immediately, the CD can be sold. The certificates of deposit market is one of the London money markets, and there is no difficulty for a CD holder to sell if the wish to do so arises. The appeal of a CD is that it offers an attractive rate of interest, *and* can be easily sold. CDs are sold on the market at a discount which reflects prevailing interest rates.

6.3 The document recognises the obligation of the amount to the **bearer** (with or without interest) at a future date. The holder of a certificate is therefore entitled to the money on deposit, usually with **interest,** on the stated date. Payment is obtained by presenting the CD on the appropriate date to a recognised bank (which will in turn present the CD for payment to the bank or building society that issued it).

6.4 CDs have one major advantage over a money-market time deposit with the same bank or building society, namely **liquidity**. Unlike a money market deposit which cannot be terminated until it matures, CDs can be liquidated *at any time* at the prevailing market rate.

6.5 There is a large and active **secondary market** in bank and building society CDs. Hence they are an ideal way to invest funds in the short term while retaining the flexibility to convert into cash at short notice if the need arises. In return for this liquidity, the investor must accept a lower yield than a money market deposit would command. This is normally either $1/16$ of 1% (6.25 basis points or 0.0625%), or $1/8$ of 1% (12.5 basis points or 0.125%) below the equivalent rate for a large deposit with the same bank or building society.

6.6 Buyers of CDs in the secondary market are banks and other companies or institutions wishing to invest at money market rates. They are attracted by the competitive rates of interest on a CD, the comparatively low credit risk (of the bank failing to repay the deposit with interest at maturity) and the continuing liquidity of CDs, which can be resold any number of times before maturity.

7 BILLS OF EXCHANGE

7.1 A **bill of exchange** is similar to a cheque although, strictly speaking, a cheque is a type of bill of exchange.

> **KEY TERM**
>
> A **bill of exchange** is an unconditional order in writing from one person or company to another, requiring the person or company to whom it is addressed to pay a specified sum of money on demand (**sight bill**) or at a future date (**term bill** - usually from two weeks to six months).

7.2 Term bills of exchange have the following features.

   (a) Their duration or maturity may be from two weeks to six months.
   (b) They can be denominated in any currency.
   (c) They can be for a value of up to £500,000 per bill.

   Bills may be drawn in any currency.

Definitions

7.3 The **bill** is **drawn** on the company or person who is being ordered to pay. The **drawer** orders payment of the money. The **drawee** is the party who is to pay, and to whom the bill is addressed. The **payee** receives the funds. Let us take the example of a cheque. A (the drawer), writes out a cheque to B (the payee). The cheque instructs A's bank (the drawee), to pay B a sum of money. The drawee of a bill of exchange does not have to be a bank, and the payment date does not have to be immediate.

7.4 The **date of the bill** is normally the date when it is signed by the drawer. The place of drawing (which might be shown just as a town or city name) is also included. The amount payable must be shown in words and figures as in a cheque).

7.5 There are three ways of specifying the **due date for payment** of a term bill.

   (a) On a stated date
   (b) A stated period after sight (sighting date is when the drawee signs his acceptance of the bill)
   (c) A stated period after the date of the bill

7.6 A bill is an unconditional order to pay, and it will always include the word 'pay' and be phrased so as to make it clear that the order is unconditional. The bill must also specify the name of the payee, which might be the drawer ('Pay... to our order') or a third party ('Pay.... to XYZ Limited or order....').

7.7 For a term bill with a future payment date, the **drawee** signs his acceptance of the order to pay (**accepts the bill** in other words, agrees to pay) and returns the bill to the drawer or the drawer's bank. When a bill is accepted, it becomes an IOU or promise to pay. Acceptance of a term bill is by signature across the front of the bill. To an accepted bill there will also be added details of where the payment will be made. For example, an accepted bill might have wording such as 'Accepted payable at Epsilon Bank, Moorgate, London, for and on behalf of Omega Tango Limited' followed by the signature of an authorised person.

7.8 An example of an accepted bill is shown below. The name of the drawee is shown in the example on the bottom left-hand side.

Part A: Cash management

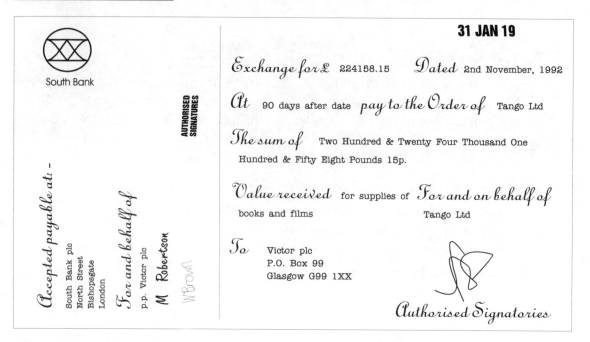

Discounting bills

7.9 As an IOU, an accepted bill of exchange is a form of debt. It is a **negotiable instrument**.

(a) The holder of the bill can hold on to the bill until maturity, then present it to the specified bank for payment.

(b) Alternatively, the bill holder can *sell* the bill before maturity, for an amount below its payment value (ie at a discount). A bill of exchange can be transferred by a simple endorsement. (An authorised signatory of the drawer or bill holder signs the back of the bill, and gives the bill to the buyer. The buyer, as the new bill holder, will claim payment at maturity, unless the bill is sold on again.)

7.10 The ability of a bill holder to sell the bill for a reasonable price depends on:

(a) The credit quality of the drawee, and

(b) The existence of a liquid secondary market in bills. Bills are used extensively as a short-term investment by banks and non-banking institutions, and larger financial institutions are able to operate a liquid two-way market for accepted term bills.

7.11 The buyer of a bill expects to make a profit by purchasing the bill at a discount to its face value and then either receiving full payment at maturity on presenting the bill for payment, or reselling the bill before maturity. The profit from buying a bill therefore represents an **interest yield** on a short-term investment (to maturity of the bill). The seller obtains immediate cash from the buyer of the bill, but in effect is borrowing short-term funds, with the interest rate for borrowing built into the discount price.

7.12 Bills of exchange are also used extensively to finance domestic and international trade, because they are tradeable instruments for short-term credit. There are two main types of sterling-denominated bills of exchange.

(a) **Trade bills** are bills drawn by one non-bank company on another company, typically demanding payment for a trade debt. The ability of the drawer (bill holder) to discount a trade bill before maturity (ie resell the bill at a discount) depends on the financial status of the two companies concerned. Institutions will only buy the 'finest' trade bills, where both companies have a high credit standing.

(b) **Bank bills** are bills of exchange drawn and payable by a bank. The most common form of bank bill is a **banker's acceptance**, whereby a bank accepts a bill on behalf of a customer, and promises to pay the bill at maturity.

7.13 Money market instruments are traded on either an interest rate basis or a discount basis.

(a) When an **interest rate** basis applies, a principal sum is lent and the borrower repays the principal plus interest at maturity. The interest rate is specified and applied to the principal amount for the term of the loan to calculate the amount of interest payable. Bank loans are made on this basis.

(b) When a **discount basis** applies, a specified sum is payable at maturity to the holder of a money market instrument. If the instrument is purchased before maturity, the price will be less than the amount payable at maturity. For example, a bill of exchange for £50,000 payable in six months' time might be discounted (sold) for £47,500.

7.14 The **size of the discount** will reflect the interest rate that the buyer of the instrument wishes to receive, and the term to the instrument's maturity.

8 OTHER COMMERCIAL STOCKS

8.1 **Bond** is a term given to any fixed interest (mostly) security, whether it be issued by the government, a company, a bank or other institution. (Gilts are therefore **UK government bonds**.) Businesses also issue bonds. They are usually for the long term. They may or may not be secured.

8.2 **Commercial paper (CP)** is the term for certificates **issued by a company**, promising to pay a fixed sum to the person bearing the note on a specified date. Like a gilt, CP is traded often at a discount reflecting the yield required. It is a type of promissory note, and companies find them useful for short term borrowing (usually 3 months), and is unsecured. It is therefore risky. Although formal **credit ratings** are not required in some countries, they do help investors make rational choices: a firm's CP is therefore given credit rating by third party agencies to assess its risk. Large companies might therefore restrict investment in CP.

8.3 **Debenture stocks** are issued in return for loans **secured on a particular asset of the business**. The factory, for example, may be offered as **security**. The loan is for the long term. Debenture holders take priority over other creditors when a business is wound-up. They can force a liquidation.

8.4 **Permanent interest bearing shares (PIBS)** are a type of security specially created to enable **building societies** to raise funds while improving their capital ratios. PIBS are quoted on the London Stock Exchange and the market totals about £1 billion.

(a) An element of risk arises from the fact that PIBS are irredeemable and subordinated to all other creditors and shareholders of the building society. Furthermore, PIBS do not qualify for compensation under the Building Society Investor Protection Fund. They bear a fixed rate of interest; however, the society must waive payment of interest if such payment would bring the society's capital adequacy below the required level.

(b) Dealings in PIBS must be in specified multiples. Although some issues have multiples as low as £1,000, others must be purchased in multiples of £50,000, making them unsuitable for the smaller investor. Dealings are transacted at the price quoted plus or minus daily accrued interest. Settlement is after seven days and brokers usually charge the same commission as for gilts.

9 MAKING INVESTMENTS

Risk and exposure

9.1 All investments possess some degree of **risk**. In some cases this may be very small indeed.

(a) Those **investments with the lowest risk** are, perhaps, fixed interest National Savings plans. Any chance that the British government might default on the payment of interest or capital is exceedingly remote. For all practical purposes, such investments are risk-free in money terms. There is, however, a real risk that both income and capital values may be eroded by inflation.

(b) At the other extreme many forms of investment are **highly speculative**. Indeed some tactics such as selling shares you do not own, have a theoretically **unlimited downside potential**.

9.2 Risk may be considered in terms of its effect on income, capital or both.

(a) **Income only**: for *most* cash investments there is virtually no risk that the *capital* invested will not be repaid. Also while there may be little doubt that the interest will be paid, those cash investments which carry a variable rate of interest also carry the risk that the rate will fall in line with conditions prevailing in the market.

(b) **Capital only**: with an investment in gilts or other 'undoubted' marketable fixed interest stocks, there is always a risk of a capital loss if prices fall, even though the payment of interest may be considered completely secure.

(c) **Capital and income**: for many investments both income and capital are at risk. Often a loss of income will precede a loss of capital. A company may reduce its ordinary share dividend, precipitating a fall in the share price.

9.3 Risk may be caused by general factors, or by factors specific to an individual security or sector.

(a) **General factors**. All investments are affected, to some extent, by changes in the political and economic climate. In October 1987 all major stockmarkets fell dramatically, apparently taking their cue from one another.

(b) **Inflation**. A fall in the value of money may affect both income and capital. Cash and other non-equity investments are particularly susceptible, although the high yield may provide some compensation.

(c) **Special factors**. The results of an individual company will be affected not only by general economic conditions but also by:

(i) Its type of products or services
(ii) Its competitive position within the industry
(iii) Management factors

Systematic and unsystematic risk

9.4 The **systematic risk** of a security is that part of its total risk stemming from those changes in the general political and economic climate which affect all securities.

Unsystematic risk is that part of the total risk caused by factors which do not affect all securities and may affect just one security (such as incorrect decisions made by a company's management) or one sector (such as falls in tobacco sales following an increase in excise duties).

The relationship between risk and return

9.5 The return expected by an investor will depend on the level of risk. The higher the risk, the higher the required return. This is illustrated in the diagram below.

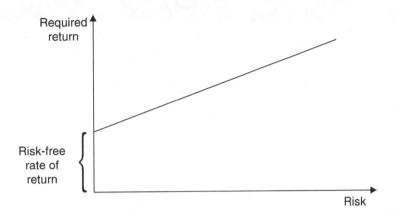

9.6 Marketable UK securities can be ranked in order of increasing risk and increasing expected return.

- Government securities
- Local authority stocks
- Other 'public' corporation stocks
- Company mortgage debentures
- Other secured loans
- Unsecured loans
- Convertible loan stocks
- Preference shares
- Equities

Low risk

High risk

9.7 The riskiness of CDs and bills of exchange varies with the **creditworthiness of the issuers**. They are riskier than government (and probably local government) securities, but less risky than shares.

9.8 **What combination of risk and return is appropriate?** Given that an investor is faced with a range of investments with differing risk/return combinations, what sort of investment should he choose? This is very difficult question to answer. Whilst it is safe to assume that most investors are risk-averse (they prefer less risk to more risk, given the same return), the intensity of that aversion varies between individuals. Some are quite happy to take a bit of a gamble in the hope of achieving a higher return. Others require a degree of safety. They are happy to accept a relatively low return.

Diversification and holding a portfolio

9.9 Holding more than one investment always carries less risk than holding only one. If only one investment is held, the investor could lose a lot if this one investment fails.

9.10 The extent to which risk can be reduced will depend on the relationship which exists between the different returns. The process of reducing risk by increasing the number of separate investments in a portfolio is known as **diversification**.

Part A: Cash management

ASSESSMENT ALERT

You need only be aware of the *reason* for having a portfolio, not of the details of how you would manage an investment portfolio.

Portfolio example

9.11 An investor is trying to decide between investing £10,000 in security A alone or £5,000 in each of security B and security C. In each case the returns from the securities will be:

Good result 15%
Bad result 5%

'Returns' in this context are a combination of income and capital gains.

Let us consider the choice between A on the one hand and B plus C on the other under three different situations.

(a) Where the returns from B and C have perfect positive correlation, this means that either *both* will have good results or *both* will have bad results.

Condition	Return from A		Returns from B and C	
Perfect positive	Good	£1,500	Both good	£1,500
correlation	Bad	£500	Both bad	£500

(b) Where the returns from B and C are *independent* of each other, B and C may both have good results or they may both have bad results or one may be good and the other bad. In this situation the combination of B plus C is the same as A alone.

Condition	Return from A		Returns from B and C	
Independence	Good	£1,500	Both good	£1,500
	Bad	£500	B good, C bad	£1,000
			C good, B bad	£1,000
			Both bad	£500

(c) Where the returns from B and C have *perfect negative correlation*, this means that if one is good the other is certain to be bad. In this case, the risk has been reduced because there is now a chance of getting a 'middle of the road' return of £1,000.

Condition	Return from A		Returns from B and C	
Perfect negative	Good	£1,500	B good, C bad	£1,000
correlation	Bad	£500	C good, B bad	£1,000

Now we see that the cash return from B and C is certain to be £1,000. The risk has been eliminated altogether.

9.12 This example is rather theoretical. The important point is that risk can be reduced by investing in securities where returns are *not* perfectly positively correlated. While it is not usually possible to find investments whose returns have perfect negative correlation, some degree of negative correlation is often possible.

Choosing investment instruments

9.13 Suppose that a company has prepared a forecast of its sterling cash flows as follows.

Date	Cash in £'000	Cash out £'000	Cash balance £'000
Week 1			
Start of week			50
Day 1	1,000	100	950
Day 2	850	300	1,500
Day 3	600	500	1,600
Day 4	1,200	1,600	1,200
Day 5	1,500	600	2,100
Week 2	6,000	4,000	4,100
Week 3	5,000	5,000	4,100
Week 4	5,000	5,100	4,000

The finance director has decided to invest the company's cash surpluses in the money markets.

9.14 The company's cash forecast will extend beyond Week 4, and if the finance director is reasonably confident that the minimum surplus for at least three months from Day 2 of Week 1 will be £1,200,000, he or she might decide to invest this amount in a money market instrument, such as three-month CDs. The balance of surplus funds in Week 1 might be held on deposit with a bank at the most favourable rate obtainable for money at call.

9.15 From Day 5 of Week 1, the finance director can review the cash situation again, in more detail for Week 2 and beyond, with a view to making further investment decisions for the cash surplus currently expected to build up.

Interest yield and risk

9.16 A company's finance director or treasurer must decide on a **target interest rate yield** for investments. This will depend largely on the anticipated level of market interest rates, but also on the skills of the company's dealers in extracting a premium rate from its counterparty banks. One element of skill or judgement is to predict the likely movement in interest rates. The directors must decide what is an acceptable level of risk.

(a) If interest rates are expected to rise in the near future, a company might prefer to hold all surplus cash temporarily on short-term deposit, and invest in longer-term money market instruments (eg three-month CDs), only after allowing time for interest rates to rise, with the aim of profiting from the higher interest yields that would then be obtainable.

(b) If rates are expected to fall, a company is more likely to invest earlier for fixed terms of several months, rather than to invest in shorter-term instruments or deposits.

Making an investment at the best time, even during the course of a single day, can earn a company substantial profits.

Activity 7.9

Your supervisor is unclear about the risks involved in holding each of: ordinary shares in UK quoted companies; bank deposit accounts; redeemable British Government stocks. Draft a note to her, describing the relative risks and suggesting how these risks may be minimised.

Part A: Cash management

Dealing direct with market-making banks

9.17 Companies with surplus cash wishing to invest short-term in the money markets can deal directly or indirectly through a broker or their bank. Large companies with substantial cash surpluses have the ability to speak directly to the main dealing centres of banks, either to make a deposit at a negotiable interest yield or to purchase selected money market instruments (eg bills, CDs).

Buying and selling marketable securities through brokers

9.18 For most companies buying gilts, shares and so on is effected through specialist firms of intermediaries. These go by the generic name of brokers, and in practice, these brokers buy and sell on their clients' behalf in the various investment markets that are available.

9.19 There is no need to go into detail, but the procedure for Stock Exchange investments will be as follows.

(a) The client contacts the broker with a specific instruction. The Treasury department may have surplus funds it needs to invest. Sometimes, it might have a definite idea as to the type of investment it wishes to make: at other times the broker will research the market and offer a price.

(b) The broker will send a contract note, once the transaction has been completed, and the date at which settlement must be made. The Stock Exchange has introduced 'rolling settlement', whereby settlement normally takes place a specified number of days (normally 10) after the transaction.

Dealing through money market brokers

9.20 The **money market brokers** in London have access to a pool of banks far greater than a small company's dealing operation could achieve, and cover virtually all active banks. They can be useful to smaller companies because they are prepared to place smaller sums than could be fed into the money markets directly through banks (as little as £50,000).

Dealing guidelines

9.21 Before telephoning a bank to ask for an interest rate, it is a good idea to calculate the financial impact of each $1/8\%$ or $1/16\%$ on the planned transaction. For example, an additional $1/16\%$ on a £10 million investment for one year equates to £6,250 - a significant amount. An additional $1/16\%$ on a £1 million overnight deposit produces only £1.71 of extra interest, and it is not worth spending time trying to extract such a small sum from a bank by insisting on a higher yield.

9.22 When a transaction is agreed by telephone, have a calculator ready, in order to agree the amount of interest receivable or payable. The interest figure verifies three elements in the transaction: the **amount invested**; the **interest rate**; and the **term of the loan**.

9.23 A company planning an investment should be comfortable with the **additional risks** associated with the higher yields on offer from any investment that might seem attractive. Equally important is to **spread the investment risk** over a number of different banks or instruments. This was a lesson from the BCCI collapse for those local authorities (such as the Western Isles of Scotland) that had invested a large proportion of their surplus funds (tax receipts) with the bank.

7: Investing money

9.24 **Smaller companies** that make money market investments through their local bank, or their bank liaison officer, can use many of the same dealing tips. For them, however, it is relatively difficult to obtain a competitive interest yield from their bank, and to access up-to-the-minute money market rates. These companies should discuss with their bank to check that the interest rate is as close to market levels (LIBID/LIBOR or base rate) as possible. Performance can then be monitored against market rates, either LIBOR (as quoted in the financial press) or the bank's base rates.

9.26 Companies can shop around for alternative investment opportunities with other banks, building societies and, if the surplus funds run into millions, with authorised money market brokers.

Safe custody

9.27 Purchased investments, with a few exceptions, can require **safe custody**. This is very important for bearer securities such as Treasury bills, bills of exchange and eurobonds, for which physical possession is taken as evidence of ownership. Safe custody is also required for certificates of deposit (but these can be stored at the company's commercial bank) and for commercial paper, but this will usually be warehoused, free of charge, with the bank selling the commercial paper.

Key learning points

- A company has a variety of opportunities for using its **cash surpluses**, but the choice of obtaining a return is determined by considerations of **profitability**, **liquidity** and **safety**.
- Surplus funds can be deposited in **interest bearing accounts** offered by banks, finance houses or building societies. Generally speaking: these are for a fixed period of time; withdrawal may not be permitted, or may result in a penalty; the principal does not decline in monetary value.
- **Securities** (ie financial instruments) can be bought or sold, and in London the markets in the main stocks are very liquid.
- The **yield** (profitability) of a money market instrument depends on: its face value; the interest rate offered; the period of time before it is redeemed (ie converted into cash) by the issuer.
- **Gilts** are securities issued by the UK government. Other fixed interest marketable securities included **local authority bonds**, and **corporate debt**.
- **Commercial paper** and **debenture stock** are debt instruments issued by companies: commercial paper is unsecured.
- A **certificate of deposit** is a certificate indicating that a sum of money has been deposited with a bank and will be repaid at a later date. As CDs can be bought and sold, they are a liquid type of investment.
- A **bill of exchange** is like a cheque, only it is not drawn on a bank. It orders the drawee to pay money.
- The relative attractiveness of investing in any of these securities derives from their **return** and the **risk**. **Diversification** across a range of separate investments can reduce risk for the investor.
- The organisation's **procedures and guidelines** need to be followed when making investments, taking into account any legal restrictions.

Quick quiz

1. What sort of investment opportunities are offered by high street banks?
2. What are gilts?
3. How can gilts be bought and sold?
4. What is meant by a yearling?

Part A: Cash management

5 What is the advantage of a CD over a time deposit?
6 Define a bill of exchange.
7 What factors affect the riskiness of investments?
8 Local authority stocks are considered riskier than equities. True or false?

Answers to quick quiz

1 Deposit accounts, high interest cheque and deposit accounts, regular income accounts, option deposits, money market deposits.

2 Marketable British Government securities.

3 Through a stockbroker, a registered agent or at post offices (through the National Savings Stock Register).

4 Local authority bonds redeemable after one or two years.

5 Liquidity: a CD can be liquidated at any time at the prevailing market rate.

6 An unconditional order in writing from one person or company to another, requiring the person or company to whom it is addressed to pay a specified sum of money on demand or at a future date.

7 (a) Market sentiment about the general political and economic climate
  (b) The rate of inflation, and the future outlook for inflation
  (c) Factors relating to the products, competitive position and management of the enterprise

8 False.

Answers to activities

Answer 7.1

The attributes that an asset must possess in order to be considered liquid are as follows.

(a) The asset must be capable of being transformed into a means of making payments quickly. Payments are made with notes and coin or by drawing on deposits in current bank accounts. There are degrees of liquidity, depending on the speed with which the asset can be transformed into cash or a current account deposit. The most liquid assets are cash itself and a current account deposit; time deposits with seven days' notice of withdrawal are slightly less liquid; and longer term deposits are less liquid still.

(b) The asset must also be convertible into a means of payment in a short time without the loss of (nominal) value. For example, if an asset with a nominal value of £100 can be turned into cash immediately (perhaps by selling it) but would realise only, say, £98, there would have been a loss of capital value of £2.

If the asset can be transformed without the loss of capital value, but at the expense of foregoing some interest on the asset, the asset would still be considered liquid.

Answer 7.2

(a) Both obviously have made the same amount of profit in the year in question. In absolute terms they are equal.

(b) However, if we examine more closely, we find that the relative performance of Steve and Andy differs.

	Steve	Andy
Profit	£1,200	£1,200
Net assets	£4,800	£3,900
%	25%	30.7%

In other words, Andy is making the same amount out of more limited resources. Steve could have easily increased his profit if he had invested his spare cash and earned interest on it.

Answer 7.3

Surplus cash flows will be earned by a company that is trading profitably and does not have high capital expenditures or other outlays to use up the cash inflows. Four possible reasons for a cash surplus are:

(a) Higher income from sales, due to an increase in sales turnover
(b) Lower costs, due perhaps to a cost-cutting exercise or improved productivity
(c) Lower capital expenditure, perhaps because of an absence of profitable new investment options
(d) Income from selling off parts of the business

The board of directors might keep the surplus in liquid form:

(a) To benefit from high interest rates that might be available from bank deposits, when returns on re-investment in the company appear to be lower
(b) To have cash available should a strategic opportunity arise, perhaps for the takeover of another company in which cash consideration might be needed
(c) To buy back shares from shareholders
(d) To pay an increased dividend to shareholders at some time in the future

Answer 7.4

A commercial bank operates with a widely varied pattern of interest rates for the following reasons.

(a) Banks will lend money at a lower rate of interest to lower-risk customers. This is apparent in short-term lending, where very low interest rates are charged on lending in the interbank market to leading banks, whereas higher interest rates are charged on similar short-term lending to even large and well-established companies. Higher interest rates will also be charged on personal loans to customers in a higher risk category.

(b) Interest rates vary with the duration of the loan or deposit. Saving schemes requiring some notice of withdrawal will attract a higher yield than an ordinary deposit account. With an ordinary current account, where customers can withdraw funds on demand, no interest at all is paid.

(c) Banks' interest rates vary with the size of loans and deposits. Generally, a lower interest rate will be charged for larger 'wholesale' loans and a higher interest rate offered for larger 'wholesale' deposits.

(d) The need to make a profit on re-lending is clearly evident in the banks' rate of interest. For example, retail loans to customers will be at an interest rate higher than the bank's base rate, whereas low or nil interest is paid on current accounts, and the rate paid on deposit accounts is less than the bank's base rate.

(e) A substantial proportion of a bank's business is conducted in foreign currencies. The interest rate in which a bank deals, in the eurocurrency markets, will vary according to the currency, and the general level of interest rates in that country.

Answer 7.5

A slightly higher return than offered by a bank: risk and reward are related.

Answer 7.6

$$\text{Interest yield} = \frac{\text{Coupon rate}}{\text{Market price}} \times 100\% = \frac{9}{134.1742} \times 100\% = 6.71\%$$

Answer 7.7

	£
Purchase consideration	
£5,000 @ £111.5064 per £100	5,575.32
Accrued interest: 56 days at 13¾% (£5,000 × 0.1375 × 56/365)	105.48
Broker's commission on consideration	
0.8% on £5,575.32	44.60
Total purchase cost	5,725.40

Part A: Cash management

Answer 7.8

The Government initially issued index-linked gilts on the basis that they could only be held by authorised pension funds (and a few others). The issue was prompted by the fact that due to the high level of inflation in the early to mid seventies, the value of many people's pensions was falling drastically in real terms. In 1974 the rate of inflation was over 25% pa, whereas pension fund investments were yielding considerably less than 20%. At the time of the first issue in 1981 it had become politic for the Government to do something.

All of the index-linked stocks offer a small real return (around 2% - 3%) depending on the stock. This is achieved by providing that both interest payments and the redemption value are index-linked. The index used is the Retail Prices Index. Many commentators have criticised this index as not being sufficiently representative of the rates of inflation suffered by the sort of investors likely to buy the stock. For example, pensioners spend a far higher proportion of their income on food than the 'average family' on which the index is based.

For the investor who is prepared to take a reasonably long-term view, index-linked gilts represent a certain way of 'beating inflation'. As with all low coupon gilts, index-linked stocks are likely to be attractive to higher rate taxpayers who prefer capital gains to income, given that capital gains on gilts are exempt from capital gains tax.

Answer 7.9

(a) An investment in the ordinary shares of UK quoted companies carries the risk that income and capital may drop or even be lost altogether. The risk will be affected by such factors as:

   (i) The general economic and political climate

   (ii) The profitability of the industry in which the company operates

   (iii) The degree of competition within the industry

   (iv) The management of the company

   (v) Its level of gearing

   (vi) The spread of shareholdings and the effect this has on the market in the company's shares and hence their market valuation

   To a large extent, an investor should be able to minimise his unsystematic risk by efficient diversification. The systematic risk associated with political and economic conditions will affect all securities to a greater or lesser extent. The effects on income and capital can, however, be minimised by active portfolio management.

(b) Capital placed in a bank deposit account has a low risk that the bank will default. Nevertheless there are other risks involved. The interest rate on the account is variable and may fall after the investment has been made. The effect of this can be reduced by switching into a fixed rate investment if it seems likely that market interest rates will fall.

   As with all cash investments, there is a risk that the buying power of the capital will be significantly eroded by inflation. Although the relatively good return which an Investment Account produces will help to compensate him for the effects of inflation, any investor who believes that the rate of inflation may rise above the interest rate should consider shifting his portfolio into equities, which over time often resist inflation rather better.

(c) The risk of default on British Government Stocks is negligible. In this case, there is no risk of the interest rate falling, although the income may not keep up with inflation. There is, however, a real risk of loss of capital both in money terms (because gilt prices may fall), and in real terms (as any increase in value to redemption or earlier sale may not compensate for the fall in the value of money). An investor can protect himself against temporary falls in value by buying only gilts which he expects to be able to hold until redemption. Some degree of protection against the risks of inflation can be obtained in the manner already outlined.

Part B
Credit control

Chapter 8 Credit control: policies and procedures

Chapter topic list

1. What is credit control?
2. Total credit
3. The credit control department
4. Legal aspects of granting credit
5. Payment terms and settlement discounts

Learning objectives

On completion of this chapter you will be able to:

	Performance criteria	Range statement
• understand legal issues relating to the granting of credit, basic contract and terms and conditions of contracts	15.3	
• understand the use of discounts for prompt payment	15.3	

Part B: Credit control

1 WHAT IS CREDIT CONTROL?

1.1 The previous chapters have discussed some of the issues of managing cash, and you will have noted the **time lag** between the provision of goods and services and the receipt of cash for them. This time lag, as we have seen, can result in a firm making considerable demands on its bank to finance its working capital. Any increase in the time lag can make it significantly more difficult for a business to pay **its** own debts as they fall due.

1.2 Many businesses, however, cannot demand payment on delivery, especially for larger items. There are two aspects to credit we shall consider.

(a) **Trade credits**. These are credits issued by a business to another business. For example, many invoices state that payment is expected within thirty days of the date of the invoice. In effect this is giving the customer thirty days credit. The customer is effectively borrowing at the supplier's expense.

(b) **Consumer credit**. This is credit offered by businesses to the end-consumer.

(i) Many businesses offer hire purchase terms, whereby the consumer takes out a loan to repay the goods purchased. Failure to repay will result in the goods being repossessed.

(ii) In practice, much of the growth in consumer credit has been driven not so much by retailers as by banks. **Credit cards** are largely responsible for the explosive growth in consumer credit. Although the retailer has to pay the credit card company a commission (up to around 4% of the value of the transaction), it is felt that credit cards encourage consumers to spend: retailers have all the benefits of offering credit with few of the risks. Although UK retailers are now permitted to offer discount for payment with cash as opposed to credit card, few actually do so.

1.3 Credit control issues are closely bound up with a firm's management of liquidity, discussed in earlier chapters. Credit is offered to enhance turnover and profitability - but this should not be to the extent that a company becomes illiquid and insolvent.

1.4 Credit is also vital in securing orders in certain specified situations.

(a) **Economic conditions** can influence the type and amount of credit offered. In 'boom times, when customers are queuing with orders' (Bass, *Credit Management Handbook*), new customers can be asked for security, and risk can be minimised. In other times, credit must be used to entice customers in, and so the credit manager's job is to control risk.

(b) **High-risk or marginal customers** require flexible payment arrangements. High risk customers are often profitable, but the risk has to be managed. The customer may require a credit limit of £50,000, on standard terms, but may only deserve £35,000. The supplier might choose instead to offer a £30,000 credit limit, together with a discount policy to encourage early payment.

1.5 Just as there is a relationship between offering credit and securing sales, so too there has to be a suitable working relationship between credit control personnel and sales and marketing staff. This is because, in the words of Bass, 'a sale is not complete until the money is in the bank' and as we discover in Chapters 10 and 11, the cost of chasing after slow payers and doubtful debts is considerable.

A firm's credit policy

1.6 A firm should have a policy for credit and credit control.

(a) This will describe in **overall** terms the principles on which a firm offers credit. (This may result in **no** credit being offered at all: how often have you seen a shop displaying a notice saying 'Please do not ask for credit as refusal often offends'?)

(i) The firm may decide only to offer credit to particular classes of customer, such as 'trade' or 'business' customers; or customers who have been doing business with the firm for a considerable length of time.

(ii) The firm may relate the total credit offered to a proportion of sales.

(b) The policy will also set out **procedures** for offering credit.

(i) Before credit is offered, the procedures might involve obtaining references (eg from the bank, other creditors), reviewing account information, customer visits etc.

(ii) Once a credit limit has been set, the customer will formally agree to it, and a written copy of the credit arrangement should be retained on file.

(iii) If the agreement is a consumer credit agreement the procedures must be designed so as to comply with the Consumer Credit Act.

(iv) The agreement might include a probationary period.

(v) The agreement will also involve settlement terms (see Section 5 of this chapter).

(c) The policy will also contain procedures for controlling credit.

(i) Reports should be designed showing debtors' ageing.

(ii) Procedures should be instituted for dealing with 'slow payers' (eg sending out statements).

2 TOTAL CREDIT

2.1 We saw in previous chapters that a bank's decision to lend money to a customer is determined by many factors over which the customer has little control. The bank, for example, might only wish to extend so much credit to firms in a particular industry.

2.2 Similarly, the firm itself has to maintain a 'global' approach to credit control in the light of the firm's objectives for **profit, cash flow, asset use** and **reducing interest costs**.

2.3 Finding a **total level of credit** which can be offered is a matter of finding the least costly balance between enticing customers, whose use of credit entails considerable costs, and refusing opportunities for profitable sales. Firstly it helps to see what debtors, which often account for 30% of the total assets of a business, actually represent.

Measuring total debtors

2.4 There are three methods of assessing how many days sales are represented by debtors.

(a) The days sales in debtors ratio, sometimes called **debtors turnover** as evidenced in analysis of financial statements. This can be calculated as an annual figure. It represents the length of the credit period taken by customers.

$$\frac{\text{Total debtors} \times 365}{\text{Sales in 365 days}} = \text{days sales}$$

For example, in 19X4 X plc made sales of £700,000 and at 31 December 19X4, debtors stood at £90,000. The comparable figures for 19X3 were £600,000 (annual sales) and £70,000 (debtors at 31.13.X3).

	19X4		19X3	
Debtors represent	$\dfrac{£90,000 \times 365}{£700,000}$	= 47 days	$\dfrac{£70,000 \times 365}{£600,000}$	= 43 days

In 19X4, the company is taking longer to collect its debts.

(b) **Count-back method**. Rather than annualising, this simply assumes that the majority of debtors are most current.

Let us take an example. Assume that at the end of March total debtors stood at £1m. Sales in March were £500,000; in February, £450,000 and in January £500,000.

	£
Total debtors at the end of March	1,000,000
Less March sales	500,000
	500,000
Less February sales	450,000
	50,000
Less January sales, unpaid portion	50,000
	-

We can calculate the days outstanding as follows.

	Days
March: entire turnover	31
February: entire turnover	28
January: $\dfrac{50,000}{500,000} \times 31$ days	3
	62 days

(c) The **partial month method** analyses each month's sales and the unpaid portion. These are then aggregated together. Assume that at the end of June, total debtors are £1.5m. Data related to the previous months are as follows.

	Sales (a)	Unpaid (b)	Days (c)	$\dfrac{b}{a} \times c$
	£	£		Days
June	500,000	500,000	30	30.00
May	450,000	400,000	31	27.50
April	500,000	300,000	30	18.00
March	600,000	150,000	31	7.75
February	400,000	50,000	28	3.50
January	500,000	100,000	31	6.20
Before January	None	None	N/A	N/A
Total	2,950,000	1,500,000	N/A	92.95

(ie Debtors)

2.5 Financial analysts will be most interested to review the **annualised figure** for debtors calculated in Paragraph 2.4(a). However, this will be of little practical interest to credit controllers. The **count-back method** also suffers perhaps because it can lead to the assumption that most debtors are necessarily recent. The **partial month method** not only provides an overall debtors ageing figure but, as importantly, it also enables an analysis broken down by month. However the **days sales outstanding** (DSO) ratio is calculated, we can examine the effect of this on profitability and cash flow.

Effect on profit of extending credit

2.6 The main cost of offering credit is the interest expense. How can we assess the effect on profit?

2.7 Let us assume that the Zygo Company sells widgets for £1,000, which enables it to earn a profit, after all other expenses except interest, of £100 (ie a 10% margin).

(a) Aibee buys a widget for £1,000 on 1 January 19X1, but does not pay until 31 December 19X1. Zygo relies on overdraft finance, which costs it 10% pa. The effect is:

	£
Net profit on sale of widget	100
Overdraft cost £1,000 × 10% pa	(100)
Actual profit after 12 months credit	Nil

In other words, the entire profit margin has been wiped out in 12 months.

(b) If Aibee had paid after six months, the effect would be:

	£
Net profit	100
Overdraft cost £1,000 × 10% pa × $^6/_{12}$ months	(50)
	50

Half the profit has been wiped out. (*Tutorial note.* The interest cost might be worked out in a more complex way to give a more accurate figure.)

(c) If the cost of borrowing had been 18%, then the profit would have been absorbed before seven months had elapsed. If the net profit were 5% and borrowing costs were 15%, the interest expense would exceed the net profit after four months.

2.8 A second general point is the relation of **total credit to bad debts**. Burt Edwards argues that there is a law of 10-to-1: 'Experience in different industries shows that the annual interest expense of borrowings to support overdue debts, ie those in excess of agreed payment terms, is at least ten times the total lost in bad debts'. This is not a 'law', but has been observed to be the case over a variety of UK businesses.

Activity 8.1

Winterson Tools Ltd has an average level of debtors of £2m at any time representing 60 days outstanding. (Their terms are thirty days.) The firm borrows money at 10% a year. The managing director is proud of the credit control: 'I only had to write off £10,000 in bad debts last year,' she says proudly. Is she right to be proud?

2.9 The level of total credit can then have a significant effect on **profitability**. That said, if credit considerations are included in pricing calculations, it may be the case that extending credit can, in fact, increase profitability. If offering credit generates extra sales, then those extra sales will have additional repercussions on:

(a) The amount of stock maintained in the warehouse, to ensure that the extra demand must be satisfied

(b) The amount of money the company owes to its creditors (as it will be increasing its supply of raw materials)

2.10 This means an increase in **working capital**. Working capital is an **investment**, just as a fixed asset (eg new machinery) is, albeit of a different kind.

Part B: Credit control

2.11 To determine whether it would be profitable to extend the level of total credit, it is necessary to assess the following.

(a) The additional sales volume which might result
(b) The profitability of the extra sales
(c) The extra length of the average debt collection period
(d) The required rate of return on the investment in additional debtors

Activity 8.2

A company is proposing to increase the credit period that it gives to customers from one calendar month to one and a half calendar months in order to raise turnover from the present annual figure of £24 million representing 4m units per annum. The price of the product is £6 and it costs £5.40 to make. The increase in the credit period is likely to generate an extra 150,000 unit sales. Is this enough to justify the extra costs given that the company's required rate of return is 20%? Assume no changes to stock levels, as the company is increasing its operating efficiency. Assume that existing debtors will take advantage of the new terms.

2.12 EXAMPLE: TOTAL INVESTMENT IN DEBTORS

Russian Beard Limited is considering a change of credit policy which will result in slowing down in the average collection period from one to two months. The relaxation in credit standards is expected to produce an increase in sales in each year amounting to 25% of the current sales volume.

Sales price per unit	£10.00
Profit per unit (before interest)	£1.50
Current sales revenue per annum	£2.4 million

The required rate of return on investment is 20%.

Assume that the 25% increase in sales would result in additional stocks of £100,000 and additional creditors of £20,000. Advise the company on whether or not it should extend the credit period offered to customers, in the following circumstances.

(a) If all customers take the longer credit of two months
(b) If existing customers do not change their payment habits, and only the new customers take a full two months' credit

2.13 SOLUTION

The change in credit policy would be justifiable, in the context of this question, if the rate of return on the additional investment in working capital exceeds 20%.

Extra profit

Profit margin $£1.50/£10$ =	15%
Increase in sales revenue £2.4m × 25%	£0.6 million
Increase in profit (15% × £0.6m)	£90,000

The total sales revenue is now £3m (£2.4m + £0.6m)

(a) *Extra investment, if all debtors take two months credit*

	£
Average debtors after the sales increase (2/12 × £3 million)	500,000
Current average debtors (1/12 × £2.4 million)	200,000
Increase in debtors	300,000
Increase in stocks	100,000
	400,000
Increase in creditors	(20,000)
Net increase in 'working capital'	380,000

$$\text{Return on extra investment } \frac{£90{,}000}{£380{,}000} = 23.7\%$$

(b) *Extra investment, if only the new debtors take two months credit*

	£
Increase in debtors (2/12 × £0.6 million)	100,000
Increase in stocks	100,000
	200,000
Increase in creditors	(20,000)
Net increase in working capital investment	180,000

$$\text{Return on extra investment } \frac{£90{,}000}{£180{,}000} = 50\%$$

In both case (a) and case (b) the new credit policy appears to be worthwhile.

Furthermore, the cost profile of the product can also support extra sales. If the firm has high fixed costs but low variable costs, the extra production and sales could provide a substantial contribution at little extra cost.

Debtor quality and liquidity

2.14 Another objective of any credit control system is to minimise any risks to **cash flow** arising from insolvent debtors. The **quality** of debtors has an important impact on a firm's overall liquidity. Debtor quality is determined by their age and risk.

2.15 Some **industries** have a higher level of risk than others, in other words, there is a higher probability that customers will fail to pay. Some markets are riskier than others, which is why export credit insurance premiums are higher for some countries than others. Selling goods to a country with possible payment difficulties is riskier than selling them in the home market.

2.16 For many customers, delaying payment is the cheapest form of finance available and there has been much publicity recently about the difficulties that delayed payments cause to small businesses. There is no easy answer to this problem.

Policing total credit

2.17 The total amount of credit offered, as well as individual accounts, should be policed to ensure that the senior management policy with regard to the total credit limits is maintained. A **credit utilisation report** can indicate the extent to which total limits are being utilised. An example is given below.

Customer	Limit £'000	Utilisation £'000	%
Alpha	100	90	90
Beta	50	35	70
Gamma	35	21	60
Delta	250	125	50
	435	271	
		62.2%	

This might also contain other information, such as days sales outstanding and so on.

2.18 Reviewed in aggregate, this can reveal the following.

(a) The number of customers who might want more credit

(b) The extent to which the company is exposed to debtors

Part B: Credit control

(c) The 'tightness' of the policy (It might be possible to increase profitable sales by offering credit. On the other hand, perhaps the firm offers credit too easily.)

2.19 It is possible to design credit utilisation reports to highlight other trends.

(a) The degree of exposure to different countries

(b) The degree of exposure to different industries (Some countries or industries may be worthy of more credit; others may be too risky.)

2.20 Credit utilisation can also be analysed by industry within country or by country within industry. It is also useful to relate credit utilisation to total sales.

Trade debtors' analysis as at 31 December

Industry	Current credit utilisation £'000	% of total debtors %	Annual sales £million	As a % of total sales %
Property	9,480	25.0	146.0	19.2
Construction	7,640	20.2	140.1	18.4
Engineering	4,350	11.5	112.6	14.8
Electricals	4,000	10.6	83.7	11.0
Electricity	2,170	5.7	49.2	6.5
Transport	3,230	8.5	79.9	10.5
Chemicals, plastics	1,860	4.9	43.3	5.7
Motors, aircraft trades	5,170	13.6	105.8	13.9
	37,900	100.0	760.6	100.0

Analysis

(a) An industry analysis of credit exposure shows in this case that over 45% of the company's trade debtors (about £17 million) are in the property and construction industries. The company's management ought to have a view about this exposure to industry risk.

(b) The size of the exposure to property and construction could seem excessive, in view of the cyclical nature of these industries, the current economic outlook, and the comparatively slow payment rate from these customers. (These industries account for only 37.6% of annual sales, but 45.2% of trade debtors.) Management might wish to consider whether the company should try to reduce this exposure.

(c) A decision might also be required about whether the company should be willing to accumulate trade debtors in these sectors, in order to sustain sales, or whether the credit risk would be too high.

Conclusion

2.21 The amount of **total credit** that a business offers is worthy of consideration at the highest management levels. Two issues are:

(a) The firm's working capital needs and the investment in debtors
(b) The management responsibility for carrying out the credit control policy

Activity 8.3

Your company is concerned about the effect of inflation, which (you should suppose) currently stands at 6%, on its credit control policy. Outline the main points to consider, for discussion with your manager.

3 THE CREDIT CONTROL DEPARTMENT

3.1 The last paragraph of the previous section of the chapter suggested that management responsibility for credit control should be defined. Some options are as follows.

(a) If the credit controller is seen as little more than a debt collector, he or she will be part of the accounts department.

(b) The credit controller might report to a sales manager or the sales director, as credit control can be seen as an integral part of marketing strategy.

(c) In some companies, particularly in the US, the credit manager might report directly to the managing director.

(d) The credit manager might report to the finance director, as an equal to the chief accountant.

3.2 The credit control function might only be a small section of a few people; on the other hand, it might be a large department.

3.3 The **roles of the credit control department** can include some or all of the following.

(a) Keeping the sales ledger up-to-date
(b) Dealing with customer queries
(c) Reporting to sales staff about new enquiries
(d) Giving references about customers to third parties (eg credit reference agencies)
(e) Checking out customers' creditworthiness
(f) Advising on payment terms

The credit cycle

3.4 The credit control function's jobs occupy a number of stages of the **order cycle** (from customer order to invoice despatch) and the **collection cycle** (from invoice despatch to the receipt of cash), which together make up the **credit cycle**. The job of the credit control department can comprise all those activities within the dotted line **in the diagram on the next page**.

(a) **Establish credit status** for new customers or customers who request a credit extension. This is the subject of the next Chapter. Does the customer deserve credit? Is it a suitable risk? What is known about the customer? Can the customer pay? Will the seller profit?

(b) **Check credit limit**. If the order is fairly routine, and there is no problem with credit status, then credit control staff examine their records or at least the sales ledger records to see if the new order will cause the customer to exceed the credit limit. There are a number of possible responses, as follows.

(i) **Authorisation**. If the credit demanded is within the credit limit, and there are no reasons to suspect any problems, then the request will be authorised.

(ii) **Referral**. It is possible that the credit demanded will exceed the limit offered in the agreement.

(1) The firm can simply refuse the request for credit, at the risk of damaging the business relationship. However, credit limits are there for a reason - to protect the business's profitability and liquidity.

Part B: Credit control

(2) The firm can offer a revised credit limit. For example, the customer may be solvent and a regular payee, therefore a low risk. The company might be able to offer a higher credit limit to this customer.

Stages in the credit cycle

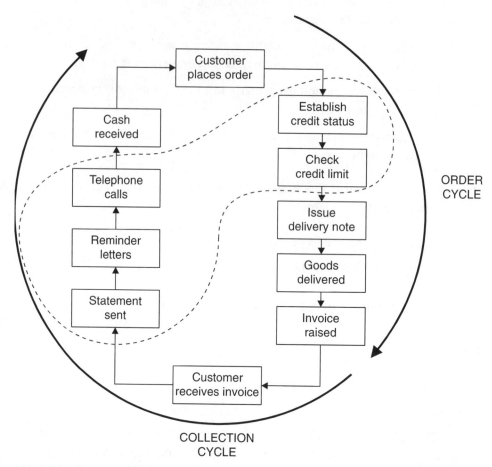

(3) The firm can contact the customer, and request that some of the outstanding debt be paid off before further credit is advanced.

(c) Issuing the delivery note, invoicing and so on is not the job of the credit control department, but the credit control department will need to have access to information such as invoice details to do its job. Indeed the credit control department might well help in the design of the invoice, to ensure issues relating to payment are given their due prominence.

(d) **Settlement**. The credit control department takes over the collection cycle, although the final payment is ultimately received by the accounts department. Collection is the subject of Chapters 10 and 11. It involves reviewing overdue debts, and chasing them.

Activity 8.4

See if you can explain the likely effects of a company's credit control policy on the control of working capital in general.

4 LEGAL ASPECTS OF GRANTING CREDIT

4.1 The credit controller's job often involves the law, especially when enforcing collection. This is mainly because the sale of goods and/or services for cash is a type of contract, and the credit controller's job is to ensure that the customer keeps his or her side of the contract.

8: Credit control: policies and procedures

You are required to have some basic understanding of the legal issues, and so they are now discussed below.

What is a contract?

> **KEY TERM**
>
> A **contract** is an agreement which legally binds the parties (ie those entering into the agreement). The essential elements to a contract (discussed in more detail below) are as follows.
>
> (a) The parties intend to create legal relations.
> (b) It is an offer and acceptance.
> (c) It is a bargain for which something is offered for consideration.

4.2 Sometimes contracts are referred to as **enforceable agreements**, as they can be enforced in a court of law.

4.3 The validity of a contract may be affected by any of the following factors.

(a) **Content**. In general the parties may enter into a contract on whatever terms they choose. But it can only be enforced if it is sufficiently complete and precise in its terms. Some terms which the parties do not express may be implied and some express terms are overridden by statutory rules.

  (i) Public policy sometimes requires that the freedom of contract should be modified. For example, the Consumer Credit Act 1974 and the Unfair Contract Terms Act 1977 both regulate the extent to which contracts can contain certain terms.

  (ii) The law will sometimes **imply** terms into contracts because the parties are expected to observe certain standards of behaviour. A person is bound by those terms even though he has never agreed to them, or never even thought of them; for example, sections 12-15 Sale of Goods Act 1979 imply terms as to title, fitness and quality of goods into all contracts for the sale of goods.

(b) **Form**. Some contracts (not all) must be made in a particular form or supported by written evidence.

(c) **Genuine consent**. Mistake, misrepresentation, duress or undue influence may affect the validity of a contract. (See below.)

(d) **Legality**. The courts will not enforce a contract which is deemed to be illegal or contrary to public policy.

(e) **Capacity**. Some persons have only restricted capacity to enter into contracts and are not bound by agreements made outside those limits.

4.4 A contract which does not satisfy the relevant tests may be either void, voidable or unenforceable.

(a) A **void contract** is not a contract at all. The parties are not bound by it.

(b) A **voidable contract** is a contract which one party may avoid, that is terminate at his option.

Part B: Credit control

(c) An **unenforceable contract** is a valid contract. But if either party refuses to perform or to complete his part of the performance of the contract, the other party cannot compel him to do so. A contract is usually unenforceable when the required evidence of its terms, for example, written evidence of a contract relating to land, is not available.

Essential elements of a contract

4.5 The essential elements of a contract were set out above: the parties to the contract intend to create **legal relations**; a contract is an **offer and acceptance**; the contract is a bargain for which something is offered in **consideration**.

Legal relations

4.6 The parties to a contract **intend to create legal relations** between themselves. In other words, the contract can be enforced or remedied by a court. The intention is judged by a person's behaviour.

(a) Any express statement **denying** such an interest is conclusive.

(b) Family arrangements (eg a parent's granting of pocket money to a child) are generally speaking **not** presumed to be contractually binding.

(c) **Most** commercial arrangements or agreements are presumed to be made with the intention of creating legal relations.

Offer and acceptance

4.7 An **offer** is a *definite* (ie not vague) promise to be bound on specific terms. It is not:

(a) The mere supply of information
(b) An invitation to negotiate
(c) An invitation to make an offer

4.8 An offer can expire after a defined period of time, if the offeror revokes (ie withdraws) it and makes this known, if the person to whom the offer (the offeree) rejects it, or if the offeree or offeror dies.

4.9 **Acceptance**, on the other hand, is an **act** by the offeree (not simply passive inaction or silence) to accept the offer. The mere fact that the offeror does not reject the offer does not guarantee acceptance. A request for information about an offer is not an acceptance.

4.10 Acceptance must be **unqualified agreement** to the terms of the offer. Acceptance which introduces any **new terms** is a **rejection and counter offer**.

4.11 The particular significance of offer (by the offer**or**) and acceptance (by the offer**ee**) is that a binding contract is thereby formed, so:

(a) New terms cannot thereafter be introduced into the contract unless both parties agree, and

(b) The terms of the contract appear from the offer and acceptance rather than from the unexpressed intentions of the parties.

8: Credit control: policies and procedures

Consideration

4.12 **Consideration** is what a person (the promisee) must give in exchange for what has been promised to him. Normally, this would be the price. All contracts are, to some degree, bargains.

(a) There are two broad types of valid consideration - **executed** and **executory**. If consideration is **past,** then it is **not enforceable**. These terms are explained below.

  (i) **Executed consideration** is an act in return for a promise. If, for example, A offers a reward for the return of lost property, his promise becomes binding when B performs the act of returning A's property to him. A is not bound to pay anything to anyone until the prescribed act is done.

  (ii) **Executory consideration** is a promise given for a promise. If, for example, a customer orders goods which a shopkeeper undertakes to obtain from the manufacturer, the shopkeeper promises to supply the goods and the customer promises to accept and pay for them. Neither has yet done anything but each has given a promise to obtain the promise of the other. It would be breach of contract if either withdrew without the consent of the other.

  (iii) Both executed and executory consideration are provided at the time when the promise is given. Anything which has already been done before a promise in return is given is **past consideration** which, as a general rule, is **not** sufficient to make the promise binding.

(b) As well as determining whether consideration is valid on the grounds of being executed or executory, the court will also seek to ensure that consideration:

  (i) Is sufficient - it must be capable in law of being regarded as consideration, and

  (ii) Has some value, though it need **not** be equal in value to the consideration received in return (The law does not judge whether a bargain is good or not.)

(c) Consideration must also be legal. A promise to pay a reward for a criminal act would be unenforceable.

Mistake and misrepresentation

4.13 The general rule regarding **mistake** is that a party to a contract is not discharged from his obligations because he is mistaken as to the terms of the contract or the relevant circumstances. The terms of the contract are established by offer and acceptance; what the parties may think or intend should not override those terms or render the contract void. There are, however, exceptional and limited categories of 'operative mistake' which render the contract **void**. Mistake is usually classified as follows.

(a) **Common mistake.** There is complete agreement between the parties but both are equally mistaken as to some fundamental point.

(b) **Mutual mistake.** The parties are at cross-purposes but each believes that the other agrees with him and does not realise that there is a misunderstanding. The terms of the contract usually settle the dispute in favour of one party or another.

(c) **Unilateral mistake.** One party is mistaken and the other (who may have induced the mistake) is aware of it. A unilateral mistake is usually (but not invariably) the result of **misrepresentation** by one party.

4.14 It is only in restricted circumstances that a mistake renders the contract void. Any such mistake must be a mistake of **fact**; a mistake of **law** can never have this effect.

4.15 A statement made in the course of negotiations may become a term of the contract. If it is a term of the contract and proves to be untrue, the party who has been misinformed may claim damages for breach of contract. If, however, the statement does not become a term of the contract and it is untrue, the party misled may be able to treat it as a **misrepresentation** and rescind (avoid) the contract, or in some cases, recover damages. The contract is **voidable** for misrepresentation; previously we saw how it may be **void** for mistake.

4.16 A misrepresentation has the following features.

(a) It is a **representation of fact** which is untrue. A statement of law, intention, opinion or mere 'sales talk' is not a representation.

(b) It is made by one party to the other **before** the contract is made. In general a misrepresentation must have been made by the misrepresentor to the misrepresentee there are two exceptions to the rule.

   (i) **Misleading advertisements**: a misrepresentation can be made to the public in general, as where an advertisement contains a misleading representation.

   (ii) The misrepresentation need not be made directly on a one-to-one basis - it is sufficient that the misrepresentor knows that the misrepresentation would be passed on to the relevant person.

(c) The party misled was induced as a result of the misrepresentation actually to enter into the contract.

4.17 Misrepresentation is classified (for the purpose of determining what remedies are available) as follows.

(a) **Fraudulent**. This is a statement made with knowledge that it is untrue, or without believing it to be true, or recklessly, careless whether it be true or false. The party misled may avoid the contract (since it is voidable), refuse to perform his part of it and/or recover damages for any loss.

(b) **Negligent**. This is a statement made in the belief that it is true but without reasonable grounds for that belief. The contract can be rescinded in some cases.

(c) **Innocent**. This is a statement made in the belief that it is true and with reasonable grounds for that belief. The contract can sometimes be rescinded.

Breach of contract

4.18 It may occur that one of the parties to an agreement does not carry out his or her side of the bargain. This is referred to as **breach of contract**. A party has a number of remedies when the other party is in breach of contract.

(a) **Damages** - as compensation for loss caused by the breach.

(b) **Termination** - he may accept the other party's repudiatory breach as discharging him from having to perform his own obligations. Alternatively he may affirm the contract (ie insist that it be performed).

(c) **Action for the price** - here the breach is failure to pay.

(d) *Quantum meruit* - payment for the value of what he has done.

(e) **Specific performance** - a court order to the defendant to perform the contract.

(f) **Injunction** - a court order for the other party to observe negative restrictions.

(g) **Rescission** - cancellation of the contract.

4.19 These are relevant to the credit controller for different reasons.

(a) **Damages** are perhaps not too relevant to the credit controller, who is trying to ensure that money owed already is paid to the firm: damages would only be rarely paid in these circumstances.

(b) **Termination**. In some cases, the other party to the contract may refuse to carry on with it. However, take the example of a jobbing firm which has spent a certain amount of time doing a job for a customer, who then decides that he has no further use for the item and repudiates the contract. The firm can **affirm** the contract (ie continue to carry out its side of the bargain and insisting that the other party keeps to the agreement).

(c) **Action for the price**. If the breach of contract arises out of one party's failure to pay the contractually agreed price due under the contract, the creditor should bring a personal action against the debtor to recover that sum. This is a fairly straight-forward procedure but is subject to two specific limitations.

(i) Action for the price (under a contract for the sale of goods) may only be brought if property has passed to the buyer (unless the price has been agreed to be payable on a specific date: s 49 Sale of Goods Act 1979).

(ii) Whilst the injured party may recover an agreed sum due **at the time** of an anticipatory breach, whether or not he continues the contract then, sums which become due **after** the anticipatory breach may not be recovered unless he **affirms** the contract, that is, he carries on with his side of the bargain. Even where he does affirm the contract, he will be **unable** to recover the price if:

(1) The other party withholds its co-operation so that he cannot continue with his side in order to make the price due, or

(2) The injured party had no other reason or 'legitimate interest' in continuing his obligations other than to claim damages. A legitimate interest may be obligations which have arisen to third parties.

(d) *Quantum meruit*. The phrase *quantum meruit* literally means 'how much it is worth'. It is a measure of the value of contractual work which has been performed. The aim of such an award is to restore the plaintiff to the position he would have been in **if the contract had never been made**. It is a **restitutory award**. (By contrast, an award of damages aims to put the plaintiff in the position he would have been in **if the contract had been performed**. It is a compensatory award.) *Quantum meruit* is likely to be sought where one party has already performed **part** of his obligations and the other party then repudiates the contract (repudiatory breach). Provided the injured party elects to treat the contract as terminated, he may claim a reasonable amount for the work done. This is clearly of relevance to a credit controller dealing with, say, payment for a construction contract.

(e) **Specific performance**. This relates more to the provision or work done, than the collection of money. The court will order that the party perform the contract - damages are not appropriate.

> **ASSESSMENT ALERT**
>
> **Injunction** and **recission** are not really relevant to the work of credit control, and therefore to your assessment. Accordingly, they are not covered here.

4.20 The right to sue for breach of contract becomes statute-barred normally after six years from the date on which the cause of action accrued, which is usually the date of the breach, not the date on which damage is suffered. The plaintiff's rights merely cease to be enforceable at law. The limitation period may be extended if the debt, or any other certain monetary amount, is either acknowledged or paid in part before the original six (or twelve) years has expired.

(a) **Acknowledgement**. The claim must be acknowledged as existing, not just as possible, but it need not be quantified. It must be in writing, signed by the debtor and addressed to the creditor.

(b) **Part payment**. To be effective, the part payment must be identifiable with the particular debt, not just a payment on a running account.

4.21 Contracts for the sale of goods and the offering of credit to customers have some special features, over and above the basics of contact law described earlier. We will go on to discuss them briefly, as they are relevant to the credit controller's job.

Sale of goods

4.22 Contracts for the sale of goods are governed by the Sale of Goods Acts 1893 and 1979. A **contract of sale** is 'a contract whereby the seller transfers or agrees to transfer the property or goods to the buyer for a monetary consideration called the price'. The seller's place of business is generally assumed to be the place where delivery is passed to the buyer. Note that the goods must be of merchantable quality.

4.23 As far as the credit controller is concerned, you should note that, **unless the contract specifies otherwise**, the Acts hold the following.

(a) Where the goods are ready for delivery (ie for the buyer and/or carrier to take), title to the property passes immediately **even if payment is delayed**.

(b) Goods sold by 'sale or return'. Title only passes when the buyer approves of the goods (eg does not state that he or she rejects them).

(c) Where the seller imposes conditions, these conditions must be met before title passes.

(d) If goods are measured or weighed, title does not pass until after this happens.

(e) If goods are specially manufactured, title passes when the goods so made are specifically allocated to the customer.

Activity 8.5

A friend of yours signs a contract with a publisher, in which he agrees to sell the manuscript of his novel for £1,000. The contract is signed on 1 July, and he hands over the manuscript. The publisher says he'll pay the £1,000 on 31 July. However, on 2 July your friend receives another offer, of £10,000, from another publisher. 'I haven't been paid, so I'll go and get my manuscript back,' he says. Can he?

4.24 What if the buyer fails to pay? Unfortunately, the credit controller is rarely entitled to wade into the buyer's premises to reclaim the goods. However, a seller who has not been paid does retain certain rights.

(a) If the buyer is **insolvent** (see Chapter 11), then the goods can be stopped in transit. Insolvency means 'unable to pay debts as they fall due' and there are legal procedures to establish it.

(b) **Lien**. Any goods which have not been paid for can be retained by the seller at the seller's premises providing the buyer has not lawfully obtained possession.

Note that the seller has **no** right to sell the goods to someone else unless the goods are perishable, or the seller has reserved the right to do so.

4.25 **Retention clauses** may be inserted in a contract to the effect that the unpaid seller can recover the goods, if they can be identified. However, these have to be precisely drafted.

4.26 Generally speaking, the principal remedy for breach of contract is '**action for the price**', and it is this which forms the basis of most debt collection procedures discussed in Chapters 10 and 11.

4.27 Remember, too, that the parties in a contract can expressly decide when they want title to pass.

Consumer credit

4.28 Certain special restrictions relate to **consumer credit**, in other words, a credit agreement between a business and an individual. The simplest form of consumer credit is a loan to a customer which he may use to purchase whatever goods or services he requires.

(a) The creditor often prefers to supply goods himself to the consumer on hire purchase terms so that the goods remain the creditor's property (and can be recovered if the debtor defaults) until the consumer has paid the price (including credit charges).

(b) It is a common business practice for a trader to sell his goods to a finance company so that the latter, in providing credit to a customer of the trader, can do so under a hire purchase or related transaction.

4.29 The Consumer Credit Act 1974 (CCA) regulates the provision of credit. 'Credit' includes a cash loan and any other form of financial benefit including hire purchase, conditional sale and credit sale agreements.

4.30 The CCA aims to protect **individual debtors** who may enter into agreements to be provided with some form of credit, either as a one-off loan or as a transaction connected with a purchase of goods. Such people may be of limited financial experience and of limited means, and in the past they were often abused by the practices of 'loan sharks' and others. One way in which the Act consistently demonstrates its commitment to their protection is by placing the burden of compliance in most cases on the creditor, for instance in relation to the filling in of forms, to cancellation rights and to the provision of copies.

4.31 The CCA applies to **regulated agreements**. Such an agreement is for less than £25,000 (but usually more than £50), is an agreement between a credit provider and an individual (not a company), excludes charge cards (but includes credit cards), involves more than four instalments, and excludes building society mortgages and loans to limited companies.

4.32 The debtor is protected in a number of ways.

(a) The debtor can withdraw at any time, until the agreement is fully executed.

(b) There are certain important formalities as to how the agreement is drawn up. The agreement must be in writing, must be signed by the debtor, must be legible and complete etc.

(c) The debtor has the right to cancel in certain cases, and must be notified of this. The debtor can cancel within five days of receiving notice.

(d) The creditor must include all relevant information.

5 PAYMENT TERMS AND SETTLEMENT DISCOUNTS

5.1 An important aspect of the credit control policy is to devise suitable **payment terms**, covering when should payment be made and how this should be achieved.

(a) Credit terms have to take into account the expected profit on the sale and the seller's cash needs.

(b) Credit terms also establish when payment is to be received, an important matter from the seller's point of view.

5.2 In addition to specifications relating to the **nature of the goods** to be supplied, the **terms and conditions of sale** normally cover the **price, delivery, date of payment, frequency of payment** (if in instalments), and **discounts**.

5.3 The credit terms the seller offers depend on many factors.

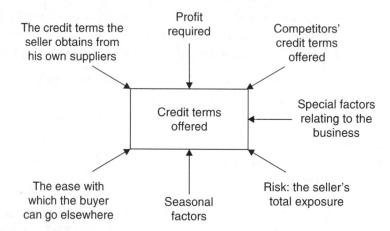

5.4 The terms must be simple to understand and easily enforceable. If the seller does not enforce his terms he is creating a precedent.

5.5 All sale agreements are **contracts**, as described earlier: credit terms are part of the contract. Although contracts do not have to be in writing, it helps if they are, and these are confirmed by the invoice.

5.6 Examples of payment terms are as follows.

(a) **Payment a specified number of days after delivery**. This might be expressed as *Net 10* (10 days).

(b) **Weekly credit**. All supplies in a week must be paid by a specified day in the next week.

(c) **Half-monthly credit**. Similar to a weekly credit, save that suppliers in the first half of the month must be paid by a specified period in the second half.

(d) **10th and 25th**. Similar to a half monthly credit: supplies received from the 16th up to the end of Month 1 must be paid for by the 10th of Month 2; supplies received in the period from the 1st and 15th of a month must be paid for by the 25th of that month.

(e) **Monthly credit**. Payment of a month's supplies must be made by a specified date in the following month. If this date is for example, the 7th of the month, this might be written *Net 7 prox*. (Do not confuse with a seven day credit Net 7 as in (a) above.) Some monthly credit is written as 1MO; a two monthly credit (2MO) means that payment must be made in the next month but one after supplies.

8: Credit control: policies and procedures

(f) **Delivery**. Certain payment terms are geared to delivery. These are self-explanatory.

    (i)   CWO: Cash with order
    (ii)   CIA: Cash in advance
    (iii)   COD: Cash on delivery
    (iv)   CND: Cash on next delivery

Methods of payment

5.7 **Payment** can be accepted in a variety of forms.

- Cash
- BACS
- Cheques
- Banker's draft
- Travellers' cheques or Eurocheques
- Postal orders
- Standing order
- Direct debit
- Credit cards
- Debit card
- Bills of exchange, promissory notes

Payment times: settlement discounts

5.8 We now come to the problem of discounts. Some firms offer a discount if payment is received early. These are called **settlement discounts**: you will have encountered them earlier in your studies. Settlement discounts have a number of uses.

(a) If sensibly priced, they encourage customers to pay earlier, thereby avoiding some of the financing costs arising out of the granting of credit. Thus they can affect **profitability**.

(b) The seller may be suffering from cash flow problems. If settlement discounts encourage earlier payment, they thus enable a company to maintain **liquidity**. In the short term, liquidity is often more important than profitability.

(c) Settlement discounts might, conceivably, affect the volume of demand if, as part of the overall credit terms offered, they encourage customers to buy.

5.9 To consider whether the offer of a discount for early payment is financially worthwhile it is necessary to compare the **cost** of the discount with the **benefit** of a reduced investment in debtors.

5.10 EXAMPLE: SETTLEMENT DISCOUNTS

Wingspan Limited currently has sales of £3m, with an average collection period of two months. No discounts are given. The management of the company are undecided as to whether to allow a discount on sales to its customers. The following estimates have been made in the event that a discount of 2% were allowed for cash buyers.

(a) The average collection period would be reduced to one month.
(b) 50% of customers would take advantage of the 2% discount.
(c) The company normally requires a 25% return on its investments.

Advise the management whether or not to introduce the discount.

Part B: Credit control

5.11 SOLUTION

In this example the offer of a discount is not expected to increase sales demand. The advantage would be in the **reduction of the collection period**, and the resulting saving in the working capital investment required.

Our solution will value debtors at sales value.

(a) *Change in debtors*

	Debtors valued at sales price £
Current value of debtors (2/12 × £3m)	500,000
New value of debtors (1/12 × £3m)	250,000
Reduction in investment in debtors	250,000

(b) The cost of reducing debtors is the cost of the discounts, ie

$$2\% \times 50\% \times £3 \text{ million} = £30,000$$

(c) The reduction in debtors of £250,000 would cost the company £30,000 per annum. If the company can earn 25% on its investments, the benefit is:

$$25\% \times £250,000 = £62,500$$

The discount policy would be worthwhile, since the benefit of £62,500 exceeds the cost of £30,000.

The percentage cost of an early settlement discount to the company giving it can be estimated by the formula:

$$\left[\frac{D}{(100-D)} \times \frac{365}{(N-S)} \right]\%$$

where:

(a) D is the discount offered (5% = 5, etc)
(b) N is the number of days credit offered net, for no discount
(c) S is the number of days credit allowed with the settlement discount

You should use this formula in the assessment (exam), which gives approximately the same result, if you find it quicker.

5.12 In the example above, the formula can be applied as follows.

$$\text{Cost of discount} = \frac{2}{(100-2)} \times \frac{365}{(60-0)}$$

$$= \frac{2}{98} \times \frac{365}{60}$$

$$= 12.4\%$$

Since 12.4% is less than the 25% by which the company judges investments, offering the discount is worthwhile.

Note that, using the formula given in Paragraph 5.11, we do not need to know how many customers will take up the discount in order to calculate the approximate percentage cost (or 'opportunity cost') of granting the discount.

Activity 8.6

Gamma grants credit terms of 60 days net to customers, but offers an early settlement discount of 2% for payment within seven days. What is the cost of the discount to Gamma?

8: Credit control: policies and procedures

5.13 As far as an **individual debtor** is concerned, the principles are similar. For example, assume Boris Ltd has an average £10,000 outstanding, representing two months sales. You offer Boris a 1% settlement discount which would reduce the average amount outstanding to £5,000 (before discounts). You borrow money at 5%. A 1% discount on annual sales of £60,000 would cost you £600. Overdraft interest saved is £250 (£5,000 × 5%) so it is not worth offering the discount.

Late payment

5.14 It has been suggested that businesses should charge interest on overdue debts. However, note the following points.

(a) **Charging for late payment** might be misconstrued. The supplier might assume that charges for late payment give the customer the authority to pay late.

(b) Statutory **rate for interest** on overdue debts has not been established in the UK.

(c) Charging for payments relates only to the effect of the late payment on **profitability**, not on liquidity.

Activity 8.7

Thinking back to topics covered in earlier chapters, explain how good cash management may realise each of the following benefits.

(a) Better control of financial risks
(b) Opportunity for profit
(c) Strengthened balance sheet
(d) Increased confidence with customers, suppliers, banks and shareholders

---

Activity 8.8

Your company has been growing rapidly over the last two years and now wishes to introduce a more formal credit control policy. You are asked to give a brief presentation on the factors involved in setting up such a policy.

Key learning points

- **Credit control** deals with a firm's management of its working capital. **Trade credit** is offered to business customers. **Consumer credit** is offered to household customers.

- **Total credit** can be measured in a variety of ways. Financial analysts use days sales in debtors, but as this is an annualised figure it gives no idea as to the make-up of total debtors. Many firms need to consider the **cost of excess credit**.

- The **total investment in debtors** has to be considered in its impact on the general investment in working capital.

- The **credit control department** is responsible for those stages in the collection cycle dealing with the offer of credit, and the collection of debts.

- A **sale of goods** is a type of contract. To be valid, a contract must result from the intention to create legal relations, must contain an offer and acceptance, and must be a 'bargain' for which consideration is offered.

- **Remedies for breach of contract** include damages, termination, action for the price, *quantum meruit*, specific performance, injunction, rescission.

- Sale of goods contracts are subject to special **legislation**. **Retention of title** clauses are rarely enforceable in practice.

- On **consumer credit arrangements** (Consumer Credit Act 1974), the potential debtor is given a number of rights.

- A firm must consider suitable **payment terms**. **Settlement discounts** can be offered, if cost effective and if they improve liquidity.

Part B: Credit control

Quick quiz

1. What is credit control?
2. Why do retailers support credit cards even though they pay a fee?
3. Describe three ways of measuring debtors ageing.
4. What should you consider if you are extending the level of total credit?
5. What can be gleaned from a credit utilisation report?
6. What factors affect the validity of a contract?
7. List the remedies for breach of contract.
8. What rule about transfer of title is assumed by the Sale of Goods Acts 1893 and 1979 for goods which are ready for delivery?
9. In brief, how does the Consumer Credit Act 1974 affect debtors?
10. What is meant by (a) Net 7; (b) 10th and 25th; (c) COD?
11. Why do firms offer settlement discounts?

Answers to quick quiz

1. Credit control is a system whereby an organisation applies controls to the amount of credit it allows to its customers, both in total and to individual customers. Credit terms offered to individual customers will include total credit allowed to the individual and an agreed period for payment after invoicing.
2. Credit cards allow retailers to offer credit with few of the risks. Turnover may be increased.
3. Calculate debtors from the financial statements; use the count-back method; use the partial month method.
4. The possible increase in sales; the profitability of extra sales achieved; the increase in the average debt collection period; the required rate of return on the additional investment in debtors.
5. An indication of the extent to which total credit limits are being utilised, and of other trends such as the degree of exposure to different countries or industries.
6. Content; form; genuineness of consent; legality; capacity.
7. Damages; termination; action for the price; *quantum meruit*; specific performance; injunction; rescission.
8. Unless the contract specifies otherwise, title to the property passes immediately even if payment is delayed.
9. It protects individual debtors on entering credit agreements, giving, for example, a right to cancel and a right to receive all relevant information.
10. (a) Payment to be made within 7 days of delivery.
    (b) Supplies received from the 1st to the 15th of the month must be paid for by the 25th of that month; supplies received from the 16th up to the end of the month must be paid for by the 10th of the following month.
    (c) Cash to be paid on delivery.
11. To encourage customers to pay early and so reduce financing costs and improve the company's liquidity.

Answers to activities

Answer 8.1

At the moment, Winterson Tools Ltd is paying $10\% \times £1m$ (ie $^{30}/_{60}$ days $\times £2m$) = £100,000 in interest caused by customers taking the extra month to pay.

Answer 8.2

The existing value of debtors is:

$$\frac{£24m}{12 \text{ months}} = £2m$$

If sales increased by 150,000 units, the value of debtors would be:

$$1\frac{1}{2} \times \frac{£24m + (150,000 \times £6)}{12 \text{ months}} = £3,112,500.$$

The debtors have to be financed somehow, and the additional £1,112,500 will cost £1,112,500 × 20% = £222,500 in financing costs.

The profit on the extra sales is: 150,000 units × (£6 – £5.40) = £90,000

The new credit policy is not worthwhile, mainly because existing customers would also take advantage of it.

Activity 8.3

Inflation accentuates the importance of credit control, because the cost of the investment in debtors, in real terms, is higher. If a company grants credit of £100,000 for 3 months, and the rate of inflation is 6% per annum, the value in 'today's money' of the eventual receipts in 3 months' time would be about 1½% less - ie about £1,500 less. If the rate of inflation went up to, say, 12%, the value of the same receipts in 3 months' time would be about £3,000 less. In other words, the cost of granting credit increases as the rate of inflation gets higher. Also, with higher inflation, customers have an increased incentive to pay late.

Activity 8.4

Working capital includes stock, debtors, creditors and cash. The effect of credit policy on working capital is that if more credit is granted, there will be a slowdown in the inflow of cash (unless the extension of credit also results in an increase in sales). Discounts for early payment would also affect cash flows. Similarly, tightening up on credit and so granting less credit will result in a speeding up of cash inflows, provided that there is no reduction in sales as a consequence of the restriction of credit.

The total amount of working capital should be kept under control because the investment in working capital must be financed, and so excessive debtors are unnecessarily costly and would reduce the organisation's return on capital employed.

Credit policy is therefore significant both from the point of view of liquidity (cash flow) and the management of finance (investment).

Activity 8.5

No. The fact he would have got a better offer is neither here nor there.

Activity 8.6

Gamma is offering customers the option of paying £98 after seven days per £100 invoiced, or payment in full after 60 days.

First, we will use the step-by-step method in Paragraph 5.11.

If we assume that all debtors take up the discount, the effect will be as follows.

Let annual sales = X.

Value of debtors with no discount policy	A = X × 60/365
Value of debtors with discount	B = X × 7/365
Reductions in debtors	= A – B
	= (60 – 7) × X/365
Cost of reducing debtors	= 2% × X

Part B: Credit control

Percentage cost $= \dfrac{2\%}{X} \div \dfrac{(60-7)X}{365}$

$= 2\% \times 365/(60-7) = 13.8\%$, ie 14% approx

Using the formula, the approximate cost of the discount to Gamma is calculated as:

$$\left[\dfrac{2}{(100-2)} \times \dfrac{365}{(60-7)}\right]\% = 14.1\%, \text{ ie 14\% approx}$$

The discount is only worthwhile financially if Gamma can save interest costs of 14% per annum or more, so that by obtaining £98 on day seven instead of £100 on day 60, more than £2 in interest costs could be saved in the time between day 7 and day 60.

Activity 8.7

(a) *Better control of financial risk.* By determining and maintaining the proper level of cash within a company in accordance with the organisation's financial procedures and within defined authorisation limits.

(b) *Opportunity for profit.* By reducing to a minimum the opportunity cost associated with maintaining cash balances in excess of company's operating needs. Earnings (or surpluses) are improved by freeing up surplus cash for investment purposes while reducing interest charged through minimising borrowing.

(c) *Strengthened balance sheet.* By reducing or eliminating cash balances in excess of target balances and putting surplus cash to work by investing it (eg in the overnight money market); by reducing or eliminating cash borrowing and keeping interest costs as low as possible.

(d) *Increased confidence with customers, suppliers, banks and shareholders.* By having access to funds to disburse to suppliers (creditors), banks (interest, fees and principal payments) and shareholders (dividends) when due. By providing good instructions to customers (debtors) to enable the organisation to convert receipts into usable bank deposits.

Activity 8.8

The factors involved in establishing a credit control policy are as follows.

(a) A total credit policy must be decided, whereby the organisation decides how much credit it can and should allow to debtors in total. Debtors should not be excessive in relation to total sales turnover, and the cost of financing debtors should also be considered. The debtor policy that is established will include maximum periods for payment.

(b) A credit policy must be set for deciding credit terms for individual customers. This will include establishing a system of credit rating, and procedures for deciding the maximum credit limit and terms for the payment period.

(c) The purpose of allowing credit is to boost sales demand. Management must consider how 'generous' credit terms should be to encourage sales, whilst at the same time avoiding excessive increases in bad debts, and problems with chasing payment from slow payers.

(d) Granting credit will inevitably mean that problems will arise with slow payers and bad debts. Procedures must be established for collecting debts from slow payers and writing off bad debts.

(e) Discounts might be offered for early payment of debts, and a decision should be taken as to how much discount, if any, should be offered to encourage early payment, thereby reducing the volume of debtors.

Chapter 9 Assessing creditworthiness

Chapter topic list

1. Minimising the risk of default
2. Externally generated information: bank and trade references, and agencies
3. Internally generated information: financial and accounting analysis
4. Internally generated information: customer visits
5. Using credit control information
6. The Data Protection Act, the Consumer Credit Act and credit control information

Learning objectives

On completion of this chapter you will be able to:

	Performance criteria	Range statement
agree credit terms with customers in accordance with the organisation's policies	15.3.1	
identify and use internal and external sources of information to evaluate the current credit status of customers and potential customers	15.3.2	15.3
open new accounts for those customers with an established credit status	15.3.3	
understand issues to do with the Data Protection Act and credit control information	15.3	
know the sources of credit status information, including external sources	15.3	15.3.2
interpret and use credit control information	15.3, 15.4	

1 MINIMISING THE RISK OF DEFAULT

1.1 The previous chapter discussed the application of the firm's credit policy overall, with a review of total credit outstanding, and total credit by industry sector. In practice, a firm's credit control policy can only be implemented at the level of the individual credit customer. A **firm's decision to grant a customer credit** depends on the firm's overall policy, the status of the particular customer, and the size and type of the customer's order. The chief consideration is the evaluation of **risk** that the debt will go bad.

> **KEY TERM**
>
> **Credit risk** means that there is a possibility that the debt will go bad.

(a) A debtor with a low credit risk is likely to be able to pay his or her debts when they fall due. Offering credit to a low risk debtor means that there is little chance that the creditor's profitability or liquidity will be threatened.

(b) A debtor who is a high credit risk is more likely to be unable to pay, and so there is a greater threat to the company's liquidity and profitability.

1.2 It has been suggested that risks can be graded, increasing in riskiness as follows.

(a) **Zero or negligible risk**. These include government institutions and major companies, but remember that governments and big companies have been known to default on their debts.

(b) **Ordinary risk**. This will include businesses with a good reputation and no history of payment problems.

(c) **Potential slow payer**. This category contains businesses which are financially sound but exploit trade credit to its maximum effect. It also includes creditworthy customers from countries where there might be problems in remitting payment.

(d) **High risk**. Such customers are responsible for most bad debt problems: but high risk sometimes entails high reward.

(e) **Unacceptable risk**. No credit should be extended to these customers.

1.3 It is not inevitable that a high risk debtor is going to default. Many firms make handsome profits from 'high risk' customers, by demanding slightly higher returns and by managing the debtors more carefully. Higher risk customers need not be shunned simply because they are higher risk.

Credit assessments

1.4 Many large companies are able to employ specialist staff, to go into considerable detail to assess a client's ability to pay. Banks, whose business is lending money after all, have sophisticated techniques for assessing the risk of any borrower, from governments and large institutions to a person requesting an overdraft.

> **KEY TERM**
>
> A **credit assessment** is a judgement about the creditworthiness of a customer. A credit assessment provides a basis for a decision as to whether credit should in fact be granted.

9: Assessing creditworthiness

1.5 The nature of the credit assessment a firm is able to carry out will therefore vary.

   (a) Some firms will simply write to the debtor's bank asking for a letter, or at best write to a credit reference agency.

   (b) Some firms, especially if lending to a large business, are able to spend time examining the customer's accounts.

1.6 Clearly, the **materiality** of the request for credit can be considered in itself.

   (a) For a multinational company, a customer who requests £100 on credit will be relative 'small-fry'.

   (b) If a customer requests £150 credit from his or her local newsagent, this is obviously much more material, simply because of the nature of the business.

1.7 Chapter 6 of this Text on borrowing money indicated a bank's canons of lending, summarised as CAMPARI. These might be relevant to the credit controller.

2 EXTERNALLY GENERATED INFORMATION: BANK AND TRADE REFERENCES, AND AGENCIES

2.1 Standard practice in the UK is often to invite the customer who is applying for credit to provide references (eg the customers bank, and/or other suppliers). Many suppliers have a standard form which prospective customers should fill in. An example of such a form is **shown on the next page**. The supplier will send it to the customer who will fill it in.

ASSESSMENT ALERT
A Unit 15 Assessment might require you to prepare a letter like the one below.

Bank references

2.2 **Bank references** are useful, but banks are naturally cautious. The prospective customer is, after all, the bank's client. However, the bank has two 'duties of care'.

   (a) **To the customer.** The bank has a duty not to give an adverse opinion without justification. Anyhow, the bank cannot break confidentiality without the customer's consent.

   (b) **To the enquirer.** In a famous case (*Hedley Byrne and Co Limited v Heller & Partners Limited 1964*), a bank can be considered *negligent*, and hence liable for damages, if the information it gives is misleading. Furthermore the bank can be liable for fraud, if the information given is so inaccurate, or if it is given with reckless disregard as to its truth, or with the knowledge that it is false. A negligent statement is made without reasonable grounds (ie insufficient supporting information) or is ambiguous.

2.3 To reconcile these two **duties of care**, banks are very cautious about the terms they use.

Part B: Credit control

> To: Britline Carriers PLC
> Sutton Lane, Liverpool
> LW6 9BC
> 0151 - 324 - 7345/6
>
> Please open a credit account in the name of:
> _____
>
> Address _____
>
> _____ Telephone _____
>
> Below are supplied the names and addresses of referees of whom the customary trade enquiries may be made.
>
> I / We note your credit terms as set out in your Standard Conditions of Sale *and agree to pay in accordance therewith for any goods services supplied by you. These terms are as follows.*
>
> | All accounts are strictly net and payable at the end of the month following the month of invoicing. |
>
> Expected maximum amount of credit required £ _____ In total*
> Weekly*
> Monthly*
>
> Signature _____
>
> (position) _____
>
> (NB: If a partnership, all partners should sign.)
>
> * delete non-applicable
>
> Our contact on accounts matters _____
>
> Bankers
> Name of bank _____ Full branch address
> _____
> _____
>
> Trade references
>
> (1) Name _____ Address _____
> _____
>
> (2) Name _____ Address _____
> _____

2.4 When writing to the bank it is necessary to be *precise* as to the credit you are offering.

Wrong

'Do you consider X Ltd to be able to pay its debts?'

Right

'Do you consider X Ltd to be good for a trade credit of £1,000 per month on terms of 30 days?'

This gives the bank manager a reasonable idea as to the amount of money required, and the terms. The manager is more able to give an opinion.

2.5 Typical bank opinions, in declining order of favour, are as follows.

	Opinion	**Notes**
Best	Undoubted.	No worries. The best opinion.
	Considered good for your figures.	Fine, but less favourable than 'undoubted'.
	Respectably constituted which should prove good for your figures.	'Should' suggests that the business is fine, but resources might be strained.
	Respectably constituted businesses whose resources would appear to be fully employed: we do not think they would undertake something they felt they could not fulfil.	This is not encouraging, as the bank makes no reference to the credit asked for.
Worst	Unable to speak for your figures.	This implies that the bank may consider the company potentially overstretched.

2.6 Other comments might qualify these statements, for example as follows.

- 'There are charges registered'. This normally implies that some of the business's assets are security for a debt (eg a bank loan).

- 'Considered good for your amount if taken in a series.' This implies that the customer will be able to pay off the sum in instalments. Some clarification might also be needed.

Trade references

2.7 The bank reference can give certain basic assurances, and for some customers, this might be all that is needed, especially if the reply from the bank suggests 'undoubted'.

2.8 However, the supplier may want additional reassurance, especially if the bank's statements are guarded. **Trade references** are obtained from other businesses that the customer deals with. The following points should be borne in mind when following them up.

(a) Some customers may name as trade references suppliers with whom they *deliberately* maintain an excellent, and otherwise untypical, payments record, simply in order to obtain good references.

(b) The trade referee should offer similar terms as the customer is requesting from the supplier.

(c) A well known company given as a referee should always be followed up. An unknown company's reference should be treated with more caution, in case of collusion.

(d) The enquiries should enclose a stamped addressed envelope, and perhaps the enquiry should be couched as a questionnaire.

Part B: Credit control

BRITLINE CARRIERS PLC
Sutton Lane
Liverpool LW6 9BC
(0151-324 7345/6)

To: Credit controller
     A Big Company plc

Dear Sir,

We have recently received a request for credit from ....Ltd ('the firm'), a customer of ours, who gave yourselves as a reference. I would be most grateful if you could help me by answering the following questions, and returning them in the stamped addressed envelope provided.

1   For how long has the firm been trading with you?
    ..... Years   .....Months

2   Did the firm supply you with suitable trade and other references when it opened its account with you?

    Yes/No

3   What are your normal credit terms for the firm?
    Amount: £.......
    Terms: Cash, weekly, monthly, other (please detail)

4   Does the firm make payments in accordance with your terms?

    Yes/No/Slow payer

5   Have you ever had to suspend credit facilities with the firm?

    Yes/No

    If Yes, when?

Please give below or overleaf any more information which you consider relevant.

Yours faithfully,

Credit ratings

2.9 **Credit ratings** are formal opinions of the creditworthiness of an entity (eg a government, government agency, financial institution or large company). They are used mainly by **investors** and **banks** to assess a company's creditworthiness.

(a) Ratings are set by specialist agencies such as IBCA (in the UK) and, in the US, Moody's and Standard & Poor's.

(b) Companies or entities are given different grades according to security they offer. Some rate commercial paper (relevant to short-term investment) according to security. AAA, for example, is very secure. C might indicate default.

2.10 Credit ratings are only of limited use to trade creditors and credit controllers, but they **do** indicate certain basic facts about a company. A company with a low credit rating is having difficulty paying its banks - trade creditors are far less important.

2.11 For trade credits, however, which require to be paid back in 30 days, and which may be owed to small customers with little clout, they are not particularly helpful.

Credit reporting agencies (credit bureaux)

2.12 **Credit bureaux** provide information about businesses so that their creditworthiness can be assessed by suppliers. Some offer background information about a client (eg copy of financial accounts). Others provide more up to date information and even offer a credit rating.

2.13 Credit reporting agencies in the UK include **CCN, Infolink, Equifax Europe,** and **Dun & Bradstreet**. Others specialise in a particular industrial or commercial sector. Although much of the information they collect is in the public domain, it would be inconvenient for the supplier to collect all of this information about a customer.

2.14 Agency reports are useful to the credit controller to the extent that they are:

(a) A summary of some, but not all, of the information available

(b) One of several sources of information which can be used to **cross-check** other information obtained, giving additional reassurance, especially where large credits are concerned

2.15 A typical agency report will contain the following details.

(a) **Legal data**

 (i) Full name and registered address of the business
 (ii) Names of directors, partners, proprietors
 (iii) Authorised and issued share capital
 (iv) Parent company, if part of a group
 (v) Secured charges
 (vi) County Court judgements recorded

 The legal status is important, if there are restrictions on operations outlined in the company's memorandum and articles.

(b) **Commercial data**

 (i) Types of business
 (ii) Location of offices, factories, branches etc
 (iii) Main features of latest annual report
 (iv) Details of latest annual report
 (v) Annual turnover
 (vi) Balance sheet abstracts

(c) **Credit data**

 (i) Bankers' opinions

 (ii) Suppliers' opinions, if available

 (iii) Possibly, the agency's:

 (1) Own credit rating of the customer
 (2) Suggested credit limit for the customer

 (iv) Possibly, the agency might keep records of credit offered by its members. *UK Infolink* is a credit reference association whose members include most UK

Part B: Credit control

(v) Dun & Bradstreet offer a **'payment' profile service**. This contains information about payments records of companies. This information is obtained from clients and fed into Dun & Bradstreet's computer database at regular intervals. A *payment score report* can be obtained from this data. This is a numerical score that rates a company's performance in paying its bills. It is based on an analysis of payment records on the agency's database. Actual payments are compared with the credit terms that were offered for each recorded transactions (eg end of month, one month from invoice date, net 14 days, 2% settlement discount on seven days, net 30 days, etc). On the scale of 100 down to zero, 100 represents a company that regularly pays in advance of the due date, 90 represents a company that regularly takes early settlement discounts, 80 represents a prompt payer and 30 a company that takes on average around three months beyond the due date.

2.16 The **problems with agency reports** are as follows.

(a) Up-to-date information which would be relevant to the credit decision may not have reached its way on to the system (eg the collapse of a major customer).

(b) Suppliers' references may be too old to be relevant.

(c) Newly established concerns will not have much of a track record on which a judgement can be made.

Activity 9.1

Clinton Ltd supplies a unique kind of herbal medicine, the Billary Pill. Each jar costs about £400 to make and is sold to chemists for £600. One day Clinton Ltd receives a request for credit from Triad Pharmaceuticals, a chain of chemist shops, comprising 20 stores in the West Midlands. They are asking for a credit limit of £6,000 on 30 days terms. They supply a bank reference, and two trade references.

(a) The bank says: 'Respectably constituted, and should prove good for your figures'.

(b) The first trade reference features a £1,000 credit limit, payable in 60 days. There have been no problems with the account.

(c) The second trade reference is not a supplier at all but one of Triad's customers. The customer's surname, Cyborg, is the same as that of the managing director of Triad Ltd.

What should Clinton Ltd do with this request?

2.17 There are a number of other sources of data about companies which can be converted into useful credit control information.

(a) **The press**. Companies produce annual financial statements and offer a half yearly report. The basics of these results, together with informed comment, is often published in papers such as the *Financial Times*.

(b) **Historical financial data**

(i) Extel became famous for Extel cards describing the basic financial data of a company, updated for important events such as recent results or rights issues.

(ii) A stock broker might conceivably offer an opinion. Some firms publish reviews for particular business sectors.

(c) **Companies Registry search**. All companies have to file certain financial information with Companies House. However, small and medium sized companies (as defined in the relevant legislation) can file accounts which omits certain information, such as the profit and loss account. However, a Companies House search provides valuable evidence as to any secured lending.

(d) **County Court records** could be inspected to see if the company has ever defaulted on a debt.

(e) **Analysing company accounts**. A company's financial statement can generate important and useful information.

(i) Most companies publish a **cash flow statement** which does indicate the extent to which a company has in the past relied on borrowing, in a prescribed accounting format. A cash flow statement is created from a company's balance sheet and profit and loss account. It gives details as to the extent that a business is a consumer of cash or a provider of it. (This is not the firm's cash budget!)

(ii) The calculation of key ratios can identify trends and difficulties in a firm's performance. We look at these in the next section of this chapter.

Credit references and the individual consumer

2.18 The above descriptions have concentrated mainly on getting credit references about **companies**. When dealing with information about **individuals**, any person running a credit reference agency needs to be licensed under the 1974 Consumer Credit Act. The terms of the Act state a credit reference agency is any business, national or local, which carries on business so as to furnish people with information relevant to the financial standing of **individuals**, having collected the information for that purpose. This last provision means that banks and building societies, for instance, are not necessarily credit reference agencies since they do not collect information with the object of passing it on.

Activity 9.2

Explain how a credit rating agency can help in providing a credit assessment of a customer.

3 INTERNALLY GENERATED INFORMATION: FINANCIAL AND ACCOUNTING ANALYSIS

Ratio analysis

3.1 The credit controller is interested in a whole variety of **accounting ratios**, to build up, where possible, a broad picture of the customer. However, the credit controller is only interested in the accounts insofar as they affect a business's ability to pay its debts on time. The credit controller has no real concern with some of the more arcane aspects of financial reporting.

3.2 Many large companies employ **credit analysts** who are able to examine in detail the performance and creditworthiness of a potential client. For example, a client might be a large company, but operating in an industry in cyclical or terminal decline. Alternatively, the company may be medium-sized, but may want an unusually large line of credit.

3.3 An assessment of a company's financial position is often based **on historical accounting information**, extracted from its annual report and accounts. Much of this information relates to profits and balance sheet values for assets and liabilities. The credit analyst is mainly concerned, however, with the probability that the company will have sufficient cash

Part B: Credit control

to pay what it owes on time. A **problem with financial ratio analysis** is that historical information about profits, assets and liabilities is used for an assessment of a *future* cash flow position, when they offer only an uncertain guide.

3.4 The analysis and interpretation of the profit and loss account and the balance sheet of a business can be done by calculating certain ratios, between one item and another, and then using the ratios for **comparison**, in terms of profitability, liquidity and efficiency, either:

(a) Between one year and the next for a particular business, in order to identify any trends, or significantly better or worse results than before, or

(b) Between one business and another, to establish which business has performed better, and in what ways.

The credit controller is mainly concerned with (a).

Profit margin, asset turnover and return on capital employed

3.5 There are **three principal ratios** which can be used to measure how the operations of a business have been managed: **profit margin**; **net asset turnover**; and **return on capital employed**.

3.6 **Profit margin**. This is the ratio of profit to sales, and may also be called 'profit percentage'.

$$\frac{\text{Profit}}{\text{Sales}} = \frac{£20,000}{£100,000} = 20\%$$

This also means that its costs are 80% of sales. A high profit margin indicates that:

(a) *Either* costs are being kept well under control
(b) *And/or* sales prices are high

3.7 **Net asset turnover**. This is the ratio of sales in a year to the amount of net assets (capital) employed. For example, if a company has sales in 19X4 of £720,000 and has assets of £360,000, the net asset turnover will be:

$$\frac{\text{Sales}}{\text{Capital employed}} = \frac{£720,000}{£360,000} = 2 \text{ times.}$$

This means that for every £1 of assets employed, the company can generate sales turnover of £2 per annum. To utilise assets more efficiently, managers should try to create a higher volume of sales for the same assets and so a higher asset turnover ratio. The significance of this improvement is that if a business can create more sales turnover from the same amount of assets it should make larger profits (because of the increase in sales) without having to increase the size of its investment.

3.8 **Return on capital employed (ROCE)** is the amount of profit as a percentage of capital employed (ie net assets).

(a) For example:

$$\frac{\text{Profit}}{\text{Capital employed}} = \frac{£40,000}{£250,000} = 16\%$$

(b) You should also realise the relation between **ROCE, profit margin** and **asset turnover**.

$$\underbrace{\frac{\text{Profit}}{\text{Capital employed}}}_{\boxed{ROCE}} = \underbrace{\frac{\text{Profit}}{\text{Sales}}}_{\boxed{Profit\ margin}} \times \underbrace{\frac{\text{Sales}}{\text{Capital employed}}}_{\boxed{Net\ asset\ turnover}}$$

An increase in sales volume can offset a decrease in the profit margin, by increasing net asset turnover, while ROCE stays the same.

3.9 Most of the providers of finance to a business expect some return on their investment.

(a) Trade creditors and most other current liabilities merely expect to be paid.
(b) A bank charges interest on overdrafts.
(c) Interest must be paid to the holders of loan stock and debentures.
(d) Ordinary shareholders also expect a dividend.

3.10 So when we refer to 'return' we must be clear in our mind about which providers of finance we are concerned with, and we should relate the return earned for those providers of finance to the amount and type of 'funds' they are providing.

3.11 For the credit controller, a firm's profitability and return are not immediately relevant to whether a debt will be paid. However, they do indicate that, overall, the company is healthy and is able to manage its operating cycle. That said, in the short term a loss-making company might be a good credit risk, and, as we have seen, a profitable company might have liquidity problems. For the credit controller profitability overall suggests the **long-term creditworthiness** of the company, providing the company maintains this in future, is assumed.

Working capital

3.12 **Working capital,** as we have seen from Chapter 1, is the difference between current assets (mainly stocks, debtors and cash) and current liabilities (such as trade creditors and a bank overdraft). Current assets and current liabilities are a necessary feature of a firm's operating cycle in (as discussed in Chapter 1). To recap:

(a) Current assets are items which are either cash already, or which will soon lead to the receipt of cash. Stocks will be sold to customers and create debtors; and debtors will soon pay in cash for their purchases.

(b) Current liabilities are items which will soon have to be paid for with cash. Trade creditors will have to be paid and bank overdraft is usually regarded as a short-term borrowing which may need to be repaid fairly quickly (or on demand).

Activity 9.3

In an article dealing with company liquidity, the statement was made that 'it is widely accepted that stronger and more profitable companies have a higher proportion of working capital'. Set out and comment on the various circumstances under which this belief might or might not be true.

Turnover periods

3.13 A **turnover period** is an (average) length of time. It is calculated from information in a firm's profit and loss account and balance sheet. In analysing a customer's financial statements, we can only go on the annual figures.

Stock turnover period

3.14 A **stock turnover period** is the length of time an item of stock is held in stores before it can be used. (Stock turnover periods can be calculated separately for raw materials stocks, work in progress, finished goods etc.) Stock turnover periods are calculated as:

Part B: Credit control

$$\frac{\text{Average stock held}}{\text{Cost of goods sold}} \times 12 \text{ months}$$

Although it is strictly correct to use average values, it is more common to use the value of *closing* stocks shown in a balance sheet - at one point in time - to estimate the turnover period. But you could use the average of the opening and closing balances in a period.

Debtors turnover period

3.15 The **debtors turnover period**, or debt collection period, is the average length of the credit period taken by customers - it is the time between the sale of an item and the receipt of cash for the sale from the customer. The debt collection period is calculated as:

$$\frac{\text{Average debtors}}{\text{Annual credit sales}} \times 12 \text{ months}$$

For example, if a company sells goods for £1,200,000 per annum in regular monthly quantities, and if debtors in the balance sheet are £150,000, the debt collection period is:

$$\frac{£150,000}{£1,200,000} \times 12 \text{ months} = 1.5 \text{ months}$$

In other words, debtors will pay for goods 1½ months on average after the time of sale. This was discussed in more detail in Chapter 8. Note, however, that if you are analysing another company's accounts you cannot do the detailed debtor breakdown which you can do for your own financial statements.

Creditors turnover period

3.16 The **creditors turnover period**, or period of credit taken from suppliers, is the length of time between the purchase of materials and the payment to suppliers. The period of credit taken from suppliers is calculated as:

$$\frac{\text{Average trade creditors}}{\text{Total purchases in one year}} \times 12 \text{ months}$$

For example, if a company sells goods for £600,000 and makes a gross profit of 40% on sales, and if the amount of trade creditors in the balance sheet is £30,000, the period of credit taken from the suppliers is:

$$\frac{£30,000}{(60\% \text{ of } £600,000)} \times 12 \text{ months} = 1 \text{ month}$$

In other words, suppliers are paid in the month following the purchase of goods. To a credit controller assessing whether a customer deserves credit, this is a very significant important ratio *in itself*, irrespective of the wider working capital position.

Activity 9.4

Legion Ltd's 20X4 accounts show the following.

	£
Sales	360,000
Cost of goods sold	180,000
Stocks	30,000
Debtors	75,000
Trade creditors	45,000

Calculate the length of the operating cycle.

Implications of turnover periods

3.17 If the stock turnover period gets longer or if the debt collection period gets longer, the total amount of stocks or of debtors will increase. (Similarly, if the period of credit taken from the suppliers gets longer, the amount of creditors will become bigger. From the point of view of the credit analyst, examining the accounts as an **outsider,** both of these developments are important as they suggest **growing liquidity problems** in the potential debtor.

3.18 The credit analyst will also be interested in other aspects of the firm's current assets.

 (a) Does the customer have high cash balances? This would indicate that the customer hoards cash, but has no problem paying in principle: not so much 'can't pay' as 'won't pay', perhaps.

 (b) Do the accounts detail any borrowing facilities and bank arrangements the debtor has? The debtor may be able to borrow substantial funds at short notice: these can be used to repay creditors.

Liquidity and working capital: the current ratio

3.19 Working capital is an indicator of liquidity. Firms can liquidate assets to pay debts.

 (a) **Current assets** are assets which can be converted into cash.

 (i) The most liquid asset, of course, is cash itself (or a bank balance).

 (ii) The next most liquid assets are short-term investments (stocks and shares) because these can be sold quickly for cash should this be necessary.

 (iii) Debtors are fairly liquid assets because they should be expected to pay their bills in the near future.

 (iv) Stocks are the least liquid current asset because they must first be sold (perhaps on credit) and the customers given a credit period in which to pay before they can be converted into cash.

 (b) **Current liabilities** are items which must be paid for in the near future.

3.20 If a company has more current liabilities than current assets, it has **negative** working capital. This means that to some extent, **current liabilities** (eg creditors - you, the supplier) are helping to finance the **fixed assets** of the business. However, a business must be able to pay its bills on time and this means that to have negative working capital would be financially unsound and dangerous. To be safe, a business should have current assets in excess of current liabilities, not just equality with current assets and current liabilities exactly the same amount.

3.21 Is there is an **ideal** amount of working capital which it is prudent to have? In other words, is there an ideal relationship between the amount of current assets and the amount of current liabilities? Should a minimum proportion of current assets be financed by the long-term funds of a business?

3.22 These questions cannot be answered with a hard-and-fast rule, but the relative size of current assets and current liabilities are measured by so-called **liquidity ratios**. There are two common liquidity ratios

 (a) The current ratio
 (b) The quick ratio or liquidity ratio

Part B: Credit control

3.23 The **current ratio** is the more commonly used and is the ratio of current assets to current liabilities.

$$\frac{\text{Current assets}}{\text{Current liabilities}}$$

A 'prudent' current ratio is sometimes said to be 2:1. In other words, current assets should be twice the size of current liabilities. This is a rather simplistic view of the matter, because particular attention needs to be paid to certain matters.

(a) **Bank overdrafts**. These are technically repayable on demand, and therefore must be classified as current liabilities. However, many companies have semi-permanent overdrafts in which case the likelihood of their having to be repaid in the near future is remote. It would also often be relevant to know a company's overdraft limit - this may give a truer indication of liquidity than a current or quick ratio.

(b) **Are the year-end figures typical of the year as a whole?** This is particularly relevant in the case of seasonal businesses. For example, many large retail companies choose an accounting year end following soon after the January sales and their balance sheets show a higher level of cash and lower levels of stock and creditors than would be usual at any other time in the year.

3.24 A credit controller might care to look at the **inverse of the current ratio**:

$$\frac{\text{Current liabilities}}{\text{Current assets}}$$

A ratio of ½ would imply that current liabilities finance half of the current assets.

3.25 In practice, many businesses operate with a much lower current ratio and in these cases, the best way to judge their liquidity would be to look at the current ratio at different dates over a period of time. If the trend is towards a lower current ratio, we would judge that the liquidity position is getting steadily worse.

For example, if the liquidity ratios of two firms A and B are as follows:

	1 Jan	1 Apr	1 July	1 Oct
Firm A	1.2 : 1	1.2 : 1	1.2 : 1	1.2 : 1
Firm B	1.3 : 1	1.2 : 1	1.1 : 1	1.0 : 1

we could say that firm A is maintaining a stable liquidity position, whereas firm B's liquidity is deteriorating. We would then begin to question firm B's continuing ability to pay its bills. A bank for instance, would need to think carefully before granting any request from firm B for an extended overdraft facility.

3.26 The **quick ratio** is used when we take the view that stocks take a long time to get ready for sale, and then there may be some delay in getting them sold, so that stocks are not particularly liquid assets. If this is the case, a firm's liquidity depends more heavily on the amount of debtors, short-term investments and cash that it has to match its current liabilities. The quick ratio is the ratio of current assets *excluding stocks* to current liabilities.

3.27 A 'prudent' quick ratio is 1 : 1. In practice, many businesses have a lower quick ratio (eg 0.5 : 1), and the best way of judging a firm's liquidity would be to look at the trend in the quick ratio over a period of time. The quick ratio is also known as the **liquidity ratio** and as the **acid test ratio**. However, no one ratio can be used in isolation, as the activity below will demonstrate.

Activity 9.5

Wing Ltd's liquidity has declined significantly over the last 12 months. The following financial information is provided:

	Year to 31 December 20X2 £	Year to 31 December 20X3 £
Sales	573,000	643,000
Cost of goods sold	420,000	460,000
Cash/(overdraft)	5,000	(10,000)
Debtors	97,100	121,500
Creditors	23,900	32,500
Stocks	121,400	189,300

All purchases and sales were made on credit.

Required

(a) Analyse the above information, which should include calculations of the operating cycle (the time lag between making payment to suppliers and collecting cash from customers) for 20X2 and 20X3.

(b) Prepare a brief report on the implications of the changes which have occurred between 20X2 and 20X3.

Notes

(a) Assume a 365 day year for the purpose of your calculations and assume that all transactions take place at an even rate.

(b) All calculations are to be made to the nearest day.

Gearing

3.28 Companies are financed by different types of capital and each type expects a return in the form of interest or dividend. **Gearing** is a method of comparing how much of the long-term capital of a business is provided by equity (ordinary shares and reserves) and how much is provided by investors who are entitled to interest or dividend before ordinary shareholders can have a dividend themselves. These sources of capital are loans and preference shares, and are sometimes known collectively as 'prior charge capital'.

3.29 The two most usual methods of measuring gearing are:

(a) $\dfrac{\text{Prior charge capital (long-term loans and preference shares)}}{\text{Equity (ordinary share plus reserves)}} \times 100\%$

  (i) A business is low-geared if the gearing is less than 100%
  (ii) It is neutrally-geared if the gearing is exactly 100%
  (iii) It is high-geared if the gearing is more than 100%

(b) $\dfrac{\text{Prior charge capital (long-term loans and preference shares)}}{\text{Total long-term capital}} \times 100\%$

A business is now low-geared if gearing is less than 50% (calculated under method (b)), neutrally-geared if gearing is exactly 50% and high-geared if it exceeds 50%.

3.30 Low gearing means that there is more equity finance in the business than there is prior charge capital. High gearing means the opposite – prior charge capital exceeds the amount of equity.

3.31 A numerical example might be helpful.

Draught Ltd has a gearing of:

$$\frac{£200,000}{£400,000} = \frac{\text{(debenture loans plus preference shares)}}{\text{(ordinary shares plus reserves)}}, \times 100\% = 50\%$$

3.32 Gearing can be important when a company wants to raise extra capital, because if its gearing is already too high, the firm might find that it is difficult to raise a loan. Would-be lenders might take the view that ordinary shareholders should provide a fair proportion of the total capital for the business and that at the moment they are not doing so. Unless ordinary shareholders are prepared to put in more money themselves (either by issuing new shares or by retaining more profits), the company might be viewed as a bad business risk.

3.33 Gearing is important to the credit controller because trade debts generally take lower priority in a company's planning than interest payments on other forms of debt. If a company becomes insolvent, it is secured loans that are dealt with first.

3.34 As mentioned earlier, gearing is important also to a bank that is considering a lending decision. The bank will usually treat **overdraft finance** as part of a company's total indebtedness.

Interest cover

3.35 **Interest cover** is a measure of financial risk which is designed to show the risks in terms of profit rather than in terms of capital values. It shows the number of times that interest payments are 'covered' by profits, and so (as mentioned in an earlier chapter) is of particular interest to a bank making lending decisions.

$$\text{Interest cover} = \frac{\text{Profit before interest and tax}}{\text{Interest payable}}$$

The reciprocal of this, the interest to profit ratio, is also sometimes used.

3.36 As a general guide, an interest cover of less than three times is considered low, indicating that profitability is too low given the gearing of the company.

Debt ratio

3.37 For the analysis of a potential customer for credit, another useful financial risk ratio is the **debt ratio**. This is a measure of the percentage amount of the company's total assets (fixed and current) that are being financed by credit of one sort or another.

$$\frac{\text{Total creditors (due for payment either within one year or after more than one year)}}{\text{Net fixed assets + total current assets}}$$

Trends in this ratio over time can be monitored. A higher ratio indicates a higher financial risk. A ratio in excess of 50% indicates a high level of total borrowing, but there is no 'ideal' maximum debt ratio within which companies should try to operate.

3.38 The company XYZ plc has the following debt ratios.

	At 31 December Year 1	At 31 December Year 2
Creditors (short and long-term)	(20,446 + 2,931)	(21,874 + 2,041)
Assets (fixed and current)	(13,848 + 17,763)	3,782 + 23,020
	= 74.0%	= 89.2%

9: Assessing creditworthiness

Analysis

The debt ratio was high in Year 1 at 74%. It worsened to 89% at the end of Year 2. This indicates that creditors are financing too much of the company's business. This company is clearly a high credit risk. Any request by its purchasing department for even more trade credit or for extra bank loans ought to be met with (at the very least) a strong reluctance, and in all probability a flat refusal.

Activity 9.6

You are given summarised information about two firms in the same line of business, A and B, as follows.

Balance sheets at 30 June

	A			B		
	£'000	£'000	£'000	£'000	£'000	£'000
Land			80			260
Buildings		120			200	
Less depreciation		40			-	
			80			200
Plant		90			150	
Less depreciation		70			40	
			20			110
			180			570
Stocks		80			100	
Debtors		100			90	
Bank		-			10	
		180			200	
Creditors	110			120		
Bank	50			-		
	160			120		
			20			80
			200			650
Capital brought forward			100			300
Profit for year (after interest)			30			100
			130			400
Less drawings			30			40
			100			360
Land revaluation			-			160
Loan (10% pa)			100			130
			200			650
Sales			1,000			3,000
Cost of sales			400			2,000

Produce a table of six ratios calculated for both businesses.

Activity 9.7

Write the material for a report briefly outlining the strengths and weaknesses of the two businesses in the previous activity. Include comment on any major areas where the simple use of the figures could be misleading.

Part B: Credit control

Cash flow and credit risk

3.39 A creditor should focus its attention on how strong the company's cash flows appear to be. We can use the classification outlined in Chapter 1. Remember that, as a creditor, you might have advanced credit for an item of capital equipment.

	Item	Comment
	Net operational cash flow	Should be positive
−	Priority payments	
=	Cash for discretionary spending	Should normally be positive
−	Investment spending	
=	Cash after investment spending	If negative, the company must obtain money from non-trading sources, perhaps by borrowing

Good times and bad times

3.40 Bear in mind that many companies go through periods of growth followed by periods of decline and cut-back, within the general business cycle for their industry. In the recession of the early 1990s, many companies experienced a severe downturn in business and had to cut operational expenditures to remain cash-positive.

Activity 9.8

What data would you look for in the financial statements of a new customer who asks for credit?

4 INTERNALLY GENERATED INFORMATION: CUSTOMER VISITS

4.1 In addition to the accounting analysis described above, it is sometimes necessary to visit the client, so that any information gaps can be filled. Such a visit has two purposes.

(a) Any specific queries arising from the credit reference data can be discussed.
(b) The credit controller can get a feel for the business and the people running it.

4.2 The sales manager might accompany the credit manager. The credit manager should take a look around the business, and needs to speak to people at a suitable level, perhaps the financial controller.

(a) Premises: do they look adequate to support the operations of the business?

(b) Are visitors treated courteously? (If a person is rudely or inefficiently dealt with on a company's own premises, this does not bode well for the company's normal client management.)

(c) Do the accounts department and purchase ledger department appear well run, with properly kept files of invoices, reports etc and a suitable system for recording transactions? If not, invoices and reminders go missing, and payment is delayed as a result of this lack of organisation.

(d) What payment systems does the company use (eg BACS)?

(e) Is the overall impression, derived from the factory and offices, that the business is prospering?

- (f) Is there an obvious build up of obsolete or slow moving stock? (This would indicate a problem with sales.)
- (g) Does the sales ledger appear efficiently run: in other words, is the business able to secure payment from its own customers?

5 USING CREDIT CONTROL INFORMATION

5.1 Having analysed the relevant accounting data, visited the client, and having received guarded assurances from a bank, we are now in a position to use this information. First of all, a new customer will be offered a set level of credit, on terms that the credit controller found appropriate.

- (a) Credit might be granted provisionally subject to a formal review at a later date.
- (b) The company may or may not wish to grant the customer's request in its entirety. For example, assume Joe Soap wanted a credit limit of £1,000 and 30 days. As a preliminary, the supplier might offer:
    - (i) £500 repayable within 30 days
    - (ii) £1,000 repayable within 15 days

Only after the customer has established a suitable payments record should this be increased. (Types of credit terms were discussed in the previous chapter.)

5.2 The **payment record** must be **monitored** continually. This depends on successful sales ledger administration.

- (a) **Invoices** must be posted at the right time.
- (b) **Receipts** should be posted when they arrive, and allocated specifically to the invoices to which they relate.
- (c) Any **queries** (eg customers debiting their own credit balance with a debit note as 'notification' to the supplier) need to be dealt with quickly.
- (d) Orders should **always** be **vetted against credit limits.** This indicates the importance of prompt updating, as above.
- (e) A **customer history analysis** can be prepared. This is like a statement, but with:
    - (i) Total annual sales, on a rolling twelve month basis
    - (ii) Outstanding amounts owed
    - (iii) Days sales outstanding at each month end

    The advantage of this is that trends in the account can be monitored, as can also the ageing of the debtor balance.

Part B: Credit control

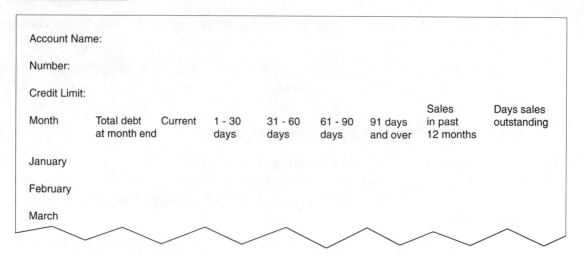

5.3 With this information it should be possible to develop in-house credit ratings.

In-house credit ratings

5.4 Credit monitoring can be simplified by a system of **in-house credit ratings**. For example, a company could have five credit-risk categories for its customers. These credit categories or ratings could be used to decide either individual credit limits for customers within that category or the frequency of the credit review. Guidelines could be provided to help credit controllers decide into which category a customer belongs.

5.5 Over time, the payment habits of a customer can be assessed, and the customer's credit rating (and credit limits) can be set accordingly. Any deterioration in a customer's payment record could raise concerns about the customer's creditworthiness.

Example

5.6 A company categorises its credit customers into the following four groups:

1. Prompt payers
2. Those who pay within 30 days of the due date
3. Those who pay between 40 and 60 days of the due date
4. Those who pay over 60 days late

The recent payment record of a regular customer, Victor, is as follows.

Invoice number	Date of invoice	Date payable	Payment received	Days overdue
3257	7 March	7 April	28 April	21
3816	26 June	26 July	1 September	37
3942	19 July	19 August	1 September	13
4185	3 September	3 October	5 November	33
				104

Average days overdue = 26 days (104 ÷ 4)

5.7 Victor would be rated in credit category 2 by the company. A review of the payment record suggests that Victor delays payment until around the end of the month following the due date. This is quite typical business practice, and although Victor is not a good payer, there is a discernible payment pattern that could persuade the company to treat Victor as an average credit risk.

5.8 A **credit taken ratio** can be used to monitor the credit limits of customers. This compares the amount currently owed by a customer with the annual sales turnover in his account. We examined this for whole industries in Chapter 8.

Example

5.9 A company has two debtors, Able and Baker. Each customer owes £20,000. Annual sales to Able are about £200,000, and annual sales to Baker are about £100,000.

5.10 The credit taken ratio is 10% for Able (20,000 ÷ 200,000 × 100%) and 20% for Baker. Baker could be regarded as a higher credit risk. The company might wish to keep the credit-taken ratio for customers below a certain limit. If this limit were 20%, a request from Baker for further credit would be refused until the outstanding debts are settled. The company would be willing, however, to consider a request from Able for more credit.

Credit reviews

5.11 A customer's payment record and the debtors aged analysis should be examined regularly, as a matter of course. Breaches of the credit limit, or attempted breaches of it, should be brought immediately to the attention of the credit controller.

5.12 Otherwise, the credit controller will not have the time to examine *each* customer's account thoroughly every month. The credit controller's efforts will be expended on more thought to be higher risk, or where there are other special factors (a debt that has gone bad). The credit situation will be reviewed more frequently, and a decision taken as to whether the credit should be extended. Illustrative internal weightings, review periods and credit offered are indicated below.

Rating	Payment record	Financial indicators	Frequency of credit reviews	Credit limit (as % of customer's annual purchases)
A Very high risk	Accounts overdue by 60 + days	Low profits Poor liquidity Highly indebted		Cash only (payment with order)
B High risk	Accounts overdue by 30 - 60 days	Deteriorating profitability, liquidity, or gearing High credit taken ratio	Monthly	Reduce to 10% of annual purchases
C Average risk	Accounts overdue up to 30 days	Stable position	Quarterly	15% of annual purchases
D Below average risk	Accounts paid on time	Stable or improving position	Six-monthly	25% of annual purchases
E Low risk	Accounts paid early Public sector customers	Strong financial position, or public sector ownership	Annually	For negotiation with the customer

Part B: Credit control

Activity 9.9

Suppose that you work for an accountancy firm, and you have been asked to advise a manufacturing company client on guidelines for a credit control system. Make brief notes for a presentation to the client on possible guidelines, covering the following points:

(a) Categorisation of debtor risk
(b) Assessment of individual customers' risk categorisation
(c) Procedures to check that the customer has received goods and an invoice

Activity 9.10

Set out more detailed notes for the same presentation as was mentioned in the previous activity on the topic of: 'The credit control approach to existing individual customers'.

6 THE DATA PROTECTION ACT, THE CONSUMER CREDIT ACT AND CREDIT CONTROL INFORMATION

6.1 The growth of information technology and the concern for civil freedoms and individual privacy has meant that legislation has been passed restricting the use of computer-held data. The relevance to consumer credit is now described.

6.2 In the UK the current legislation is the **Data Protection Act 1998**. This Act replaced the Data Protection Act 1984, although there is a transitional period (see paragraph 6.11).

6.3 The Data Protection Act 1998 is an attempt to protect the **individual**. The terms of the Act cover data about individuals - **not data about corporate bodies**.

6.4 In order to understand the Act it is necessary to know some of the technical terms used in it.

KEY TERMS

Personal data is information about a living individual, including expressions of opinion about him or her. Data about other organisations (eg supplier or customer companies) is not personal data, unless it contains data about individuals who belong to those other organisations.

Data users are organisations or individuals who control the contents of files of personal data and the use of personal data which is processed (or intended to be processed) automatically - ie who use personal data which is covered by the terms of the Act.

A **computer bureau** is an organisation (or individual) which processes personal data for data users, or allows data users to process personal data on its equipment. An organisation or an individual may be classified as a computer bureau under the Act even though not actually in business as a computer bureau.

A **data subject** is an individual who is the subject of personal data.

Activity 9.11

One of the basic problems with the Act is understanding what is meant by personal data 'held' by a data user. Try answering the following question.

9: Assessing creditworthiness

A company keeps a mailing list of customers on computer. All its customers are companies, but the data records include the name and department reference code of the 'contact' inside the customer organisation. Is the data about these individual contacts 'personal data held by the data user'?

The data protection principles

6.5 There are certain Data Protection Principles which registered data users must comply with.

> **DATA PROTECTION PRINCIPLES (1998 ACT)**
>
> Schedule 1 of the Act contains the revised data protection principles.
>
> 1 Personal data shall be processed fairly and lawfully and, in particular, shall not be processed unless:
>
>   (a) At least one of the conditions in Schedule 2 is met (see item (d) above), and
>
>   (b) In the case of sensitive personal data, at least one of the conditions in Schedule 3 is also met (see item (e) above)
>
> 2 Personal data shall be obtained only for one or more specified and lawful purposes, and shall not be further processed in any manner incompatible with that purpose or those purposes.
>
> 3 Personal data shall be adequate, relevant and not excessive in relation to the purpose or purposes for which they are processed.
>
> 4 Personal data shall be accurate and, where necessary, kept up to date.
>
> 5 Personal data processed for any purpose or purposes shall not be kept for longer than is necessary for that purpose or those purposes.
>
> 6 Personal data shall be processed in accordance with the rights of data subjects under this Act.
>
> 7 Appropriate technical and organisational measures shall be taken against unauthorised or unlawful processing of personal data and against accidental loss or destruction of, or damage to, personal data.
>
> 8 Personal data shall not be transferred to a country or territory outside the European Economic Area unless that country or territory ensures an adequate level of protection for the rights and freedoms of data subjects in relation to the processing of personal data.

6.6 The earlier (1984) Data Protection Act was brought in to bring the UK's laws into line with the minimum requirements laid down by the European Union (EU). In July 1995, however, the European Parliament adopted a **Directive on Data Protection**, with two main purposes.

(a) To protect **individual privacy**. Previous UK law only applied to **computer-based** information. The directive applies to **all personal data, in any form.**

(b) To **harmonise data protection legislation** so that, in the interests of improving the operation of the single European market, there can be a **free flow of personal data** between the member states of the EU.

This directive led to the introduction of the Data Protection Act 1998.

The coverage of the Act

6.7 Key points of the Act can be summarised as follows.

(a) With certain exceptions, all **data users** and all computer bureaux have had to **register** under the Act with the **Data Protection Registrar**.

(b) **Individuals** (data subjects) are awarded certain **legal rights**.

(c) **Data holders** must adhere to the **data protection principles**.

Part B: Credit control

Registration under the Act

6.8 The Data Protection Registrar keeps a Register of all data users. Each entry in the Register relates to a data user or computer bureau. Unless a data user has an entry in the Register he may not hold personal data. Even if the data user is registered, he must only hold data and use data for the **purposes** which are registered. A data user must apply to be registered.

The rights of data subjects

6.9 The Act establishes the following rights for data subjects.

(a) A data subject may seek **compensation** through the courts for damage and any associated distress caused by the **loss, destruction** or **unauthorised disclosure** of data about himself or herself or by **inaccurate data** about himself or herself.

(b) A data subject may apply to the courts for **inaccurate data** to be **put right** or even **wiped off** the data user's files altogether. Such applications may also be made to the Registrar.

(c) A data subject may obtain **access** to personal data of which he is the subject. (This is known as the 'subject access' provision.) In other words, a data subject can ask to see his or her personal data that the data user is holding.

(d) A data subject can **sue** a data user (or bureau) for any **damage or distress** caused to him by personal data about him which is **incorrect** or **misleading** as to matter of **fact** (rather than opinion).

6.10 **Features of the 1998 legislation**

(a) It spells out the **conditions under which processing is lawful**. (This was not at all clear under the 1984 Act.)

(b) Everyone now has the right to go to court to seek redress for **any breach** of data protection law, rather than just for certain aspects of it.

(c) Filing systems that are structured so as to facilitate access to information about a particular person now fall within the legislation. This includes systems that are **paper-based** or on **microfilm** or **microfiche**. Personnel records meet this classification.

(d) Processing of personal data is **forbidden** except in the following circumstances.

(i) With the **consent** of the subject (Consent cannot be implied: it must be by freely given, specific and informed agreement.)

(ii) As a result of a **contractual arrangement**

(iii) Because of a **legal obligation**

(iv) To **protect the vital interests** of the subject

(v) Where processing is in the **public interest**

(vi) Where processing is required to exercise **official authority**

(e) The processing of '**sensitive data**' is forbidden, unless express consent has been obtained or there are conflicting obligations under employment law. Sensitive data includes data relating to **racial origin, political opinions, religious beliefs,** physical or mental **health, sexual proclivities** and **trade union** membership.

(f) If data about a data subject is **obtained from a third party** the data subject must be given:

(i) The identity of the **controller** of the data
(ii) The **purposes** for which the data are being processed
(iii) **What data** will be disclosed and **to whom**
(iv) The existence of a right of subject **access** to the data

(g) Data subjects have a right not only to have a **copy of data** held about them but also the right to know **why** the data are being processed and **what is the logic** behind the processing.

6.11 The new Act provides for a transitional period which data controllers can bring existing systems into line with the new law. Manual and automated data where processing was already underway before 24 October 1998 will not have to comply with the new Act until 2001.

Credit reference agencies and the individual consumer

6.12 Any person running a credit reference agency needs to be **licensed under the Consumer Credit Act**. Such reference agencies were brought within the Consumer Credit Act's scope so as to ensure that people were able to access and correct information held about them. These provisions cover some of the same ground as is covered by the Data Protection Act 1998.

6.13 The extent of the **information held by credit reference agencies** is great and its use can have a great effect on an individual; he may find that credit is not extended to him for reasons which are stated by the agency but of which he may not be aware or which may be wrong. However, the 1974 Act gives the individual access and correction rights.

(a) Any consumer is entitled to be told by the creditor, owner or negotiator with whom he deals of the name and address of the credit reference agency being used. He does not have to be seeking credit at the time. If the request is made in writing, it is an offence not to comply.

(b) The consumer is then entitled to make a written request to the credit reference agency for a copy of the file relating to him. If a trader is approached for credit, the consumer has a right to be given the name and address of any agency which he intends to contact.

(c) A consumer may require the agency to correct or remove information held about him if he feels he is likely to be prejudiced by it not being corrected or removed. The agency should do so and report that it has done so within 28 days; alternatively the debtor may require the agency to file a correcting notice, of not more than 200 words, drawn up by the consumer, who may seek an order from the Director General of Fair Trading if the agency does not comply. Disobeying such an order is a criminal offence.

Part B: Credit control

Key learning points

- **Credit risk** is the possibility that a debt will go bad. High risk customers can be profitable, but need to be managed carefully.
- **Data about potential debtors** can be obtained from a number of sources.
    - Banks owe a **duty of care** to their customers and to the enquirer: their assessments of a debtor's credit status are likely to be precisely worded.
    - **Trade references** are useful, but should not be used uncritically.
    - **Credit reference agencies** supply a variety of legal and business information thereby saving time for the enquirer. An agency might give its own suggested rating.
- Some companies are able to employ **credit analysts** to examine a firm's **financial accounts**. As these are historical statements, they are no guide to a debtor's **future creditworthiness**. However, **ratio analysis** can give some idea as to trends and highlight areas for further investigation.
    - The **current ratio** is the ratio of current assets to liabilities. The **quick ratio** measures liquidity more precisely.
    - The **creditors payment period** indicates the average length of time a company takes to pay its debts. Together with **debtors turnover** and **stock turnover** this gives some idea as to the operations cycle.
    - **Gearing ratios** put trade creditors in the context of the firm's overall borrowing: trade creditors are frequently unsecured.
- **Visits to the customer's premises** can provide useful information.
- The **Data Protection Act** makes certain restrictions about the use of data about **individual customers** and the use of **personal data**. **Credit reference agencies** are exempt from the Data Protection Act, but are covered by the **Consumer Credit Act 1974**.

Quick quiz

1. Give an example of grading customers by risk.
2. What are a bank's duties of care in giving credit reference information?
3. What should you bear in mind when following up trade references?
4. What might a report from a credit reference agency typically contain?
5. What is the problem with using published financial accounts for credit control information?
6. What is the current ratio?
7. What is the debt ratio?
8. Does the Data Protection Act apply to data held about limited companies?
9. What legislation applies to credit reference agencies?

Answers to quick quiz

1. Risks might be classified as: zero or negligible risk; ordinary risk; potential slow payers; high risk; unacceptable risk.
2. Not to give an adverse opinion on a customer without justification; not to give misleading information to an enquirer.
3. Suppliers may maintain an untypically good payment record with those they nominate as referees; referees who are not well known businesses should be treated with caution; the referee should ideally be on similar terms as those applied for by the customer.
4. Legal, commercial and credit information.
5. Historical information is an unacceptable guide for the future.
6. The ratio of current assets to current liabilities.
7. The ratio of total creditors to: net fixed assets plus total current assets.
8. No: it covers data about individuals, held on computer, only.
9. The Consumer Credit Act 1974.

9: Assessing creditworthiness

Answers to activities

Answer 9.1

The bank reference is hardly damning, but it is not an overwhelming endorsement either: Triad *should* prove to be a good customer. Therefore the quality of the trade reference is more important. The first reference, while indicating no problems, is of limited usefulness as the credit facility offered is much lower than that which Clinton Ltd is asked to provide. The second credit reference, from Triad's customer, who may be a relative, is worthless.

The request should not be dismissed out of hand, but more investigation is needed.

Answer 9.2

Credit rating agencies, of which Dun and Bradstreet is perhaps one of the best known, can provide:

(a) A same day analysis, if required, perhaps by an on-line computer link on to a VDU in the credit controller's office

(b) Ratio analysis of the business of the customer being assessed, plus

(c) Comment on the customer's credit position

Individual customers (especially non-corporate customers) can be asked to provide the names of referees who can be approached for references. One referee will usually be the customer's *bank*. Another might be the customer's accountant. The initial procedure is for the referee to be asked if in his opinion the individual is reliable up to certain levels of credit. Usually, this is a low amount to start with, but as confidence develops, so the amount may well be increased.

Answer 9.3

In order to carry on a business successfully a company cannot just invest in capital projects and fixed assets. It must also invest in and exercise control over working capital: stocks, debtors and creditors. This working capital has an important bearing on a company's cash needs and cash flows, and therefore on its liquidity, which is as important as its profitability.

Different companies will have different working capital needs depending on the nature of the company's business. The statement in the question that 'stronger and more profitable companies have a higher proportion of working capital' may well be true for a manufacturing company. A manufacturing company will need substantial levels of stocks and will probably have high levels of debtors and creditors as well. However, an equally profitable service company may have a much lower proportion of working capital because, although it may have debtors and some creditors, a service company is unlikely to have large stocks.

Even in manufacturing companies, a decision to use Just in Time techniques of production, if implemented successfully, would result in lower stocks, with smaller batches being produced and so smaller stocks of finished goods.

So a company need not necessarily have a high proportion of working capital in order to be profitable or strong. Conversely companies with high proportions of working capital are not necessarily profitable, well managed companies. It may be that in some companies the reason for high working capital is bad management. Stock control and credit control may be lax whilst not enough advantage is being taken of available trade credit. A much more profitable company may have lower levels of working capital due to an efficient stockholding policy, tight credit and minimum cash holdings.

Answer 9.4

Stock turnover	Debt collection period	Credit taken from suppliers
$\dfrac{30{,}000}{180{,}000} \times 12$	$\dfrac{75{,}000}{360{,}000} \times 12$	$\dfrac{45{,}000}{180{,}000} \times 12$
= 2 months	= 2½ months	= 3 months

Part B: Credit control

The cash cycle is:

	Months
Stock turnover period	2.0
Credit taken from suppliers	(3.0)
Debt collection period	2.5
Operating cycle	1.5

In this example, Legion Ltd pays its suppliers one month after the stocks have been sold, since the stock turnover is two months but credit taken is three months.

Answer 9.5

(a) The information should be analysed in as many ways as possible, and you should not omit any important items. For example, the current and quick ratios are fine, when compared with the guidelines above. However, these only tell part of the story, as the dramatic change in turnover periods indicate. The relevant calculations would seem to be as follows.

(i)

	20X2 £	20X3 £
Sales	573,000	643,000
Cost of goods sold	(420,000)	(460,000)
Gross profit	153,000	183,000
Gross profit percentage	26.7%	28.5%

(ii) Size of *working capital and liquidity ratios* (in 20X3, the bank overdraft has been added to creditors):

	£	£
Cash	5,000	(10,000)
Debtors	97,100	121,500
Stocks:	121,400	189,300
	223,500	300,800
Creditors	(23,900)	(32,500)
Working capital	199,600	268,300

Current ratio: $\dfrac{£223,500}{£23,900} = 9.3:1$ $\dfrac{£310,800}{£42,500} = 7.3:1$

Quick ratio: $\dfrac{£102,100}{£23,900} = 4.2:1$ $\dfrac{£121,500}{£42,500} = 2.8:1$

(iii) *Turnover periods*

	20X2 days		20X3 days	
Stock	$\dfrac{121,400}{420,000} \times 365$	= 105	$\dfrac{189,300}{460,000} \times 365$	= 150
Debtors' collection period	$\dfrac{97,100}{573,000} \times 365$	= 62	$\dfrac{121,500}{643,000} \times 365$	= 69
Creditors' payment period	$\dfrac{23,900}{420,000} \times 365$	= (21)	$\dfrac{32,500}{460,000} \times 365$	= (26)
Operating cycle		146		193

(b) Sales were about 12% higher in 20X3 than in 20X2 and the cost of sales was about 9% higher. The investments in stocks and debtors minus creditors (ie working capital ignoring cash) rose from £194,600 to £278,300, ie by £83,700 or nearly 44%. This is completely out of proportion to the volume of increase in trade, which indicates that working capital turnover periods are not being properly controlled.

The increase in working capital by £83,700 means that the net cash receipts from profits in 20X3 were £83,700 less than they would have been if there had been no increase at all in stocks and debtors (less creditors) during 20X3. The company's overdraft of £10,000 is therefore unnecessary. Furthermore, arguably the current ratio is excessive. Although the current and quick ratios appear healthy as they stand, the trend is worrying, with the quick ratio declining rapidly. This would not be necessary, if the company controlled debtors and stock better.

The causes of the increase in working capital in 20X3 are:

(i) The increase in sales, but mainly
(ii) The increased length of turnover periods

Debtors, already allowed 62 days to pay in 20X2, were allowed 69 days in 20X3 and this would seem to be an excessive length of time. The most serious change, however, is the increase in the finished goods stock turnover period from 105 days to 150 days and it is difficult to see an obvious reason why this should have occurred, although there may have been a temporary build-up at the end of 20X3 in preparation for a big sales drive.

Part of the increase in stocks and debtors has been financed by an increase in the creditors payment period, from 21 to 26 days. This doesn't seem too bad, but in practice it might be worse. Cost of goods sold includes more than just raw materials, and if we knew the level of raw materials purchases, say, the position might appear worse. For the credit controller there are two worries:

(i) The increase in the creditors' payment period
(ii) The overall change in working capital out of all proportion to the growth of business activities, suggesting growing problems in liquidity, even though the current and quick ratios are healthy in themselves at the moment

Answer 9.6

> *Tutorial note.* More than six ratios can be calculated from the information given; we have given all of the most obvious ratios.

			A	B
1	Gross profit margin =	$\dfrac{\text{Gross profit}}{\text{Sales}}$	$\dfrac{1{,}000 - 400}{1{,}000}$ = 60%	$\dfrac{3{,}000 - 2{,}000}{3{,}000}$ = 33%
2	Net profit margin =	$\dfrac{\text{Net profit}}{\text{Sales}}$	$\dfrac{30}{1{,}000}$ = 3%	$\dfrac{100}{3{,}000}$ = 3.3%
3	Asset turnover =	$\dfrac{\text{Sales}}{\text{Capital employed}}$	$\dfrac{1{,}000}{200}$ = 5 times	$\dfrac{3{,}000}{650}$ = 4.6 times
4	Return on capital employed (ROCE) = $\dfrac{\text{Net profit before interest}}{\text{Total long term capital}}$		$\dfrac{30 + 10(10\% \times 100)}{200}$ = 20%	$\dfrac{100 + 13(10\% \times 130)}{650}$ = 17.3%
5	Gearing =	$\dfrac{\text{Debt}}{\text{Equity}}$	$\dfrac{100}{100}$ = 100%	$\dfrac{130}{520 \,(160 + 360)}$ = 25%
	or	$\dfrac{\text{Debt}}{\text{Total capital}}$	$\dfrac{100}{200}$ = 50%	$\dfrac{130}{650}$ = 20%
6	Current ratio =	$\dfrac{\text{Current assets}}{\text{Current liabilities}}$	$\dfrac{180}{160}$ = 1.125	$\dfrac{200}{120}$ = 1.667

Part B: Credit control

7	Quick ratio = $\dfrac{\text{Current assets - stock}}{\text{Current liabilities}}$		$\dfrac{100}{160}$ = 0.625	$\dfrac{100}{120}$ = 0.833
8	Debtors turnover period = $\dfrac{\text{Debtors} \times 365}{\text{Sales}}$		$\dfrac{100 \times 365}{1,000}$ = 36½ days	$\dfrac{90 \times 365}{3,000}$ = 11 days
9	Stock turnover period = $\dfrac{\text{Stock} \times 365}{\text{Cost of sales}}$		$\dfrac{80 \times 365}{400}$ = 73 days	$\dfrac{100 \times 365}{2,000}$ = 18 days
10	Creditors turnover period = $\dfrac{\text{Creditors}}{\text{Cost of sales}}$		$\dfrac{110 \times 365}{400}$ = 100 days	$\dfrac{120 \times 365}{2,000}$ = 22 days

Answer 9.7

Although A and B have similar net profit margins, B has a lower gross profit margin. A must therefore have a much higher percentage of overheads than B. A's turnover is, however, much lower than B's and so its net profit is also much lower in absolute terms.

A also has a higher ROCE. This is because it makes more efficient use of its assets, as shown by its high asset turnover. However, B's asset turnover is reduced by the revaluation of its land.

A is considerably more highly geared than B because its long-term debt is currently as high as its proprietors' equity, whereas B's capital is nearly four times higher than its debt. Thus, A is a higher risk for a potential investor or lender.

B appears to manage its working capital much more efficiently than A. A turns its stock over five times a year but B is about four times as efficient. It may be as a result of this difference in working capital management that B does *not* have an overdraft while A's is quite high. B's liquidity is very much better.

However, we are not told in which industry A and B operate. If, for instance, they are both retailers, it may be that A is an antiques shop while B is selling food or clothes, which turn over much faster but at a lower margin. We are also ignorant of the ownership of each business. If the owners of one business work in it, then part of their drawings are effectively wages and so their profits should be adjusted to be comparable with the other firm.

Another proviso is that A's bank overdraft may effectively be part of its long-term debt, in which case ROCE and gearing should all be adjusted accordingly. This leads on to the problem that one balance sheet on its own is not necessarily representative. Ideally, a series should be examined, so that trends can be identified and conclusions can be considered better founded.

A further difficulty in looking at the accounts of unincorporated businesses is that they are not required to give a true and fair view and so are not governed by SSAPs. The accounting policies applied may therefore be quite different in each case.

Finally, we have no idea whether or not A's assets could also be revalued upwards. If so, its ROCE is almost certainly overstated, and its asset turnover deceptively high.

A tentative conclusion, in spite of the above reservations, would be that A is a more profitable but less solvent firm than B. This makes it a riskier proposition for lending or investing, especially as it has a much smaller capital base.

Answer 9.8

For *new customers* about whom nothing is known the credit controller can go to Companies House to obtain financial statements on a corporate customer (ie copies of past annual reports and accounts of the customer which have been filed at Companies House). These accounts can then be analysed to assess the financial position of the customer, and changes in this position over time.

Items that might be studied and ratios that might be calculated are:

(a)   The amount of annual profit

(b)   The net assets of the customer's business

9: Assessing creditworthiness

(c) The return on capital employed achieved by the customer

(d) The profit/sales ratio

(e) Asset turnover ratios, in particular

    (i) The current ratio (current assets: current liabilities);
    (ii) The acid test ratio (current assets excluding stock: current liabilities)
    (iii) Debtors' payment period;
    (iv) Credit period taken from creditors (estimated as $\frac{\text{creditors}}{\text{cost of sales}} \times 365$ days)
    (v) Stock turnover period

(f) Gearing ratio (the ratio of 'prior charge capital' to equity capital)

(g) Debt ratio (the ratio of current and long term debts to total assets)

(h) The percentage increase in annual sales turnover

The weaknesses of this approach to credit risk assessment are that:

(a) The reports and accounts filed at Companies House show an out-of-date situation (The customer's financial position might now be completely different.)

(b) Sending someone to Companies House to make the investigation takes time

(c) Not all customers are corporate customers, and so information about them will not be held at Companies House

Answer 9.9

(a) A simple system for categorising debtor risk would be to establish four categories of debtor:

    (i) Strong
    (ii) Average
    (iii) Marginal
    (iv) Weak/poor

Different credit terms might then be offered to a customer according to how that customer is categorised, with strong customers being allowed most credit and weak customers not being allowed any credit at all (ie cash sales only).

(b) Procedures should be in place for assessing any individual customer's risk categorisation. Since circumstances change over time, the risk category of existing customers should be reviewed from time to time. All new customers should be put into one of the credit controller's categories.

(c) Procedures should exist for checking that goods and an invoice have been sent to the customer, and when customers pay any invoice so that:

    (i) The credit control section is kept up-to-date about the current debt position for every customer
    (ii) The debt collection staff can be notified when debts become overdue.

Answer 9.10

For existing customers, credit risk categorisation should be reassessed periodically. If a customer's position seems to be stronger, the credit controller should be prepared to put the customer into a different risk category and grant more credit if required. If on the other hand a customer's position seems to have worsened, the steps to be taken might include:

(a) Notifying the staff responsible for debt collection that existing debts should be pursued if they are overdue

(b) In the case of important customers, the credit manager should discuss the changing situation with the customer, to try to find out what is happening with the customer's business (As a result of these discussions, different (stricter) credit terms might be agreed.)

One way of checking on existing customers is to conduct a regular review to see if customer payment patterns are changing. This will give an early warning that events are forcing the customer to finance his business through taking longer credit periods. The review is easily done through a regular ratio analysis of sales to outstanding balances.

Answer 9.11

If the mailing list is simply used to send letters or mailshots to the customer's organisation, and the individual names and department codes are only needed to direct the letters to the right part of the organisation, then the data about the individuals is not personal data held by the data user. This is because the data is not processed by reference to the individual.

However, if the mailing list file also contains data about the individual contacts which are intended to help with marketing (for example, data about attendances at open days or other events held by the data user) then it will be personal data held by the data user, since it might be processed by reference to the individuals themselves.

Chapter 10 Managing debtors

Chapter topic list

1   Maintaining information on debtors
2   Collecting debts
3   Default insurance, factoring and invoice discounting
4   Debt collection from difficult customers

Learning objectives

On completion of this chapter you will be able to:

	Performance criteria	Range statement
• discuss the reasons for refusing credit with customers in a tactful manner	15.3.4	
• monitor regularly information relating to the current state of debtors' accounts and take appropriate action	15.4.1	
• contact debtors and make arrangements for the recovery of the debt, passing information and recommendations for action to the appropriate individual within your organisation	15.4.2	15.4.2
• discuss factoring arrangements and debt insurance	15.4	
• analyse information on debtors	15.4	15.4.1
• evaluate different collection methods	15.4	

Part B: Credit control

1 MAINTAINING INFORMATION ON DEBTORS

1.1 We have already seen that the credit controller should obtain information from a variety of sources in order to decide whether or not to grant credit and, if credit is granted, what that level should be. The credit controller's job does not end there, however. After all, a customer may become less (or more) creditworthy over time. One of the principal instruments a credit controller uses is the **aged debtors listing**.

Debtors age analysis

1.2 An **aged debtors listing** will probably look very much like the schedule illustrated below. The analysis splits up the total balance on the account of each customer across different columns according to the dates of the transactions which make up the total balance. Thus, the amount of an invoice which was raised 14 days ago will form part of the figure in the column headed 'up to 30 days', while an invoice which was raised 36 days ago will form part of the figure in the column headed 'up to 60 days'. (In the schedule below, 'up to 60 days' is used as shorthand for 'more than 30 days but less than 60 days'.)

HEATH LIMITED

AGE ANALYSIS OF DEBTORS AS AT 31.1.X2

Account number	Customer name	Balance	Up to 30 days	Up to 60 days	Up to 90 days	Over 90 days
B004	Brilliant Ltd	804.95	649.90	121.00	0.00	34.05
E008	Easimat Ltd	272.10	192.90	72.40	6.80	0.00
H002	Hampstead Ltd	1,818.42	0.00	0.00	724.24	1,094.18
M024	Martlesham Ltd	284.45	192.21	92.24	0.00	0.00
N030	Nyfen Ltd	1,217.54	1,008.24	124.50	0.00	84.80
T002	Todmorden College	914.50	842.00	0.00	72.50	0.00
T004	Tricorn Ltd	94.80	0.00	0.00	0.00	94.80
V010	Volux Ltd	997.06	413.66	342.15	241.25	0.00
Y020	Yardsley Smith & Co	341.77	321.17	20.60	0.00	0.00
Totals		6,745.59	3,620.08	772.89	1,044.79	1,307.83
Percentage		100%	53.6%	11.5%	15.5%	19.4%

1.3 An age analysis of debtors can be prepared manually or, more easily, by computer. In theory this should represent actual invoices outstanding, but there are problems, which we shall discuss later in this chapter, of unmatched or 'unallocated' cash and payments on account.

1.4 The age analysis of debtors may be used to help decide what action to take about older debts. Going down each column in turn starting from the column furthest to the right and working across, we can see that there are some rather old debts which ought to be investigated. Correspondence may of course already exist on some of these items. Perhaps some older invoices are still in dispute. Perhaps some debtors are known to be in financial difficulties. (If there are newer invoices also for customers who could be in financial difficulties, we should perhaps be asking whether we ought to be continuing to supply goods to these customers.)

1.5 A number of **refinements** can be suggested to the aged debtors listing to make it easier to use.

(a) A report can be printed in which **overdue accounts** are seen first: this highlights attention on these items.

(b) It can help to aggregate data by **class of customer**. In this case, a report would be printed containing, for debtors aggregated into regions, type of customer, industry sectors etc, the:

    (i)   Sales revenue
    (ii) Outstanding amount owed, broken down into age
    (iii) Days' sales outstanding

(c) There is no reason why this should not apply to individual debtor accounts as below. You could also include the date of the last transaction on the account (eg last invoice, last payment).

Account number	Customer name	Balance	Up to 30 days	Up to 60 days	Up to 90 days	Over 90 days	Sales revenue in last 12 months	Days sales outstanding
B004	Brilliant Ltd	804.95	649.90	121.00	0.00	34.05	6,789.00	43

1.6 We can see from the age analysis of Heath Ltd's debtors given earlier that the relatively high proportion of debts over 90 days (19.4%) is largely due to the debts of Hampstead Ltd. Other customers with debts of this age are Brilliant Ltd, Nyfen Ltd and Tricorn Ltd.

Debtors' ageing and liquidity

1.7 Also of interest to the credit controller is the *total* percentage figure calculated at the bottom of each column. In practice the credit controller will be concerned to look at this figure first of all, in order to keep the ageing figures consistent. Why might a credit controller be worried by an increase in the ageing? If the credit controller knows the customers are going to pay, should it matter?

1.8 Think back to your work on cash forecasting. This is based on the expectation that a company's debts will be paid within, say, 30 days after payment. In other words revenue booked in Month 1 would be followed up by cash in Month 2. The cash forecast also has an outflow side. Any reduction in the inflow caused by an overall increase in the debtors period affects the company's ability to pay its debts and increases its use of overdraft finance: unauthorised overdrafts carry a hefty fee as well as interest.

1.9 A simple example will make this clear. The cash flow forecast of Perrith Ltd for January to March 19X5 is as follows.

	January £	February £	March £
Receipts from debtors	1,500	1,000	1,400
Payments	(1,200)	(1,300)	(900)
Surplus/deficit for the month	300	(300)	500
Cash at bank/(overdraft) brought forward	(400)	(100)	(400)
Cash at bank/(overdraft) carried forward	(100)	(400)	100

At the end of March, there is a forecast surplus of £100. Let us assume that all customers take exactly one month credit (ie January cash receipts reflect December sales). Squidgee Ltd has an arranged overdraft facility of £700, which it seems to be well within. The facility is reviewed at the end of each period, and excess borrowing over £700 costs 10% of the amount over that limit.

Part B: Credit control

1.10 Let us now assume that customers suddenly take longer to pay. There are no bad debts, but customers now pay two months after the sale. In other words, December invoices sales are paid for in February, and so on.

	January £	February £	March £
Receipts from debtors	-	1,500	1,000
Payments	(1,200)	(1,300)	(900)
Bank charges*		(90)	(79)
Surplus/(deficit)	(1,200)	110	21
Cash at bank/(overdraft) brought forward	(400)	(1,600)	(1,490)
Cash at bank/(overdraft) carried forward	(1,600)	(1,490)	(1,469)

* Bank charges in February are £1 for every £10 over the overdraft limit at the end of January and so on.

1.11 What this very simple example goes to show is the dramatic impact that fluctuations in the debtors ageing, even a one-off change, can have on a firm's cash position.

(a) From working comfortably within the agreed overdraft, the firm has found itself carrying a long-term overdraft which is quite expensive.

(b) The firm's own creditworthiness is likely to suffer.

(c) The firm pays more in overdraft fees and interest.

1.12 Of course, most fluctuations are unlikely to be as violent, but any upward trend should be brought to a halt.

1.13 It may be the case that an increase in the overall debtors ageing is caused by the activities of one customer, and there is always the possibility that cut-off dates for producing the report can generate anomalies. (For example, a customer might pay invoices at the end of every calendar month, whereas the debtors ageing analysis might be run every 30 days.)

1.14 However, the credit controller should try and avoid situations when a customer starts to delay payment. He or she should review information from:

(a) Sales staff regarding how the company is doing
(b) The press for any stories relevant to the company
(c) Competitors
(d) The trade 'grapevine'

These can supply early warning signals.

1.15 If, however, there is a persistent problem, the credit controller might have to insist on a **refusal of credit**.

(a) This is likely to be resented by sales staff who will possibly receive less commission as a result of lower sales.

(b) However, if there is a possibility of default, the loss of a **potential** sale is surely less severe than the failure of **actual** money to arrive.

1.16 **Additional ratios** which might be useful in debtor management, in addition to day's sales outstanding, are as follows.

(a) **Overdues as a percentage of total debt**. For example, assume that if Heath Limited (Paragraph 1.2) offers credit on 30 day terms. Brilliant Ltd's debt could be analysed as:

$$\frac{£121.00 + £34.05}{£804.95} = 19.3\% \text{ overdue.}$$

(b) **If debts are disputed**, it is helpful to see what a proportion these are of the total debtors and the total overdue. If, of Heath's total debtors of £6,745.59, an amount of £973.06 related to disputed items, the ratio of disputed debts to total outstanding would be:

$$\frac{£973.06}{£6,745.59} = 14.4\%$$

As a percentage of total items *over* 30 days old:

$$\frac{£973.06}{£6,745.59 - £3,620.08} = 31\%$$

An increasing disputes ratio can indicate:

(i) Invoicing problems
(ii) Operational problems

Activity 10.1

Briefly describe the format and content of the aged debtors listing.

2 COLLECTING DEBTS

ASSESSMENT ALERT

An assessment task might require you to evaluate different methods of debt collection and to recommend the most appropriate method.

2.1 Collecting debts is a two-stage process.

(a) Having agreed credit terms with a customer, a business should issue an invoice and expect to receive payment when it is due. **Issuing invoices** and **receiving payments** is the task of sales ledger staff. They should ensure that:

(i) The customer is fully aware of the terms
(ii) The invoice is correctly drawn up
(iii) They are aware of any potential quirks in the customer's system

(b) If payments become overdue, they should be 'chased'. **Chasing late payers** might be a responsibility of credit control staff. Alternatively, depending on the size of the organisation, the work might be handed over to specialist debt collection staff, under the supervision of the credit manager. In the case of very late payers, the services of an external debt collection agency might be employed. **Procedures** for pursuing overdue debts must be established, for example:

(i) Issuing reminders or final demands
(ii) Chasing payment by telephone
(iii) Making a personal approach for payment from the credit manager or a salesman
(iv) Notifying the debt collection section about what debts are overdue so that further credit will not be given to the customer until he has paid the due amounts
(v) Handing over the task of debt collection from the sales ledger staff to a specialist debt collection section

Part B: Credit control

(vi) Instituting legal action to recover a debt

(vii) Hiring an external debt collection agency to collect the debt

2.2 Sales **paperwork** should be dealt with promptly and accurately.

(a) Invoices should be sent out immediately after delivery of goods.

(b) Checks should be carried out to ensure that invoices are accurate.

(c) The investigation of queries and complaints and, if appropriate, the issue of credit notes should be carried out promptly.

(d) If practical, monthly statements should be issued early so that all items on the statement might then be included in customers' monthly settlements of bills.

Customer awareness of terms

2.3 Many larger companies and public sector organisations have a reputation for being slow payers. Small businesses in particular appear to suffer at the hands of larger companies which take as long a time to pay as possible. This practice can severely damage a small business, especially if the value of the invoice, in relation to the small business's expected cash flow, is large. A small business can be thrown on to the mercy of its bankers if its bills are not paid. Any business can increase its chances of getting paid by ensuring, at various stages, that **the customer has no right to plead ignorance** of the due date, or that the seller attaches no importance to it.

(a) Payment dates and terms should be discussed during the initial negotiations as to the price on the grounds that, for the supplier, payment terms can be costed into pricing calculations.

(b) When the order is confirmed in writing, payment terms should be clearly stated, not left to the small print.

(c) When a customer account is set up, the credit agreement should contain a clause whereby a customer acknowledges agreement to the supplier's terms and conditions.

(d) The invoice should state boldly the payment terms.

(e) Payment terms should also be prominently displayed on the final statement.

Proper invoicing

2.4 Slip-ups in invoicing by a supplier might create delays in payment by a customer, because the internal controls in the customer's procedures for paying the debt prevent the debt from being paid because of the discrepancies or faults. So, when issuing an invoice sales ledger staff should check the following.

(a) The customer's name and address: are they correct and current?

(b) Is the invoice being sent to the right place? Many companies have a central purchasing area and central purchases ledger area. Invoices, if they are to get to the purchase ledger staff, must be sent to where the customer requests them to be sent.

(c) Is the invoice recognisable and how is it to be sent? An invoice sent with the goods that is not immediately recognisable might sit on an advice note file of the stores and never get to the staff responsible for paying the invoice.

(d) Does the invoice have the customer's authorisation reference on it? If it is to be matched with a purchase order, then it must quote the purchase order number.

(e) Are the details on the invoice correct as to quantities, descriptions and details, and arithmetic total? The customer organisation's staff will be authorised to reject the invoice if the details are not correct.

(f) Having delivered the goods, the invoice should be submitted to the customer promptly.

Knowledge of customer payment systems

2.5 It helps to have some ideas as to **how customers pay**.

(a) Some customers have an invoice run on a monthly basis. There is an inevitable cut-off point after which data cannot be input to the system. Delays might be caused by a bureaucratic backlog.

(b) Other customers, regardless of their actual obligations, ration the amount paid out per month. Personal customers with financial problems have to ration scarce resources, paying essentials (ie food, mortgage) before servicing other debts (especially non-secured loans like credit cards). Many businesses need to conserve cash and act in this way.

(c) Some customers will only pay when sent a reminder or when specifically asked by suppliers.

(d) Other customers will not pay until threatened with legal action.

Statements, reminders and final demands

2.6 Invoices are usually followed by a **monthly statement** to customers which will:

(a) List the new invoices during the month
(b) Indicate the cash received
(c) Indicate the outstanding balance due
(d) Analyse the debts by age
(e) Serve as a reminder to the customer about payment

2.7 Instead of statements, a business might issue **reminder notices** to slow payers. The reminder would be intended to prompt the customer into making the payment. An example is given **on the next page**.

2.8 **Final demands** are sent when an invoice is overdue for payment, warning the customer that unless payment is received within a certain period of time, steps will be taken to pursue the debt by 'legal methods'. The threat of legal action should then persuade the customer to pay (if he can afford to!)

Part B: Credit control

BRITLINE CARRIERS PLC
Sutton Lane, Liverpool LW6 9BC
Telephone: 0151 - 324 7345/6

Directors:
D Smith (Managing)
P Patel
C Wilkes

Registered office:
Sutton Lane Liverpl LW6 9BC
Reg. No 34567
Reg. in England

Ref: NC/nn TO 16

21 June 19--

Accounts Department
Tradewell Office Products & Services Ltd
Easy St
MANCHESTER M12 7SL

Dear Sir

OVERDUE ACCOUNT: 33521

Further to the statement sent to you on 16 May 19-- it appears that your account for April 19-- totalling £1,402.70 remains outstanding. Please find enclosed a copy statement.

The terms of credit extended to your company were agreed as 30 days from receipt of statement.

Please settle the above account by return of post.

Yours faithfully,

N Competent, Receivables Officer
Credit Control Department (extension 916)

enc

Special cases

'Key account' customers

2.9 In most businesses, major **'key account' customers** will receive special treatment in the sales effort, and it is appropriate that special treatment is also given in managing the debts in these cases. In such circumstances, a more personal approach to debt collection is advisable, with the salesman or a debt collection officer (perhaps the credit manager himself) making an approach to the customer to request payment.

Reconciliation and 'on account' payments

2.10 A problem you might encounter is a customer who pays a round sum to cover a variety of invoices. The round sum may be a **payment 'on account'**: in other words, the customer might not state which invoices the payment refers to. This might occur because the customer is having liquidity problems. Unallocated payments on account, which have not been agreed, should be investigated.

Receipts on long-term contracts

2.11 You may have read or heard about the disputes between Eurotunnel plc and TransManche Link, the consortium which carried out the construction work on the Channel Tunnel. This was an example of some of the problems that might be encountered on **long-term contracts** of any kind. Such long-term contracts generally feature **precise terms**, and a **requirement of third-party verification** (eg an architect's certification) for payments to be made.

2.12 There is always scope for argument, and the normal conditions of credit control do not necessarily apply. Simply refusing to continue to provide a service to a customer who is a slow payer may involve significant costs, especially if resources have been allocated to the project. Furthermore, the creditor firm is still concerned to maintain a healthy commercial relationship for the duration of the project.

2.13 As contracting firms devote substantial resources to certain contracts, the results of not being paid for work done can be catastrophic. The person running the cash and credit control side of the business needs to be aware of the implications in cash flow terms and perhaps needs to demand regular payments.

Customer queries

2.14 Many problems with debtors do not arise out of insolvency or liquidity but for **operational reasons**.

(a) Invoices might be disputed.
(b) Goods may be returned if they do not accord with the specified order.

2.15 Many customer queries are not therefore the province of the credit control department. However, any customer query should be investigated, before the firm starts instituting its bad debt procedures. **Courtesy** should be maintained at all times. It might also help to do a **reconciliation** of items in the debtor's and the creditor's accounting records.

3 DEFAULT INSURANCE, FACTORING AND INVOICE DISCOUNTING

Default insurance

3.1 Companies might be able to obtain **default insurance** against certain approved debts going bad through a specialist credit insurance firm. A company cannot insure against all its bad debt losses, but may be able to insure against losses above the normal level.

3.2 When a company arranges credit insurance, it must submit specific proposals for credit to the insurance company, stating the name of each customer to which it wants to give credit and the amount of credit it wants to give. The insurance company will accept, amend or refuse these proposals, depending on its assessment of each of these customers.

3.3 Credit insurance is normally available for only up to about 75% of a company's potential bad debt loss. The remaining 25% of any bad debt costs are borne by the company itself. This is to ensure that the company does not become slack with its credit control and debt collection procedures, for example by indulging in overtrading and not chasing slow payers hard enough.

Part B: Credit control

Domestic credit insurance

3.4 **Credit insurance** for **domestic** (ie not export) businesses is available from a number of sources including the following.

- Trade Indemnity plc
- AIG Europe (UK) Ltd
- Credit and Guarantee Insurance Co Ltd
- Panfinancial Insurance Co Ltd
- Sun Alliance

3.5 Insurance companies such as those listed above are prepared to assume for themselves the risk of the debt going bad, and they hope to profit from this. Furthermore, they are less vulnerable, as institutions, to the possibility that debt will ruin their business.

3.6 It is (sadly) not possible simply for a firm to unload all its doubtful receivables on to an insurance company. The insurance company, after all, is in the business of making a profit. Therefore, most insurance companies will spend a considerable effort in examining a company's books and systems before they will accept any of the risks.

(a) The insurer will examine the entire sales ledger to look at the overall portfolio of risk, if, for example, insurance is provided against the entire sales ledger.

(b) The firm's credit control, debt collection and sales ledger administration will also be scrutinised to ensure that the firm is not lax in its credit control policy and that all efforts are taken to reduce the possibility of debts going bad.

3.7 There are several types of credit insurance on offer. These are briefly described below.

'Whole turnover' policies

3.8 **Whole turnover policies** can be used in two ways.

(a) It can cover the firm's entire sales ledger, although, normally speaking, the actual amount paid out will rarely be more than 80% of the total loss for any specific claim.

(b) Alternatively, the client can select a proportion of its debtors and insure these for their entire amount.

In other words, perhaps 80% of each debt is insured; or the entire amount of the debts incurred, say, by perhaps 80% of the customers.

3.9 Premiums on a whole turnover policy are usually 1% of the insured sales. Although strictly speaking, the payment is calculated in arrears, the firm normally pays a deposit in advance for each quarter.

Activity 10.2

Gibbony Whey Ltd has a whole turnover policy for its debts. The policy is underwritten by Broaken Amis Assurance plc and is on a whole turnover basis, whereby 80% of the sales ledger is covered, provided that the total credit offered to customers does not exceed £1m. In the first quarter of 19X4, the company made total sales of £4m: at the end of the quarter debtors for credit sales stood at £1.4m. Gibbony Whey has traded with Sloe Pears Ltd: the underwriters approved a credit limit for Sloe Pears of £1,700. At the end of the quarter, Sloe Pears had outstanding debts of £2,100. Sloe Pears turns into a 'bad debtor' when the company's buildings are completely destroyed by a falling asteroid.

Gibbony Whey writes to Broaken Amis claiming for the bad debt. How much will Gibbony Whey be entitled to as compensation?

Annual aggregate: excess of loss

3.10 Under an **annual aggregate excess of loss policy,** the insurer pays 100% of debts above an agreed limit. This is similar to motor insurers requiring that the first amount (eg £50) of a loss is borne by the insured.

Specific account policies

3.11 Insurance can be purchased to cover a **specific debtor account** in the event of some contingency. For example, a policy might depend on the debtor being formally declared insolvent.

Export credit insurance

3.12 The credit risks which an **exporter** must consider come under two headings.

(a) **Buyer risks** also known as **commercial risks**. These are similar to those risks encountered in domestic sales, except that the credit period on export sales is often longer. Also, suing someone overseas is often a much harder, longer and more expensive process than suing a domestic customer in the County Court.

(b) **Country risks** also known as **market risks** or **political risks**. These include not only risks in the buyer's country, but also obstacles in the UK (eg cancellation or non-renewal of an export licence) or in a third country through which payment must be made.

3.13 Cover for short-term business (up to 180 days, or, subject to individual discussion, up to two years) is provided by private-sector insurers, most notably NCM Credit Insurance Ltd, a UK subsidiary of Nederlandsche Credietverzekering Maatschappij. For short we shall refer to NCM Credit Insurance Ltd as NCM. **NCM** offers:

(a) An **international guarantee** offering cover of around 90% in respect of various buyer and country risks

(b) A **domestic policy** in respect of buyer risks only (the country risks not being relevant)

3.14 The Government's **Export Credits Guarantee Department (ECGD)** provides longer term help to UK firms in the following main ways.

(a) ECGD issues **guarantees to banks**. Against the strength of this security, the bank provides, usually at favourable interest rates, finance to support the export contract.

(b) ECGD offers **specific guarantees** to exporters who want to finance sales either out of their own funds or by way of ordinary borrowings.

(c) ECGD supports the issue of third-party guarantees/bonds by **indemnifying** the bondgiver.

Factoring

3.15 Some businesses might have difficulties in financing the amounts owed by customers (debtors). There are two main reasons for this.

(a) If a business's sales are rising rapidly, its total debtors will rise quickly too. Selling more on credit will put a strain on the company's cash flow. The business, although making profits, might find itself in difficulties because it has too many debtors and not enough cash.

(b) If a business grants long credit to its customers, it might run into cash flow difficulties for much the same reason. Exporting businesses must often allow long periods of credit to foreign buyers, before eventually receiving payment, and their problem of financing debtors adequately can be a critical one.

3.16 **Factors** are organisations that offer their clients a financing service to overcome these problems. They are prepared to advance cash to the client against the security of the client's debtors. The business will assign its debtors to the factor and will typically ask for an advance of funds against the debts which the factor has purchased, usually up to 80% of the value of the debts.

3.17 For example, if a business makes credit sales of £100,000 per month, the factor might be willing to advance up to 80% of the invoice value (here £80,000) in return for a commission charge, and interest will be charged on the amount of funds advanced. The balance of the money will be paid to the business when the customers have paid the factor, or after an agreed period.

3.18 This service gives the business immediate cash in place of a debt (which a promise of cash in the future). If the business needs money to finance operations, borrowing against trade debts is therefore an alternative to asking a bank for an overdraft.

> **KEY TERM**
>
> **Factoring**: an arrangement to have debts collected by a factor company, which advances a proportion of the money it is due to collect.

3.19 The main aspects of **factoring** are:

(a) Administration of the client's invoicing, sales accounting and debt collection service

(b) Credit protection for the client's debts, whereby the factor takes over the risk of loss from bad debts and so 'insures' the client against such losses (This service is also referred to as 'debt underwriting' or the 'purchase of a client's debts'. The factor usually purchases these debts 'without recourse' to the client, which means that if the client's debtors do not pay what they owe, the factor will not ask for his money back from the client.)

(c) Making payments to the client in advance of collecting the debts (This is sometimes referred to as 'factor finance' because the factor is providing cash to the client against outstanding debts.)

3.20 The appeal of factor financing to **growing firms** is that factors might advance money when a bank is reluctant to consider granting a larger overdraft. Advances from a factor are therefore particularly useful for companies needing more and more cash to expand their business quickly, by purchasing more stocks and allowing more credit sales. However, factoring companies are generally reluctant to assist companies with less than a year's trading behind them, and so which do not have much of a track record in business yet, because of the strong risk that a new company might get into financial difficulties.

The advantages of factoring

3.21 The **benefits of factoring** for a business customer can be set out as follows.

(a) The business can pay its suppliers promptly, and so be able to take advantage of any early payment discounts that are available.

(b) Optimum stock levels can be maintained, because the business will have enough cash to pay for the stocks it needs.

(c) Growth can be financed through sales rather than by injecting fresh external capital.

(d) The business gets finance linked to its volume of sales. In contrast, overdraft limits tend to be determined by historical balance sheets.

(e) The managers of the business do not have to spend their time on the problems of slow paying debtors.

(f) The business does not incur the costs of running its own sales ledger department.

3.22 An important **disadvantage of factoring** is that debtors will be making payments direct to the factor, which is likely to present a **negative picture of the firm**.

Invoice discounting

3.23 **Invoice discounting** is related to factoring and many factors will provide an invoice discounting service. Invoice discounting is the purchase of a selection of invoices, at a discount. For example, if your business had just redecorated the Town Hall it might have sent the Council an invoice for £5,000. This would be an easy invoice to sell on for cash because the Council are very likely to pay. An invoice for £5,000 sent to 'A Cowboy & Co' would not be so easy to sell for immediate cash!

3.24 The invoice discounter does **not** take over the administration of the client's sales ledger, and the arrangement is purely for the advance of cash. A business should only want to have some invoices discounted when it has a temporary cash shortage, and so invoice discounting tends to consist of 'one-off' deals. Since the discounter does not control debt administration, and relies on the client to collect the debts for him, it is a more risky operation than factoring and so the discounter might only agree to offer an invoice discounting service to reliable, well established companies.

> **KEY TERM**
>
> **Invoice discounting**: the purchase (by the provider of the discounting service) of trade debts at a discount. Invoice discounting enables the company from which the debts are purchased to raise working capital.

3.25 **Confidential invoice discounting** is an arrangement whereby a debt is confidentially assigned to the factor, and the client's customer will only become aware of the arrangement if he does not pay his debt to the client.

Activity 10.3

The Managing Director, the Chief Accountant and the Chief Internal Auditor were meeting to discuss problems over debt collection recently identified in the Forward Company. One point made strongly by the Chief Internal Auditor was that his staff should be involved in much more than the routine verification tasks normally undertaken. It is, therefore, agreed that the internal audit section should look at the problem and consider the possibility of using the services of a factor to take over some, or all, of the work of the debtors credit section.

Part B: Credit control

Task

Outline the advantages and disadvantages of using the services of a factor.

4 DEBT COLLECTION FROM DIFFICULT CUSTOMERS

4.1 The last chapter mentioned that different customers take different views as to paying their bills. Some who are perfectly able to pay are happy to withhold payment until they have received correspondence, solicitors' letters and so on. The last chapter outlined a sample reminder letter. This section describes some of the techniques employed where a credit controller has to be more persistent.

4.2 First of all, it is necessary to identify those customers whose payment records leave something to be desired.

(a) The largest outstanding balances and the accounts with most arrears can be examined first. This focuses attention on value.

(b) A list can also be prepared of 'live accounts' which have not received payments in the preceding month.

4.3 If neither the invoice nor the statement elicit any response the firm has a number of alternative techniques. These include the following.

(a) **Letters**: cheap but not very effective
(b) **Telephoning**: expensive, but fairly effective
(c) **Fax transmission**: medium cost, medium effectiveness
(d) **Personal visit**: very expensive, but very effective

Each of these methods is appropriate to different circumstances. Broadly speaking, the higher the value of the debt the more personal should be the intervention.

Lower value ─────────────────→ Higher value

Letter → Fax (or telex) → Telephone ─────→ Personal visit

4.4 The credit control department's own records are an important way of controlling the proceedings. The **customer record card** can be used to keep track as to how the collection process is going.

Account no Account name Address				Telephone Fax Contact name Extension		
Date and time	Phone	Letter	Spoke to	Date promised	Amount promised	Details

Such a card can be prepared from a daily telephone log of all calls.

Letters

4.5 An example of a simple reminder letter can be found in a previous chapter, but here is a checklist you can consult for the contents of any letter.

(a) The letter should be addressed to a **named individual** (or job title at the very least).

(b) The sender should indicate his or her **job title** and **telephone extension**, and the sender should **sign** it personally.

(c) The **amount overdue** should be prominently displayed.

(d) Ask for **payment by return of post**.

(e) A **final letter** should **be** final: in other words it should be followed by the matter being put into the hands of a third party, such as a solicitor or debt collector.

(f) It often helps to **copy the letter** to the person who is responsible for ordering the supplies in the first place. This can result in additional pressure on the accounts department.

(g) Be specific about any further action to be taken.

(h) Do not make threats you are not prepared to implement.

(i) Customers might soon learn your collection procedures, so it helps to vary the content and timing of letters.

4.6 The first reminder should be like the one you encountered in the previous chapter.

Final letters

4.7 If the **first reminder** fails to elicit an appropriate response, the firm may:

(a) Issue a **second reminder**, then a **third reminder**
(b) Issue a **final demand**, after which legal action is taken

4.8 Given that the customer has already received an invoice, a statement and a reminder, there may seem to be little point in adding a second, gently worded reminder letter, which will be ignored just like the first. However, it may be the case that the company wishes to increase the pressure gradually. After all, legal action may unnecessarily antagonise an important customer. There may be advantages in this approach.

(a) The debtor may only have paid part of the bill. This can be used as an excuse to demand payment of the rest. Short payment could mean any number of things:

  (i) Invoices not input to the sales ledger system before a cheque run
  (ii) Deduction of a disputed amount
  (iii) Agreement with sales staff
  (iv) Deliberate under-payment

(b) A valued customer might be goaded into action perhaps if the supplier threatens to refuse to sell any more goods on credit until the debt is cleared. This is less serious than legal action, but still significant.

4.9 **Examples of final demands** are given **on the next page**. One states that failure to pay will result in court action, the other that the matter will be put in the hands of a debt collection agency.

(a)

BRITLINE CARRIERS PLC
Sutton Lane, Liverpool LW6 9BC
Telephone: 0151 - 324 7345/6

Directors:
D Smith (Managing)
P Patel
C Wilkes

Registered office:
Sutton Lane Liverpl LW6 9BC
Reg. No 34567
Reg. in England

Ref: NC/nn TO 16

21 July 19--

Chief Accountant
Tradewell Office Products & Services Ltd
Easy St
MANCHESTER M12 7SL

FINAL DEMAND

Dear Mr X

Re: OVERDUE AMOUNT: £1,402.70 (Account 33521)

We regret to note that you have not replied to our previous reminder of 21 June when we requested payment of the above overdue amount.

Your account has now been transferred to A & B Ltd for collection, with any additional costs chargeable to you. Immediate payment of the full amount by return can avoid this distasteful action.

Yours faithfully

Edith Threadneedle
Chief Credit Controller (Extension 600)

(b)

BRITLINE CARRIERS PLC
Sutton Lane, Liverpool LW6 9BC
Telephone: 0151 - 324 7345/6

Directors:
D Smith (Managing)
P Patel
C Wilkes

Registered office:
Sutton Lane Liverpl LW6 9BC
Reg. No 34567
Reg. in England

Ref: NC/nn TO 16

21 July 19--

Financial Director
Tradewell Office Products & Services Ltd
Easy St
MANCHESTER M12 7SL

FINAL DEMAND

Dear Mr X

Re: OVERDUE AMOUNT: £1,402.70 (Account 33521)

We regret to note that you have not replied to our previous reminder of 21 June when we requested payment of the above overdue amount.

We would advise you that should the debt remain unpaid within seven days we will immediately place your account with the County Court. Full payment by return will avoid the need for this distasteful action.

Yours faithfully

Elizabeth Valmouth
Financial Director

ASSESSMENT ALERT

Drafting of reminder and subsequent demand letters is very likely to be an assessment task for Unit 15.

Activity 10.4

You have recently been employed by Schtrappter Vorcash Ltd of Dombey House, Newgate Street, London E23 4AR. One of the company's customers is an individual, a Mr Millfield. He owes £750 for the supply of Elbow Grease, and this amount has been outstanding for some time. You have already sent an invoice (reference X123), a statement (on 3 June 20X8) for this amount and a first reminder letter (on 14 July). The invoice date was 1 June and was payable by 30 June.

Draft a letter to Mr Millfield, reminding him of the debt, and saying that you might have to consider taking him to court. Mr Millfield's address is 20, Roedene Street, London N1 4PR. Today's date is 21 August. Schtrappter Vorcash Ltd's terms are that payment should be received 30 days after invoice date; and Mr Millfield was aware of this when he was offered credit.

Telephone

4.10 The **telephone** is now accepted as a means of collecting payment. It certainly provides greater nuisance value than a letter, and the greater immediacy can encourage a response. However telephone calls may more expensive than letters and the telephone may take up more of the credit controller's time. There may also be problems of getting through to the right person. A person collecting by telephone must also be prepared to put up with stalling, excuses and so on.

4.11 Some useful hints for collecting by telephone are outlined below.

(a) **Be prepared**. Have all relevant information to hand so you do not have to call back, or hunt through files.

(b) During the call, keep calm, make notes and, most importantly, guide, if you can, the conversation towards a suitable **close**, whereby the customer repeats back what is agreed, how much is to be paid, and the timing of payment.

4.12 A successful collector will know how to deal with the variety of excuses or evasions he or she might be faced with.

(a) **Customer denies receiving the invoice**. The collector can offer to fax a copy immediately, and can therefore ask the customer to confirm there and then that payment will be authorised.

(b) **'The cheque is in the post.'** The collector should ask for the cheque number, the date it was posted and the address to which it was sent. Supplementary questions include requests to stop the cheque and post a new one (eg if incorrectly addressed) etc.

(c) **'The cheque has been drawn up, but the chief accountant has yet to sign it.'** The collector should ask to speak directly to the chief accountant, ask for the cheque number, when it was passed for payment etc.

(d) **'The computer is run on a monthly basis.'** In that case, you can ask if a manual cheque can be raised. This is perfectly possible for most firms. For example, a firm might employ weekly-paid staff who have to be paid somehow.

Part B: Credit control

(e) **'The chief accountant is ill', 'on holiday'** etc. Ask if there are any other signatories. There must be some.

(f) **'We have a problem with our cash flow.'** You should immediately try to find out whether this is a genuine problem (eg impending appointment of a receiver/insolvency) or just an excuse.

4.13 Some other guidelines on telephone calls are as follows.

(a) The **switchboard operator** is often the gatekeeper to the organisation as a whole. If the switchboard operator has obviously been given instructions to stall calls to the purchase ledger, then you know there are problems. If the switchboard operator refuses to put you through, you can ask to speak to other people. This will prevent the switchboard operator from getting on with other work.

(b) Once you have reached the **decision-maker** you need to **put your case firmly and politely.**

(i) Approach the decision-maker (surname etc) and ensure this is the right person with whom to deal.

(ii) Do not be too informal, as this might imply a lack of professionalism.

(iii) The call should be timed for when the debtor is at his or her most vulnerable - at the beginning of the working day, for example.

(iv) Ensure beforehand that the customer has not been offered a special arrangement.

(v) Ensure that the customer agrees the amount and timing of the payment.

(vi) There is *no* need to be apologetic: the credit controller is merely exercising a right to receive payment.

4.14 In some circumstances, it may be necessary to consider calling the debtor at home, although section 40 of the Administration of Justice Act 1970 outlaws harassment of debtors likely to subject the debtor or the debtors' family to 'alarm, distress or humiliation'.

4.15 The following '**Ten Commandments**' are suggested by Pauline Malandine (in *Credit Management Handbook*, edited by Burt Edwards).

- Be **courteous**
- Be **urgent**
- Be **repetitive** (ie keep mentioning the sum required)

- Be **businesslike**
- Be **prompt**
- Be **prepared**

- **Remember** that 'your chasing call is not only the end of one sales chain but the start of another'
- Be **tactful**
- Be **persistent**

- Be **co-operative**

> **Mnemonic**
> the CURB PaPeR TaPe Co

Fax transmission

4.16 A **fax** can be used to demand payment: as a supplement to a phone call, or to give a sense of 'urgency'. Fax can also inconvenience the customer slightly: fax paper costs money, and your (repeated) requests may prevent other faxes coming through.

10: Managing debtors

Personal visits

4.17 **Personal visits** are time consuming.

- They should never be made without an appointment.
- They should only be made to important customers who are worth the effort.
- Any agreement should be quickly confirmed in writing.

Personnel issues

4.18 As a rule of thumb, the older the debt, and the more problems with collecting it, the more senior should be the company official sending the letters, and the more senior should be the proposed recipient.

Activity 10.5

What collection techniques would you recommend for the following debtors, assuming you have offered 30 days credit?

(a) A customer with a good payment record is a week late.

(b) A major customer is two months late, and already an invoice, a statement and a reminder have been sent.

ASSESSMENT ALERT

The management of debtors and other elements of working capital gets right down to the day-to-day practicalities of running a business. In assessments involving working capital management, you should always consider whether any proposed course of action really makes business sense.

Key learning points

- In managing **debtors**, the **creditworthiness** of customers needs to be assessed. The risks and costs of a customer defaulting will need to be balanced against the profitability of the business provided by that customer.

- For control purposes, **debtors** are generally analysed by age of debt.

- There should be efficiently organised procedures for ensuring that **overdue debts** and **slow payers** are dealt with effectively.

- The earlier debtors pay the better. **Early payment** can be encouraged by good administration and by discount policies. The risk that some debtors will never pay can be partly guarded against by insurance.

- **Credit insurance** can be obtained against some bad debts. However, the insurers will rarely insure an entire bad debt portfolio - as they are unwilling to bear the entire risk. Also the client's credit control procedures should be of a suitable standard to avoid any unnecessary exposure.

- Some companies use **factoring** and **invoice discounting** to help short-term liquidity or to reduce administration costs

- Some customers are **reluctant** to pay. The debt collector should keep a record of every communication. A **staged process** of reminders and demands, culminating in debt collection or legal action, is necessary.

223

Part B: Credit control

Quick quiz

1. What is a bad debt?
2. How might the creditworthiness of a potential new customer be checked?
3. What is a debtors age analysis?
4. What is default insurance?
5. What is a 'whole turnover' policy?
6. A particular credit insurance policy pays 100% of unrecovered debts above an agreed limit. What is the name for this type of policy?
7. What policies are offered by NCM to exporters?
8. What services do factors provide?
9. What is invoice discounting?
10. Draft guidelines for writing letters to slow payers.

Answers to quick quiz

1. A debt that is never repaid.
2. References; credit ratings agency; annual report and accounts; visits to customer.
3. A listing of the balances on debtors' accounts, showing, usually in bands, how long debts have been due.
4. Default insurance or credit insurance is insurance against certain debts going bad.
5. A credit insurance policy covering the whole, or the whole of a specified part, of a firm's sales ledger.
6. Aggregate turnover: excess of loss.
7. Credit insurance cover for short-term business.
8. Debtor administration; credit protection; advance payments.
9. The purchase of a selection of invoices, at a discount.
10. (a) Address to a named individual
    (b) State sender's job title
    (c) Sender to sign personally
    (d) Show amount overdue prominently
    (e) Ask for payment by return of post
    (f) If a letter is stated as final (prior to third party involvement), then it should be treated as such
    (g) Be specific about the further action to be taken
    (h) Vary the content and timing of letters.

Answers to activities

Answer 10.1

The aged debtors analysis splits up the total balance on the account of each customer across different columns according to the dates of the transactions which make up the total balance. Thus, the amount of an invoice which was raised 14 days ago will form part of the figure in the column headed 'up to 30 days', while an invoice which was raised 36 days ago will form part of the figure in the column headed 'up to 60 days'.

Answer 10.2

£1,700 × 80% = £1,360.

Gibbony Whey gave more credit than was underwritten by the insurance company.

Answer 10.3

The decision to factor the debts should only be taken once a wide ranging assessment of the costs and benefits of so doing has been carried out. This will involve the following steps.

(a) Find out which organisations provide debt factoring services. These may include the firm's own bankers, but there might be specialist agencies available who could also do the job.

(b) Some assessment of the services provided should also be made. Factors take on the responsibility of collecting the client firm's debts. There is a variety of factoring services.

  (i) *With recourse factoring*. This is the most basic service, whereby the bank undertakes to collect the debts and offer an advance, perhaps 80% thereon. The remainder is paid over once the cash has been received from customers. If the debt cannot be collected, the bank can claim back the advance from the client firm.

  (ii) *No recourse factoring*. The bank undertakes to pay the debts, but cannot claim the advance back from the client if the debt does not prove collectable.

  (iii) Some factors are willing to purchase a number of invoices, at a substantial discount. The factor would not be taking responsibility for the client's overall credit administration. In a way, this is like receiving an advance from a debt collector.

(c) The costs of the factoring service can then be assessed. The cost is often calculated as a percentage of the book value of the debts factored, so that if the factor took over £1,000,000 of debt at a factoring cost of 1.5%, then the client would pay a fee of £15,000. Moreover interest might also be charged on the advance, in some cases, before the debt was recovered.

(d) This can then be compared with the costs of doing nothing. If the choice is between either employing a factor or leaving things as they are, then the costs included in the decision include administration, salaries, interest costs on the overdraft, and other cash flow problems (eg delayed expenditure on purchases owing to bad debts, might mean that the company cannot take advantage of settlement discounts offered).

(e) However, before any final decision is taken, the organisation can try to ensure that factoring is still better value than other choices. These can include:

  (i) The introduction of settlement discounts as an inducement to pay early might improve the collection period, and hence reduce the outstanding debt

  (ii) The use of credit insurance in some cases

  (iii) A stronger credit control policy

  (iv) Perhaps appointing more credit control staff might in the long run be cheaper than factoring if the collection rate increases

There may well be operational or management solutions to this problem. These should be investigated first as customers might not like dealing with a third party.

Answer 10.4

Schtrappter Vorcash Ltd
Dombey House
Newgate Street
London E23 4AR

Mr Millfield
20 Roedene Street
London N1 4PR

21 August 20X8

Dear Mr Millfield,

Re: Outstanding amount £750
     Due 30 June 20X4

We regret to note that you have not replied to our reminder letter of 14 July requesting immediate payment of the above overdue amount, which represents Elbow Grease supplied on 1 June, invoice ref X123.

Our terms require payment within 30 days of invoice, and you did accede to them.

We would advise you that should the debt remain unpaid within seven days, we will immediately place your account with the County Court. Full payment by return will avoid the need for this unfortunate action.

Yours sincerely

Answer 10.5

(a) At this stage, a quick phone call to the accounts department might identify any problems, as the customer is normally reliable.

(b) A more senior official, such as the finance director should write to someone of equivalent rank in the debtor company. The creditor's sales director might also bring up the issue with the debtor's purchasing manager.

Chapter 11 Remedies for bad debts

Chapter topic list

1. Bad and doubtful debts
2. Third party involvement and going to Court
3. Bankruptcy: an outline
4. Insolvency: an outline
5. Provisions and write-offs

Learning objectives

On completion of this chapter you will be able to:

	Performance criteria	Range statement
• monitor information on the incidence of bad and doubtful debts	15.4.2	15.4.1
• send information regarding significant outstanding accounts and potential bad debts promptly to relevant individuals within the organisation	15.4.2	15.4.2
• conduct discussions and negotiations with debtors courteously and achieve the desired outcome	15.4.3	
• use debt recovery methods which are appropriate to the circumstances of individual cases and are in accordance with the organisation's procedures	15.4.4	
• base recommendations to write off bad and doubtful debts on a realistic analysis of all known factors	15.4.5	
• understand legal and administrative procedures for the collection of debts, and remedies for breach of contract	15.4	
• understand the effect of bankrupcy and insolvency on organisations	15.4	

Part B: Credit control

1 BAD AND DOUBTFUL DEBTS

1.1 **Credit control** necessarily involves an **expense** to the business. Its costs include the salary of credit control staff, the extra time spent in administration, and the extra expense of obtaining other sources of working capital to cope with the delays in receiving payment.

1.2 All this can be justified for two reasons.

 (a) It enables customers to spend.

 (b) The extra administration can be compensated for by savings in time and inconvenience spent handling cash, cheques etc.

1.3 Even the best-run credit control system, however, cannot ensure that a business which is offered credit **is never** exposed to the risk of bad and doubtful debts, which increase the cost to a business of offering credit. It might be helpful to distinguish between doubtful debts and bad debts: not all doubtful debts turn bad. They entail different costs for the business.

1.4 A debt is said to be **doubtful** when there is some uncertainty as to whether it will be paid: the key criterion is **uncertainty**. The debtor might still pay up but this is obviously much less certain than when the debtor was offered credit. In other words, the debt appears to be more risky than it appeared when the credit was first offered.

1.5 A **bad debt**, on the other hand, is a debt which will not be paid.

KEY TERMS

A **doubtful debt** is a debt for which there is some uncertainty as to whether it will be paid. A **bad debt** is a debt which will not be paid.

1.6 Doubtful debts and bad debts reduce profits. (Normally, a debtor is defined as a 'current asset' which should be liquidated within 12 months.)

 (a) A **provision** may have to be made **against doubtful debtors** in the accounts, either against specific debtors or as a percentage of total debtors, based on past experience.

 (b) Even if the doubtful debt is eventually repaid in full, there will still be **additional expenses** relating to:

  (i) The effect on cash flow, especially if the debt is large
  (ii) The administration expenses of debt recovery procedures

 (c) Bad debts, which will never be recovered, can be **written off against profits**. Bad debts relating to a specific customer are allowable for tax purposes, although general provisions are not.

1.7 It should also be noted that the expense of 'chasing' some small debtors to the extent, for example, of taking them to court may well exceed the debt itself. Although offensive to principle, it might be **expedient** just to write them off.

Warning signs

1.8 We have dealt with establishing credit risk in an earlier chapter. Circumstances change, however and, as has been suggested, the risk offered by a particular debtor may increase for any number of reasons which could not have been easily foreseen at the time. Here are some examples.

Personal customers

1.9 Many businesses have accounts with many personal customers: gas, electricity and telephone companies are examples, which generally offer supplies on credit over a three month billing cycle. Obviously, they cannot keep track of the personal circumstances of each of their customers. That said, many do *encourage* customers to speak to them about any problems they might have meeting the bills, to help deal with the problem or come to an arrangement.

1.10 **Warning signs** of 'bad debts' relating to debts incurred by personal customers might include the following.

(a) Any sudden or unexpected change in payment patterns
(b) Requests for credit extension
(c) Notice of court action for personal bankruptcy
(d) Refusal to communicate or reply to correspondence and/or phone calls

Activity 11.1

Jot down as many factors as you can think of which would increase the risk of a debt from a personal customer going 'bad'.

Business customers

1.11 With **business customers**, a debt can become doubtful or go 'bad' for any number of reasons. Some examples are provided below.

(a) The sudden loss of a major customer, hurting your customer's own cash flow
(b) The failure of your customer's own customers to pay on time in a timely fashion
(c) Disaster, such as a fire
(d) Industrial action, in some cases
(e) Sudden changes in overdraft terms, affecting the business customer's liquidity

1.12 Many of these events may not be easily predicted either by the credit controller or by the business customer. However, a business can become a bad debtor owing to a 'creeping' insolvency, a trend in poor cash management which finally leads to selling up. **Insolvency** (the inability of a business to meet its debts as they fall due) can result from a slow decline. The following tell-tale signs can indicate to the credit controller that there are problems with an account.

(a) Some customers who are always 'slow payers': we have identified elsewhere that this is harmful to the business. However, a previously good customer can become slower, or a slow company even worse. Slow payment might also indicate persistent cash flow problems.

(b) Other suppliers reporting similar payment difficulties.

(c) The supplier's sales representatives acquiring information 'on the grapevine'.

(d) A sense of impending doom, poor morale etc, at the customer's place of business, combined, perhaps with evident management complacency, indicates problems.

(e) Newspaper articles highlighting closures, reorganisation, profitability.

(f) County court judgements.

(g) Adverse comments from credit vetting agencies.

Part B: Credit control

(h) Cheques that 'bounce', indicating liquidity problems.

1.13 In addition, some bad signs for the future ability of a business to pay its debts include:

(a) Accounts lodged late at Companies House
(b) Auditors' report qualifications on the accounts
(c) Ratio analysis reveals declining performance

1.14 You know, of course, that there is going to be trouble if a **receiver** is appointed, if there is a meeting of creditors, or if the court is presented with a petition to wind up the company. These measures are drastic and sudden. Many creditors, especially unsecured creditors with no title over the goods or no security (unlike the bank), will be left with little to show for their debts.

Warning signs in financial statements

1.15 The credit controller, with the good fortune to have enough time, can pore over a firm's **annual financial statements** for any warning signs. A problem, though, is that when a company is having difficulties, financial statements are at their least reliable.

(a) The accounts might be late.

(b) There might be pressure on auditors to sanction imprudent accounting policies.

(c) Some of the accounting ratios calculated may be contradictory. For example, the company may post an increase in *sales* whereas in fact it is overtrading and running out of cash.

(d) Financial statements need only be published annually, and so might be out of date for the credit controller's purposes.

1.16 Other more sophisticated techniques can be used which take into account other aspects of the business's behaviour.

1.17 **Z-scoring** is a technique where a 'solvency model' is developed and chosen ratios are input to it to give the company a Z-score: the higher the score, the safer the company. A declining score indicates increasing riskiness. There is no need to go into any great detail here, except to say that Z-scoring:

(a) Has been successful as a predictor of corporate failure

(b) Is based on published financial data and so suffers from the drawbacks as in 1.15 above

(c) Can be used to compare a company's performance with others in the same industry

1.18 **A-scoring** is more subjective, but is based on three main pillars.

(a) **Defects**. Before they collapse, companies display a number of defects, which include the following.

(i) The company is dominated by a single individual.
(ii) The posts of Chairman and Chief Executive are combined.
(iii) Other directors do not have much of a say.
(iv) The Board of Directors does not contain a broad spectrum of expertise.
(v) The Finance Director is weak.
(vi) There are few professional managers below Board level.
(vii) The company has poor accounting systems.
(viii) The company is not responsive to change in certain key areas.

(b) **Mistakes**. The company perhaps:

   (i) Borrows too much so that it is vulnerable to sudden misfortune
   (ii) Expands faster than it really can afford to (overtrading)
   (iii) Depends on the success of a big project

(c) **Symptoms**

   (i) Financial ratios, Z-scores etc are in decline.
   (ii) Sudden changes of accounting policies.
   (iii) Non-financial signs (eg fall in market share).

1.19 In practice, few credit controllers have the time to perform any such analysis on most of their customers. After all, some sales ledgers contain over a thousand customers. If there is a high volume of orders that have to be assessed, this more detailed financial analysis may be put to one side. The **original** assessment for creditworthiness, done when credit was first offered, may therefore remain unquestioned for far too long.

Warning signs revealed in internal review

1.20 It is likely that the first indication that a debt is going bad will come from a company's own sales ledger, through a review of the aged debtors' listing or late payments. A suggested procedure is as follows.

(a) Maintain a list of customers to which the firm is most exposed (ie important clients). **ABC analysis** is a technique of focusing on the most important customers.

(b) Any unusual or delayed transactions should be followed up more closely.

1.21 The credit controller needs to ensure that this information is conveyed to the appropriate personnel.

(a) The **finance department** should be told so that:

   (i) Any necessary accounting entries can be made to provide against or write off the debt
   (ii) The firm's cash flow forecast can be altered, and any new borrowing arranged

(b) If the debt is large, then the **Finance Director** might also be told if it has a material effect on profits.

(c) The **sales department** needs to know, so that no further losses arising from trading with this particular debtor are made.

Activity 11.2

You have just been given the aged debtors listing, which no-one has looked at for ages. The account for one of your customers, who is not normally a slow payer, shows some peculiarities.

	\multicolumn{4}{c}{Days}	
	Current	30+	60+	90+	Total
Amount outstanding	1,000	-	-	400	1,600

You investigate further and find out that the customer always pays within the 30 day period and has paid all recent invoices, so the £400 outstanding seems rather odd.

What should you do?

Part B: Credit control

Activity 11.3

The Lax Company began trading in 20X7 and makes all its sales on credit. The company suffers from a high level of bad debts and a provision for doubtful debts of 3% of outstanding debtors is made at the end of each year.

Information for 20X7, 20X8 and 20X9 is as follows.

	Year to 31 December		
	20X7	20X8	20X9
	£	£	£
Outstanding debtors at 31 December	44,000	55,000	47,000
Bad debts written off during year	7,000	10,000	8,000

Tasks

(a) State the amount to be shown in the profit and loss account for bad debts and provision for doubtful debts for the years ended 31 December 20X7, 20X8 and 20X9.

(b) State the value of debtors which would be shown in the balance sheet as at 31 December in each of these years.

(This Activity revises your bookkeeping knowledge and also reinforces the need for sound credit control.)

2 THIRD PARTY INVOLVEMENT AND GOING TO COURT

2.1 There comes a point when the debtor has no alternative but to threaten **legal action** and, if this does not produce a suitable result, has to take a variety of measures to collect a debt. The firm may go to court immediately, but it is often cheaper to use a debt collection agency first of all.

Debt collection agencies

2.2 **Debt collection agencies** (alternatively called 'credit collection agencies') are the most effective way of pursuing debts. Some debt collection agencies offer a variety of credit control services, include running the credit control department in its entirety. There are over 250 such agencies in the UK. The **Credit Services Association** is a professional body for debt collectors.

2.3 Unlike other sources of third party assistance, most debt collection agencies are happy to be **paid by results**. In other words, **most** debt collectors offer a 'no collection, no fee' basis. (There are some exceptions, such as the **trade protection societies**, which are associations set up by businesses in the same industry for their mutual benefit.) Some agencies require an advance subscription to be paid for their services, or require clients to submit a 'coupon' for each case submitted. Most, however, receive a straight percentage. Commissions can vary between 1% and 25%, depending on the value of the debt. Some clients use debt collection agencies as a matter of course, largely as an alternative to having an inhouse credit control department. Others will only go to agencies as a last resort. The agency chosen must be licensed under the **Consumer Credit Act**. Ideally, the agency will be a member of the **Credit Services Association**.

2.4 Any collection agency will employ suitable techniques, depending on the client.

(a) Some collect on a letter and telephone basis. This is often the case where the client has passed on a large number of **consumer debts**.

(b) Others, especially for more difficult cases, collect 'on the doorstep'.

2.5 Here are some of the practices you might expect to see in a debt collection agency.

(a) Meticulous recording of all telephone conversations is necessary.
(b) Collectors can sometimes negotiate a payment plan with individual debtors.
(c) Clients are presented with a report every month.

Activity 11.4

You are considering employing the services of a debt collection agency. List the main considerations in this decision.

Specialist solicitors

2.6 A business might choose to use a firm of **specialist solicitors**. Using non-specialist solicitors may not be as effective as a collection agency and will probably cost more. Debt collection agencies are considered to be normal business services, and the use of a collection agency is unlikely to result in the end of a commercial relationship. Rightly or wrongly, however, employing a solicitor is seen as being more serious. To use a solicitor effectively, the following should be noted.

(a) The debt should be undisputed.
(b) The approach to any action in court will depend on whether the debtor is an individual (ie consumer) a sole trader or partnership (ie an unincorporated business) or a limited company (ie a firm with the letters Ltd, Limited, or plc after its name).
(c) The individual's full name should be supplied.
(d) For an unincorporated business, the firm's trading name and the name of the proprietor(s) should be supplied.
(e) For a limited company, the name of the firm should be that registered at Companies House.

Many court cases fail because the respondents in the case have not been named correctly.

Going to court

ASSESSMENT ALERT

A typical assessment task might require you to outline the best means of recovering a long-overdue debt using the courts, perhaps devising an internal procedure for such a process.

2.7 Before going to the expense and hassle of going to court, a firm must be sure of its case, and should therefore do the following.

(a) Be sure that the debtor is a genuine **debtor** rather than a dissatisfied customer: if the latter, the customer's complaints should be examined and dealt with if possible.
(b) Check who the debtor is (individual, firm, limited company).
(c) Ensure the name is correct. For unincorporated businesses, it is helpful to use a form of words such as 'Joe Bloggs trading as Bloggs Enterprises'.
(d) Before suing, it is advisable to check the original credit information. Is the customer likely to have sufficient assets?

Part B: Credit control

2.8 When instructing a solicitor to sue, an appropriate letter should be sent *in brief*. You should let the solicitor know the following.

(a) Whether goods, services, materials or any combination of them were supplied

(b) The date(s) when the liability arose (Generally speaking this will be the date when the goods/services/materials were supplied. The invoice date should also be provided for reference.)

(c) The debtor's legal status

(d) General background information (eg if the debtor has raised any complaints, whether or not these were genuine, and how they were resolved)

(e) Copy invoice, agreeing with the amount claimed

Which court?

2.9 The **Small Claims Court** generally deals with amounts under £3,000. The parties can refer the case to an **arbitrator**, whose award is recorded as a county court judgement.

2.10 **County Courts** deal with all actions in contract below £25,000, and some between £25,000 and £50,000. The **High Court** deals with amounts over £50,000 and some cases where the amounts disputed lie between £25,000 and £50,000. The decision as to whether the action shall go to the High Court or the County Court depends on:

(a) The type of transaction
(b) Any public interest issues
(c) The legal and factual complexity of the case
(d) The speed at which the case can be tried

2.11 Each County Court covers a fixed area. Actions to recover a debt may be commenced in the County Court in which the debtor resides or carries on a business, or in the County Court in the area in which the contract was made.

2.12 A **default summons** must be issued. This has to be requested by the plaintiff (ie the person bringing the case to court, in this case the creditor). The Small Claims Court will provide you with copies. Once the court has received the necessary paperwork, it will issue a **summons**, normally by post, but for a fee the Court bailiff will deliver it personally.

2.13 If the **debtor** does nothing (ie does not reply to the summons) judgement goes against him. That is why the writ requires an acknowledgement of service. The debtor can admit the claim: in other words the debtor accepts the amounts owing. If the debtor admits the claim, the debtor may offer to pay by instalments. The creditor can accept this, or, if not, has the right for the court to fix a suitable means of payment.

2.14 The debtor might defend the action. Small amounts (eg below £500) can be dealt with by **arbitration**. The debtor can defend in court, perhaps issuing a **counterclaim**.

2.15 A **pre-trial review** is a preliminary review of the case, conducted by the registrar to ensure that all the relevant material is available. The registrar may even order that the debtor pay part of the claim. On the day fixed for the **trial**, the creditors will be required to bring evidence to prove the claim and to defend against any counterclaim the debtor might bring. A **summary judgement** is when the creditor draws up an **affidavit** (a statement of the facts of the case). If the defendant does not appear, the judgement may well go against him.

Enforcement

2.16 Whilst obtaining a county court judgement is fine in itself, we must not forget the purpose of the exercise, which is to collect money. The county court judgement must therefore be enforced, which may need to be achieved by one of the following methods.

(a) **Warrant of execution**. The court bailiff can seize the debtor's goods and sell them by public auction. However, a debtor might remove or destroy the assets. The debtor's assets may be transferred to a spouse where they cannot be reached. Such assets must be **tangible, moveable assets**. This is called a **writ of fi fa**.

(b) **Attachment of earnings**. The court can order a specific weekly amount to be deducted from the debtor's wages. This might take some time to implement, as the court must contact the employer for details.

(c) **Garnishee order**. A person owing money to the debtor is instructed to pay it instead to the creditor. In other words, assume that A owes money to B, and B owes money to C. B does not pay C, and C serves judgement against B and obtains a garnishee order on A. A therefore pays money to C. It is possible for bank accounts to be garnisheed, but an exemption has been made for post office savings accounts.

(d) **Petition for bankruptcy**. This is described in Section 3 of this Chapter.

(e) **Administrative order**. A debtor with multiple debts not exceeding £5,000, at least one of which is a judgement debt they are unable to settle immediately, discharges all obligations by making regular payments into court. These are distributed among creditors on a *pro rata* basis.

(f) **Charging order**. If the courts orders a charge on the debtor's property, for example their house, this means that the property cannot be sold or transferred by the debtor: if the debt is not settled within six month, the creditor can have the property sold.

Other remedies: sale of goods

2.17 A contract for the sale of goods is covered by the Sale of Goods Acts. It does provide certain remedies, providing the contract is drawn up in the right way.

(a) **Lien**. A seller who is unpaid and who still has possession of the goods can hold on to them (eg in case of insolvency).

(b) **Retention of title**. Some contracts specify that the supplier retains title to the goods until the supplier has been paid. However, this is subject to many restrictions.

Commercial arbitration

2.18 **Arbitration** is an alternative to litigation in commercial disputes. As a process, it has much more in common with a business's other commercial activities than does litigation. It is often preferred by business people for that reason. A matter may be referred to arbitration in four ways:

(a) By order of the court
(b) By Act of Parliament
(c) By agreement of the parties
(d) By way of arbitration proceedings in the County Court (small claims procedure)

We are concerned mainly with category (c).

Part B: Credit control

> **KEY TERM**
>
> An **arbitration agreement** is defined in the Arbitration Act 1950 as 'a written agreement to submit present or future differences to arbitration, whether an arbitrator is named therein or not'.

2.19 The Arbitration Act has been amended in 1975, 1979 and by the Consumer Arbitration Agreements Act 1988. Relevant provisions are as follows.

(a) The parties to the agreement must submit to being examined on oath by the arbitrator and must produce all relevant documents which may be called for.

(b) The award made by the arbitrator can be considered final and binding on the parties. The 1979 Act allows for the right of appeal to be expressly *excluded* by agreement between the parties, provided this is agreed after arbitration has begun (unless under international law).

(c) The arbitrator can normally offer **specific performance** of a contract, as a remedy.

(d) An interim award may be made.

(e) The Arbitration Act 1979 limited the right of parties to an arbitration to apply to a court in the event of disagreement over the outcome of arbitration. In addition to (b) above, the Act:

   (i) Limits the right to refer a preliminary point of law to the High Court
   (ii) Limits the right of appeal on a point of law
   (iii) Requires the arbitrator in certain cases to state reasons for his awards

2.20 Some of the **advantages** of arbitration are set out below.

(a) The proceedings are less formal and more flexible than litigation, and are cheaper.

(b) In some cases, arbitration may be quicker and cheaper than litigation.

(c) The parties can **select** an arbitrator in whom they have confidence (eg an expert).

(d) The arbitrator is likely to be familiar with the commercial activities of the parties.

(e) The hearing is most often in private, so avoiding publicity.

(f) The atmosphere of an arbitration is more friendly than that of a court action. This is a point of some importance if the parties are intending to continue their commercial dealings with each other.

2.21 Nevertheless, arbitration suffers from some **disadvantages** compared with litigation.

(a) Plaintiff and defendant in an action are bound to observe certain time limits in preparing their cases, and so an arbitration procedure may provide more scope for deliberate time-wasting by a defendant.

(b) A judge has power to grant interim relief (eg an injunction) to the parties or curtail proceedings by means of a summary judgement. An arbitrator's powers are less extensive.

(c) Judges exercise their profession after many years of training in the process of weighing evidence and interpreting law. Arbitrators may be unqualified in such matters, and hence their decision may be subjective.

Negotiated settlements

2.22 Most commercial disputes do not make it to court. Apart from cases covered by arbitration procedures negotiations between the parties may be conducted at any time. They may even occur during trial. A defendant who wishes to reach a settlement without waiting for judgement has various courses open to him. The possibilities include the following.

(a) A **payment into court** may be made by a defendant of a sum less than the full amount claimed by the plaintiff. The plaintiff must then decide whether to accept the amount paid in, or to press on with his case in the hope of eventually being awarded a greater amount. Continuing the action at this stage carries risks for the plaintiff: not only may the eventual judgement be for less than the amount paid in (indeed, he may even lose the case) but he may also have to pay the defendant's costs incurred after the payment into court was made.

(b) Instead of paying money into court, the defendant may make a **without prejudice offer**. If the offer is accepted it becomes binding on both parties. If it is not accepted, the court must **not** be informed of it. This is to prevent the judge from forming an unfavourable view of the defendant.

(c) **Open offers** are uncommon. They differ from 'without prejudice' offers in that they may be brought to the notice of the court, with the risk that the judge may be inclined against the defendant. Their advantage over 'without prejudice' offers is that, like payments into court, they place the plaintiff under the risk of having to pay the defendant's subsequent costs if the offer is refused.

Activity 11.5

Why as a credit controller might you be reluctant to go to arbitration, assuming there is no dispute about the goods and services supplied?

3 BANKRUPTCY: AN OUTLINE

3.1 There may come a time whereby, for whatever reason, a person or business is unable to serve the debts that have been incurred. Sometimes, the only course available to a creditor or group of creditors is to use bankruptcy and insolvency legislation to obtain payment or, perhaps at best, part-payment. This means that the assets of the person administered by someone else can be sold. Such legislation exists because: the debtor may have more debts than assets which can be sold to pay them; there may be many different creditors, each of whom requires fair treatment; and not all creditors have the same rights.

3.2 The procedures dealing with an individual's bankruptcy on the one hand and a limited company's insolvency on the other differ significantly. You are only required to have an outline knowledge of these topics. Insolvency and bankruptcy legislation in the UK is based on the Insolvency Act 1986 and subsequent amendments.

Voluntary arrangements

3.3 A **voluntary arrangement** enables an individual to make binding agreements with creditors, minimising official involvement.

(a) The debtor formulates a proposal. The proposal explains why the arrangement is necessary, the debtor's liabilities and the assets to meet them. The information

Part B: Credit control

includes: the duration of the scheme; proposed dates of distribution; and interim credit facilities.

(b) A qualified insolvency practitioner (to act as supervisor) is nominated by the debtor. Before the arrangement is accepted by creditors, the supervisor is known as the **nominee**.

(c) The debtor applies for an interim order: this will not be granted if a bankruptcy petition is pending. The purpose of the interim order is to protect the debtor's property, but it will only be granted if the debtor could alternatively have petitioned for bankruptcy.

(d) The nominee should submit a report on the proposals to the court. This might conclude that a meeting of creditors be summoned to consider the proposals. (The meeting must be between 14 - 28 days of the report being submitted.) A report of the meeting is then sent to the court, and the court can review the report for unfairness. The amount of a creditor's vote depends on the size of the debt, and the proposal must be accepted with a **three-quarters majority in value**. (Other resolutions are passed with a simple majority, providing that those who vote against it represent more than half the value of the debt outstanding.)

   (i) A creditor meeting may suggest **modifications** (eg replacing the nominee), but there can be no modification which would cause the scheme to be outside the Act, and any modification must be **approved by the debtor**.

   (ii) The meeting's decision might be challenged in certain cases by the debtor, the nominee, or any other person entitled to vote at the meeting or, in some cases, by the trustee of an undischarged bankrupt (see below).

(e) If the proposal is approved and not challenged, the nominee, now called the **supervisor**, takes possession of all the assets and sells or distributes as necessary.

3.4 A voluntary arrangement can either be an alternative to bankruptcy, before it gets started; or a way of ending a situation of bankruptcy, so that the voluntary arrangement takes over from the bankruptcy proceedings.

Bankruptcy petition

3.5 Three weeks before creditors petition a court for a bankruptcy order, they must issue a **statutory demand**. The debtor might offer a settlement. The court will refuse to declare the debtor bankrupt if the creditor 'unreasonably' refuses. Otherwise the court will issue a bankruptcy order, once the **petition** is received.

(a) For the petition to be granted, the debt must be at least £750, and unsecured. The debtor must be domiciled or present in England and Wales (different legislation applies to Scotland).

(b) The petition will be dismissed if the statutory demand has been complied with, or there is reasonable prospect of paying the debt.

(c) A supervisor of a voluntary arrangement can petition for bankruptcy if the debtor has not complied with his or her obligations under the arrangement, or if the debtor supplied false information.

(d) The debtor can petition for bankruptcy in certain cases.

3.6 The consequences of the petition are as follows.

(a) With a few exceptions, if the debtor pays money to creditors or disposes of property, such transactions are void.

(b) Any other legal proceedings relating to the debts or the debtor's property are held in abeyance.

(c) An **interim receiver** is appointed. This may be the official receiver (a civil servant) or another qualified insolvency practitioner. The interim receiver is mainly concerned to protect the estate (eg by selling goods that will diminish in value).

The process of bankruptcy

3.7 Once the petition is granted, the consequences of a bankruptcy order are as follows.

(a) The **official receiver** takes custody and control of the bankrupt's property, until (d) below.

(b) A **statement of affairs**, detailing the bankrupt's assets and liabilities is drawn up within 21 days.

(c) Within 12 weeks of the date of the order, the official receiver summons a meeting of creditors.

(d) These **creditors** (or on occasion the court or the Secretary of State) appoint a **trustee in bankruptcy** (normally within 12 weeks of the order). The trustee has a number of powers, similar to those that the debtor had over his or her own property, before being made bankrupt. The trustee has the power to 'disclaim onerous property', in other words unprofitable contracts, property that cannot be sold etc. The functions of the trustee are basically: to dispose of the bankrupt's property; to keep records; to convene creditors meetings; to distribute proceeds to creditors; to summon final meetings.

(e) The debtor's assets are realised.

   (i) Tools, books, vehicles and other equipment necessary for the bankrupt's business or basic domestic needs are excluded (unless these can be replaced by cheaper substitutes).

   (ii) The bankrupt's income may be paid into court, with a reasonable amount left for the bankrupt's subsistence.

   (iii) If the bankrupt is owed any money by other people, the bankrupt cannot assign the debts (eg give them to a friend).

   (iv) If the trustee in bankruptcy wishes to sell the family home in which the spouse and perhaps the bankrupt's children are living, the court will take their needs into account. If children under 18 are living in the house, the bankrupt cannot be evicted without a court order.

(f) A distribution is made to creditors.

3.8 Once the bankruptcy order is made, the debtor is termed an **undischarged bankrupt**. The debtor:

(a) Is deprived of the ownership of his or her property

(b) Must hand over any relevant records

(c) Must make an inventory

(d) Must provide the official receiver (or the trustee in bankruptcy) with any information

Part B: Credit control

(e) Is liable to be arrested if he or she fails to appear in court without excuse, or is believed to be intent on destroying the property or has removed property to the value of £500

(f) May have his or her mail redirected

The creditor's position

3.9 Creditors should submit a written claim to the trustee, detailing how the debt is made up. The creditor may also need to substantiate any claim with documentary evidence. Creditors will be sent a form on which details can be given.

(a) **Trade discounts** and so on should be deducted.

(b) The **rate of exchange** will be that prevailing at the date of the bankruptcy.

(c) If a creditor is **late** in making a claim, no adjustment can be made to previous distributions.

3.10 Different groups of creditors have different claims and are ranked in order. Claims are paid in rank order, as follows.

(a) Fees paid by an apprentice or articled clerk relating to an unexpired period of training - these are reimbursed first.

(b) **Preferential creditors**:
   (i) The Inland Revenue for PAYE (12 months)
   (ii) Subcontractors in the building industry
   (iii) Customs and Excise for VAT
   (iv) Car tax, and other excise duties
   (v) National insurance contributions
   (vi) Pension scheme contributions
   (vii) Employees' wages for four months, up to £800 per employee

(c) **Ordinary creditors** (all others)

(d) Any remainder is allocated as follows:
   (i) Statutory interest
   (ii) Debts incurred between spouses
   (iii) The bankrupt

Discharge

3.11 Bankruptcy as a legal state is ended by **discharge**. Normally, the bankrupt is discharged automatically three years after the order was made, unless the court determines otherwise. The bankrupt receives a **certificate of discharge**. Discharge releases the bankrupt from his bankruptcy debts, although secured creditors may realise their security (eg the building society may repossess the bankrupt's house) and the bankrupt remains liable for certain other debts (eg personal injury, matrimonial proceedings).

Activity 11.6

You receive information that one of your customers, a sole trader, has successfully petitioned the court to make himself bankrupt. He cannot pay his debts as they fall due. He owes your company the sum of £1,000 for raw materials which he has used up. You learn that the bank has a fixed charge.

(a) Briefly outline the main stages of bankruptcy procedure.

(b) Along with other trade creditors, you hope to get a substantial amount of the £1,000 back. You learn, however, that the customer has bank debts of £40,000. His house is worth £40,000. How optimistic are you of recovery?

4 INSOLVENCY: AN OUTLINE

4.1 A company is **insolvent** when it cannot pay its debts as they fall due. The term '**unable to pay its debts**' is defined in s 123 of the Insolvency Act 1986 as follows.

(a) A creditor (owed over £750) has served on the company, by leaving it at the company's registered office, a written demand (in the prescribed form) requiring the company to pay the sum and the company has for three weeks has failed to do so.

(b) A court order in favour of a creditor of the company is returned unsatisfied in whole or in part.

(c) It is demonstrated to the satisfaction of the court that the company is unable to pay its debts as they fall due.

(d) A company is also deemed unable to pay its debts if it is proved to the satisfaction of the court that the value of the company's assets is less than the amount of its liabilities.

4.2 Soon its creditors may want to recover their money from the company in some way. There are three main routes.

(a) **Liquidation**. This means winding the company up, in other words selling off its assets, and closing it down.

(b) **Receivership** or **administrative receivership**. Secured creditors (see Paragraph 4.3 below) call in the receiver to run the business so that they can be paid. The business is then handed back to the directors.

(c) **Administration.**

4.3 In the last section, we noted that different classes of creditors have different rights in respect of the bankrupt's assets. In a company this is also true.

(a) **Secured creditors** have a **charge** of the assets of a business. For example, a bank may lend a business money secured on its factory premises so that if the loan is not repaid, the bank has the right, subject to other legal issues, to sell the factory. There are two kinds of charge, which were mentioned in an earlier chapter.

KEY TERMS

A **fixed charge** refers to a specific item, such as a factory.

A **floating charge**, on the other hand, does not relate to a specific item: it might cover 'the company's assets to the value of £100,000' for example. It is said to 'crystallise' when the company is wound up.

(b) **Unsecured creditors** have no such charge.

Compulsory liquidation

> **KEY TERM**
>
> In a **liquidation,** the company is dissolved, the asset are realised, debts are paid out of the proceeds and any surplus amounts are returned to shareholders.

4.4 **Compulsory winding up or liquidation** is carried out by a **liquidator**, on behalf of the shareholders and/or creditors of the firm. The court decides that the company should be liquidated, usually as a result of a petition from a shareholder or creditor. Generally speaking a compulsory winding up occurs because a company is unable to pay its debts, or that the court considers it 'just and equitable'.

(a) A compulsory liquidation may be brought by a single individual creditor.

(b) A **provisional liquidator** is appointed after the petition, but it is by no means certain that the order will be granted. The person who petitioned might then have to compensate the company for any expense incurred.

(c) Once the order has been made, the assets of the company remain the company's assets, but **under the liquidator's control**, unless the court determines otherwise. The company must present the liquidator with a **statement of affairs** detailing assets and liabilities.

(d) The liquidator's job is to ensure that the creditors will be paid. The liquidator is under *no* obligation to carry on the business, although the liquidator may do so if this is the most effective way of satisfying creditors.

(e) Once the liquidator's work is done, the company can be wound up.

Voluntary liquidation

4.5 A **voluntary winding up** or **liquidation** occurs when shareholders and/or creditors decide to do so. Creditors have the decisive role, however, as they have prior claim over the company's assets, to the extent that their debts are paid.

(a) Although shareholders and creditors have the right to liquidate a company, it is the creditors that concern us in this Unit. (Note only that a voluntary winding up by shareholders requires the directors to make a statutory declaration that the company can pay its debts. In a shareholders' winding up, creditors play no part.)

(b) A meeting of creditors is held, and the company's directors, having ensured the assent of the shareholders, present a **statement of affairs** before the creditors' meeting.

(c) The creditors may appoint a **liquidator**: sometimes the members can nominate a liquidator, but the powers of the members' nominee are limited.

The liquidation committee

4.6 A **liquidation committee** may be appointed in a compulsory liquidation and in a creditors' voluntary liquidation. It usually comprises an equal number of representatives of members and of creditors (in a creditors' voluntary liquidation, five from each side). The committee meets once a month unless otherwise agreed and may be summoned at any time by the liquidator or by a member of the committee. The general function of the committee is to work with the liquidator, to supervise his accounts, to approve the exercise of certain of his statutory powers and to fix his remuneration.

Powers of liquidators

4.7 The liquidator's basic function is to obtain and realise the company's assets to pay off its debts. All liquidators may, with the relevant sanctions:

(a) Pay any class of creditors in full
(b) Make compromises or arrangements with creditors
(c) Compromise any debt or questions relating to assets
(d) Take security
(e) Bring or defend legal proceedings
(f) Carry on the business in a way beneficial to the winding-up

The liquidator's subsidiary powers, given to enable him to perform the above, include selling assets, giving receipts (often under seal), receiving dividends, drawing bills of exchange, raising money, appointing agents and doing any other necessary things.

Duties of liquidators

4.8 Given the wide ranging **powers** invested in a liquidator, he has certain **duties**.

(a) He must exercise discretion in application of his powers. Although he may delegate clerical tasks and those which he cannot perform personally (for which he can appoint agents), a liquidator **cannot delegate his duty** to use his judgement, even to the court.

(b) He stands in a **fiduciary relationship** to the company, its creditors and contributories (ie a relationship of trust).

(c) He must **co-operate with the official receiver**.

(d) He must **notify the liquidation committee** of relevant matters.

(e) He must **keep records** of proceedings, receipts and payments, and if the company continues trading, a trading account should be kept.

(f) The official receiver in a **compulsory liquidation** must investigate the causes of a company's failure. He must also report to creditors and contributories on the liquidation's progress.

(g) A liquidator must **act quickly** in carrying out his duties, and not delay for lack of obvious funds.

(h) Liquidators must **keep minutes** of the proceedings and resolutions of creditors', contributories' and liquidation committee meetings.

(i) The liquidator must pay the balance of funds not required for day-to-day running of the liquidation into a special account at the Bank of England (the **Insolvency Services Account**).

(j) The **registrar is entitled to receive reports** on a voluntary liquidation at the end of twelve months and every six months thereafter.

Proof of debts

4.9 The liquidator must obviously require satisfactory evidence that a creditor's claim is properly admissible as a liability. This is done (where necessary) by a formal procedure for **proof of debts.**

(a) A **statute barred debt** (ie a debt so old it cannot be enforced) should be rejected since it is not legally enforceable. But in a members' voluntary winding up the liquidator may with the consent of all contributories pay such a debt. The general rules on statute barred debts are as follows.

   (i) A debt becomes statute barred (the creditor may no longer take legal proceedings to enforce payment) if it remains unpaid for six years (12 in some cases) and the creditor does not within that time commence legal proceedings to recover it.

   (ii) The company becomes liable again to pay a statute-barred debt (after six years) if it issues to the creditor a written acknowledgement of its indebtedness.

(b) In liquidation a **secured creditor** with a fixed charge has a variety of options open to him. In practice secured creditors are likely to be the bank or debenture holders, not trade creditors.

Order of application of assets in liquidation

4.10 The **order of application of assets in liquidation** is as follows.

   (a) **Secured creditors** who have **fixed charges** are entitled to be paid out of their security so far as it suffices. If the security is insufficient in value to pay the debt in full the creditor ranks as an unsecured creditor for the balance.

   (b) The **costs of winding up** are paid next. They rank before floating charges.

   (c) **Preferential unsecured debts** are paid next. They rank equally. If there are insufficient funds to pay them all, they are pro-rated. They include:

   (i) PAYE and VAT owing (for the last 12 and 6 months respectively)
   (ii) Wages, up to £800 per employee or four months pay
   (iii) Excise duties etc

   (d) **Debts secured by floating charges** come next in order.

   (e) **Unsecured non-preferential debts** come next (eg trade).

   (f) **Deferred debts** (eg unpaid dividends to shareholders) come last in order.

Alternatives to liquidation

4.11 We have seen that winding up a company is a fairly drastic step involving the cessation of trading, the disposal of assets and the final dissolution of the company. In many cases, these steps arise from the fact that the company cannot pay its debts, even though such inability to pay may be temporary or as a result of a 'one-off' disaster from which the company is basically sound enough to recover. What then are the alternatives to full-blown liquidation when a company is insolvent to some degree?

   (a) **Administrative receivership:** a company's secured creditor, in preference to presenting a winding up petition, may appoint a **receiver** (under a fixed charge) or an **administrative receiver** (under a floating charge). This may well result in the secured creditor receiving payment but it can often result in a healthy company being destroyed for the sake of the secured creditors when it could have continued trading to the benefit of all concerned.

   (b) **Administration:** under this procedure a moratorium is imposed by the court on creditors' actions against the company while an insolvency practitioner attempts to secure a good resolution.

(c) **Voluntary arrangement with creditors:** by means of this the company itself, under the supervision of an insolvency practitioner, arranges with creditors for a way of sorting out the problems surrounding it.

Administrative receivership

4.12 Under a fixed or a floating charge a secured creditor can appoint a receiver. The receiver takes charge of the assets subject to the charge as a means of enforcing the security for the benefit of the secured creditor. The receiver must be a **qualified insolvency practitioner**. The **debenture**, the instrument which creates a floating charge gives a power to appoint a receiver, and specifies the precise circumstances when the receiver can be appointed.

Powers of an administrative receiver

4.13 An **administrative receiver** is automatically given a long list of **statutory powers**, unless the debenture provides to the contrary. These include powers:

(a) To borrow money and give security
(b) To carry on the business of the company
(c) To sell the company's property
(d) To transfer the business of the company (or part of it) to a subsidiary

The effect of the administrative receiver's appointment

4.14 The immediate effect of any appointment of an administrative receiver is as follows.

(a) He assumes control of the assets subject to the charge and the directors' powers in respect of those assets are suspended during the receivership.

(b) Every letter, order, invoice and so on issued by the company must state that a receiver has been appointed.

(c) If he is appointed by the court or by the debentureholders as their agent, not the company's, his appointment operates to dismiss employees of the company automatically (though he may re-engage them if he wishes). If he is the company's agent his appointment does not usually dismiss them.

(d) Any floating charge crystallises.

(e) Within 28 days of being appointed he must send a notice of his appointment to all known creditors of the company.

(f) The receiver within three months sends a copy of the statement of affairs (assets and liabilities) and of his comments on it (or of a summary) to the registrar, the company and the debentureholders (and also to the court if he was appointed by the Court), and if he is an administrative receiver, send a copy to unsecured creditors and convene a meeting where they can consider it.

4.15 The function of a receiver is to manage or to realise the assets which are the security with a view to paying out of those assets what is due to the secured creditors whom he represents (plus the expenses including his own remuneration). If he is able to discharge these debts he vacates his office of receiver and the **directors resume full control**. A receiver rarely acts on behalf of **normal trade creditors**. (On the other hand a liquidator is appointed to realise all the assets, to pay all the debts of the company and to distribute any surplus remaining to the shareholders.

Part B: Credit control

Administration orders

4.16 The two main drawbacks to administrative receivership are as follows.

(a) Only a **secured creditor** can make or obtain the appointment of a receiver.

(b) The appointment of an administrative receiver does not prevent an **unsecured creditor** from exerting pressure, for example by presenting a petition for compulsory liquidation, which may wreck the receiver's effort to salvage the business.

4.17 The procedure for obtaining a court **administration order** is intended to offer an alternative to receivership (they cannot exist simultaneously) and incidentally to avoid some at least of the problems outlined above.

4.18 If a company is not yet in liquidation but is already, or is likely to become, unable to pay its debts the company itself, its directors, or any of its creditors, including unsecured creditors, may present a petition to the court to make an **administration order** in respect of the company. The broad effect of such an order is to put an insolvency practitioner in control of the company with a defined programme, and meanwhile to insulate it from pressure by creditors.

(a) The **administration order** provides for the **unsecured creditor** an alternative to suing for the debt in the courts or petitioning for winding up; for the secured creditor, an alternative to both these solutions and to putting in a receiver.

(b) An important effect of an administration order is that it results in a **freezing of collection of debts** by the creditors. This provides the administrator with a breathing space, not available to a receiver, in which perhaps to save the company for the benefit of all the creditors including the secured creditor.

4.19 Effectively **the secured creditors have a right of veto** over the making of an administration order. The secured creditor on receiving the notice can then appoint a receiver. If he does, an administration order cannot be made.

4.20 **Administration orders and liquidations are mutually exclusive.** Once a winding up resolution has been passed or the court has ordered the company to be wound up, an administration order can no longer be made. On the other hand, once an administration order has been made it will no longer be possible to petition the court for a liquidation order.

The petition for administration

4.21 The company itself, its directors or its creditors (including a contingent or prospective creditor) may present a **petition to the court** for an administration order. In order to make it, the court must be satisfied that:

(a) The company is or is likely to become unable to pay its debts, and

(b) The making of an administration order is likely to achieve one or more of the following objectives:

(i) The survival of the company and its undertaking (the whole or part) as a going concern

(ii) The approval of a voluntary arrangement

(iii) The sanctioning of a scheme of arrangement, or

(iv) A more advantageous realisation of the company's assets than would be effected in a liquidation.

Objectives (ii) and (iii) are different methods, short-term and long-term, of adjusting creditors' claims against a company which is unable to meet them in full.

4.22 The **effect of the administration petition** is to impose a standstill on any move:

(a) For voluntary liquidation

(b) For seizure of the company's goods in execution of a judgement for debt

(c) To re-possess goods obtained on hire purchase, rental or retention of title arrangements, or

(d) For the institution of any legal proceedings against the company

4.23 It does not, however, prevent the presentation of a petition for compulsory liquidation - though no *order* may be made while the petition for an administration order is pending - nor does it prevent an administrative receiver from being appointed.

The administration order

4.24 A '**ring fence**' is put round the company to hold off its creditors. Other effects of an **administration order** are as follows.

(a) An administrator may challenge past transactions of the company with a view to having them reversed by court order.

(b) An administrator may, with the sanction of the court or with the charge-holder's agreement, sell property of the company subject to a fixed charge.

(c) A supplier of goods etc on hire purchase or retention of title terms may not, unless the administrator consents or the court gives leave, re-possess those goods.

(d) As regards contracts, the administrator can be prevented by injunction from refusing to carry on with a contract made by the company: *Astor Chemical Ltd v Synthetic Technology Ltd 1990*. This contrasts with the position of the receiver.

The administrator

4.25 The **administrator** may remove any director from office, appoint directors and call meetings of creditors and of members. With the approval of the court he may also dispose of, free of encumbrance, property of the company until then subject to a charge and also property in its possession under a hire purchase, rental or retention of title agreement.

4.26 On taking up his appointment, the administrator's main concern will be to implement the purpose of the order. Like an administrative receiver, with whom he has much in common, he is entitled to receive a statement of affairs. **Within three months** (or such longer time as the court may allow) the administrator must produce and circulate a statement of his proposals for implementing the purpose of the administration order.

4.27 At any time while the administration order is in force, a creditor or a member of the company may petition the court, basically on grounds of unfair prejudice to the interests of members or of creditors (including himself). The court may grant relief in such way as it sees fit, if it finds that the petition discloses adequate grounds for doing so.

Part B: Credit control

4.28 In approving the administrator's proposals, the creditors' meeting may resolve to appoint a creditors' committee to work with the administrator. They may modify his proposals, but only if he agrees to each change.

Voluntary arrangements

4.29 The insolvency of a company may of itself increase its debts and/or reduce its resources. An insolvent company may cease to trade, it may default on its commercial contracts because its suppliers will no longer do business with it, or it may dismiss its employees who are thereby entitled to redundancy payments. Hence it can be in the interest of creditors to accept a compromise with a company rather than insist on its adopting formal insolvency procedure. They are particularly likely to agree to hold their hand if there is a prospect of selling off the company's business as a going concern or of pulling it back into solvency by reorganisation or improved management.

4.30 The above methods of promoting a compromise did not work well and so a system of **voluntary arrangement** was introduced in 1986. A voluntary arrangement is either a composition (part payment) in satisfaction of a company's debts or a scheme of arrangement of its affairs. A scheme of arrangement might, for example, be an agreed postponement or rescheduling of payment of debts pending reorganisation or sale of the business.

4.31 The initiative in proposing a voluntary arrangement may be taken either **by the directors**, if the company is not already in liquidation nor subject to an administration order; providing an insolvency practitioner is appointed and agrees; or **by a liquidator or administrator** in office at the time.

4.32 The nominee holds separate meetings of **members** and of **creditors** and lays before them his proposals for a voluntary arrangement. If both meetings approve it, the voluntary arrangement becomes binding on the company and on all creditors concerned.

(a) In this way a single unsecured creditor cannot wreck the scheme at the outset by trying to exhort more advantageous treatment of his claim than is given to other creditors.

(b) Any secured or preferential creditor whose rights are modified by the arrangement is not bound by the scheme unless he has expressly consented to it.

(c) Any creditor or member of the company may raise objections to the scheme before the court by showing *either* that it is 'unfairly prejudicial' - it discriminates against him - *or* there has been a 'material irregularity' in relation to one or other of the meetings.

5 PROVISIONS AND WRITE-OFFS

5.1 It is reasonable to assume that, if matters have gone as far as receivership, administration or liquidation that the company cannot pay off all its debts. In many liquidations, receiverships and administrations, the creditors are unlikely to receive in full the amount they are owed, especially if they are unsecured or non-preferential creditors.

There are two alternatives to dealing with bad and doubtful debts in the accounts and accounting records.

(a) They can be written off completely.

(b) They can be provided against. This means that the gross debtor is still maintained, in the sales ledger control account and in the sales ledger, but that a counterbalance credit is set up to provide against them.

5.2 The double entry for **writing off a bad debt** is as follows:

Debit: Profit and loss account
Credit: Sales ledger control account

with the amount of the debt written off. The records in the sales ledger (memorandum accounts) would also be cancelled.

5.3 For example, Improvident Ltd has a sales ledger totalling £1,000. (There are no reconciling items between this total and the balance on the sales ledger control account.) One of its debtors, Cowboys Ltd, collapses and the management of Improvident Ltd are convinced that Cowboys Ltd's £150 debt cannot be recovered and they therefore resolve to write off.

(a) The double entry is:

	£	£
Dr Bad and doubtful debt expense (profit and loss)	150	
Cr Sales ledger control account (balance sheet)		150

The balance on the sales ledger control account is now £850.

(b) There would also be an entry to the sales ledger to that effect, which would also reduce its total by £150, ie so that it equals £850.

5.4 As an alternative, the company might prefer to **set up a provision**. In other words, the company's management cannot be *sure* that no money is available.

5.5 The firm sets up a new balance sheet account for the provision of bad and doubtful debts.

Debit: Bad and doubtful debts expenses (P & L)
Credit: Provision for bad and doubtful debts (balance sheet)

5.6 The sales ledger control account will continue to show the gross figure as will the sales ledger. But for financial reporting purposes, the figure for debtors will be the total on the sales ledger control account *less* the provision.

5.7 In financial reporting terms, the result is similar: profit has been reduced by the amount of the bad or doubtful debt, but the way in which it is done is different.

(a) Setting up a provision is prudent; but there is still the possibility that the debt will be recovered.

(b) Part of a debt can be provided against.

(c) The continued existence of the debt in the sales ledger is perhaps a spur to collect it: if it were written off it would be forgotten.

5.8 If Improvident Ltd were to provide against the £150 debt, the entries would be:

	£	£
Dr Bad and doubtful debt expense (profit and loss) account	150	
Cr Provision for bad and doubtful debts		150

No entry would be made to the sales ledger.

However, to calculate the figure for debtors in the balance sheet:

	£
Sales ledger control account	1,000
Provision for bad and doubtful debts	(150)
	850

Part B: Credit control

5.9 Sometimes, the doubtful debt which had been provided against will have to be written off. The profit and loss account has already been debited, so there is no extra expense. However, the double entry is:

	£	£
Dr Provision for bad and doubtful debts	150	
Cr Sales ledger control account		150

The sales ledger entry is also amended to account for the write off.

5.10 Clearly **provisions and write offs** should only be made after consideration of all suitable factors. It is too easy to be hasty, and a slight delay in receiving payment is no excuse for writing off the debt. Factors to be considered are: the success of attempts to collect the debt; the expense of pursuing the debt (which may well be more than the debt is worth); likelihood of insolvency proceedings and communication from liquidators, receivers or administrators as to the collectibility of the debt.

Monitoring bad debts: bad debts/sales ratios

5.11 It is helpful for the credit controller to monitor the overall level of bad debts encountered by a firm. The following report format might be adopted.

	Jan	Feb	March	April
Sales	£1,000	£2,000	£1,000	£4,000
Bad debts recognised	£20	£50	-	£10
% of sales	2%	2½%	-	0.25%
Bad debts originated	£50	£30	£40	?
% sales	5%	1.5%	4%	N/A

(a) **Bad debts recognised** refers to the time when the debt went bad.
(b) **Bad debts originated** refers to the date when the sale was initially made.

5.12 The purpose of such a report is to record the bad debt expense in the correct period, and to monitor the effectiveness of credit control in certain months. An increasing ratio of bad debts to sales implies a deteriorating quality of credit control, unless it results from policy to sell to higher risk customers.

Key learning points

- A **debt** can go **bad** for a variety of reasons. It might have been **'high risk'** in the first place. **Unforeseen circumstances** can arise, although for both business and personal customers, it is often possible to detect warning signs of impending disaster. Existing customers might take longer to pay.

- There are some sophisticated **scoring systems** available for analysing companies, which input data from financial accounts into a model.

- **Debt collection agencies** collect debts, for a commission.

- If it comes to **court**, a county court may issue a default summons. The judgement may be enforced in a variety of ways, including bailiffs, garnishee orders, or insolvency proceedings.

- **Bankruptcy** is where an individual's property is sold for creditors' benefit. **Insolvency** is when the assets of a company are taken over by a third party appointed by creditors. The company is run until the debts are paid, or may be wound up.

11: Remedies for bad debts

Quick quiz

1. What is Z-scoring?
2. How are debt collectors paid?
3. How is a County Court judgement enforced?
4. What are the advantages of arbitration?
5. What are the functions of the trustee in bankruptcy?
6. What is the effect of an administration petition?
7. What factors should govern a firm's decision whether to write off a debt?

Answers to quick quiz

1. A technique for evaluating the solvency of a business which produces a score calculated from a number of ratios.

2. Most receive a percentage commission on the value of the debt that they collect.

3. By one of the following methods: warrant of execution, attachment of earnings order, garnishee order, petition for bankruptcy, administrative order, charging order.

4. Less formal and more friendly atmosphere than litigation; the arbitrator is an expert; the hearing is in private.

5. To dispose of the bankrupt's property, to keep records, to convene creditors meetings, to distribute proceeds to creditors, and to summon final meetings.

6. To stop moves towards voluntary liquidation, seizure of the company's goods, repossession of goods and legal proceedings against the company.

7. Success in attempts to collect the debt; the expense of pursuing the debt; the likelihood of insolvency proceedings.

Answers to activities

Answer 11.1

Here are some examples.

(a) Divorce: joint financial arrangements are unwound; both parties suffer hardship
(b) Long-term illness, resulting in a fall in the customer's income
(c) Redundancy, leading to a reliance on state benefits
(d) The income of a self-employed person might in poor economic conditions
(e) Bankruptcy
(f) Death (obviously)
(g) Redundancy of one partner can adversely affect the income of the entire family unit
(h) Fines or imprisonment imposed by the court, or substantial civil damages
(i) Other factors (eg a rise in interest rates and hence mortgage payments)

Answer 11.2

Before contacting the customer and accusing the customer of default, it is best to eliminate other explanations for the discrepancy.

(a) Is there any unallocated cash? In other words, have payments been received which, for whatever reason, have not been matched with the invoice? (In some computer systems an error of 1p prevents matching.)

(b) Have invoices been posted correctly? In other words, does the discrepancy arise out of a clerical error? Payment might inadvertently have been posted to the wrong account.

(c) Are there matters in dispute? Review of the file should indicate existing correspondence on any items.

(d) Did the customer return the goods and send a debit note, which has not reached the system?

Once you are sure of the case, assemble all the relevant information and contact the customer: this customer is generally reliable, so it is best to act to preserve the commercial relationship.

Part B: Credit control

Answer 11.3

(a) *Initial working: provision for doubtful debts*

31 December		£	£
20X7 Provision required	= £44,000 × 3%	1,320	
20X8 Provision required	= £55,000 × 3%	1,650	
Increase in provision - charge to P & L			330
20X9 Provision required	= £47,000 × 3%	1,410	
Decrease in provision - credit to P & L			(240)

	Profit and loss account charge Year ended 31 December		
	20X7 £	20X8 £	20X9 £
Bad debts	7,000	10,000	8,000
Provision for doubtful debts	1,320	330	(240) credit

(b)

	Balance sheet extracts as at 31 December		
	20X7 £	20X8 £	20X9 £
Debtors	44,000	55,000	47,000
Less provision for doubtful debts	1,320	1,650	1,410
Balance sheet value	42,680	53,350	45,590

Answer 11.4

A debt collection agency provides a variety of services, but these have their costs.

(a) What commission is charged by the agency? Debts which are harder to collect might require a higher price.

(b) The mere involvement of a third party might encourage some debtors to pay.

(c) The cost of a solicitor should be compared with the cost of the debt collector if legal action has to be taken.

(d) The collection agency should keep the client informed about progress.

Answer 11.5

If there is no dispute, then the money is yours anyway. If the debtor is insolvent, you are likely to be overtaken by events.

Answer 11.6

(a) A petition is presented to the court, usually by a creditor or the debtor.

A bankruptcy order is made by the court.

A trustee in bankruptcy is appointed.

Once the administration is complete the bankrupt will be discharged.

(b) It is likely that the bank is a secured creditor: in other words the bank debt will be paid off before trade creditors get a look in.

List of Key Terms and Index

List of key terms

Accruals concept, 18
Arbitration agreement, 236

Bad debt, 228
Banker, 90
Banker's acceptance facilities, 104
Bill of exchange, 135
Budget period, 25

Cash budget, 25
Cash flow budget, 25
Central bank, 76
Certificate of deposit, 134
Cheque, 95
Collecting bank, 95
Committed facility, 104
Compound annual rate of interest, 126
Computer bureau, 194
Contract, 159
Convertible loan stock, 118
Credit assessment, 174
Credit risk, 174
Current assets, 4
Current liabilities, 4
Customer, 90
Cyclical variations, 52

Data subject, 194
Data users, 194
Debentures, 118
Disintermediation, 82
Doubtful debt, 228

Factoring, 216
Financial intermediary, 72
Fixed charge, 241
Flat yield, 129
Floating charge, 241

Gilts, 130

Index, 59
Interest yield, 129
Invoice discounting, 217

Liquidation, 242

Matching concept, 18
Money markets, 80
Moving average, 52

Overdraft facility, 104

Paying bank, 95
Personal data, 194
Primary banks, 73

Residual, 58
Revolving facility, 104
Running yield, 129

Secondary banks, 73
Sight bill, 135

Term bill, 135
Term loan, 104
Time series, 50
Treasury management, 19
Trend, 50

Uncommitted facility, 104
Unsecured loan stock, 118

Working capital, 4

Index

ABC analysis, 231
Account payee, 96
Accruals, 16
Accruals concept, 16, 18
Accruals or matching concept, 18
Acid test ratio, 186
Action for the price, 162
Additive model, 56
Administration of Justice Act 1970, 222
Administration order, 235, 246, 247
Administrative receivership, 244
Advances, 75
Amortising loan, 114
Amount of the loan, 106
Annual disbursement, 8
Arbitration, 235
A-scoring, 230
Asset turnover, 182
Attachment of earnings, 235

BACS, 99
Bad debts, 153, 229
Bailor/bailee relationship, 91
Balance sheet, 39
Balance sheet based forecasts, 26
Balloon repayment loan, 114
Bank of England, 76
Bank overdrafts, 186
Bank references, 175
Banker's acceptance facilities, 104
Banker's draft, 98
Banking Act 1987, 77, 90, 128
Bankruptcy, 237
Banks, 24
    duties, 93
    income and expenses, 75
    rights, 92
Base period, 60
Bilateral loans, 118
Bill of exchange, 78, 134, 135
Bills, 74, 80
Borrowing, 24
Breach of contract, 162
Buffer, 122
Building societies, 79
Building Societies Act 1986, 79, 128
Building societies deposits, 128
Bullet repayment loan, 114
Business customers, 229
Buyer risks, 215

CAMPARI, 105
Canons of lending, 105
Cash, 12
Cash budget, 25, 27
Cash cycle, 6

Cash flow based forecasts, 25
Cash flow control reports, 42
Cash flow cycle, 6
Cash flow statement, 10
Cash forecasting, 24
Cash inflows, 9
Cash investment, 126
Cash management models, 123
Cash management policy, 122
Cash outflows, 8
Categorised cash flow, 10
Central bank, 76
Certificate of deposit (CD), 134
Certificates of deposit, 80
Certificates of deposit market, 82
Character of the borrower, 105
Charging order, 235
Cheque guarantee cards, 97
Cheque guarantee scheme, 97
Cheques, 95
Cleared funds cash forecast, 37
Clearing House Automated Payments
    System (CHAPS), 99
Code of Banking Practice, 94
Collecting debts, 209
Collection cycle, 157
Commercial bills of exchange, 75
Commercial paper, 80, 137, 178
Commercial paper market, 82
Commercial risks, 215
Committed facility, 104
Compound annual rate of interest, 126
Compulsory winding up, 242
Computer bureau, 194
Consideration, 161
Consumer credit, 150
Consumer Credit Act 1974, 159, 165, 197
Contingency funding, 24
Contract, 159
Contract of sale, 164
Control of bank lending, 77
Country risks, 215
County Court, 181, 234
Covenants, 114
Creative accounting, 10
Credit assessment, 174
Credit cards, 97
Credit control, 16, 150
Credit control department, 157
Credit cycle, 157
Credit in the economy, 84
Credit insurance, 214
Credit policy, 151
Credit ratings, 137, 192
Credit reference agency, 179
Credit risk, 228
Credit utilisation report, 155

Index

Creditors turnover period, 184
Crossings, 96
Currency deposits, 74
Current assets, 4, 5, 183, 185
Current liabilities, 4, 5, 183, 185
Current ratio, 186
Customer payment systems, 211
Customer record card, 218
Cyclical variations, 52

Damages, 162
Data Protection Act, 196
Data protection principles, 195
Data subject, 194
    rights of, 196
Data users, 194
Days sales outstanding, 152
Days-in-the-month effect, 30
Days-in-the-week effect, 30
Debentures, 118, 245
Debit cards, 97
Debt collection agencies, 232
Debt collection period, 184
Debtor/creditor relationship, 91
Debtors age analysis, 206
Debtors turnover period, 184
Default insurance, 213
Default summons, 234
Deposit accounts, 127
Deposit Protection Scheme, 128
Direct debits, 98
Discount houses, 81
Discount market, 80
Discounting bills, 136
Discounts, 167
Discretionary cash flows, 10
Disintermediation, 82
Dividends, 122
Duties of care, 175

Earnings per share, 122
Eligible bills, 75
Eurocurrency markets, 82
Exceptional items, 8
Excess of loss, 215
Exchange rate, 77
Exchange rate policy, 78
Ex-dividend, 132
Executed consideration, 161
Executory consideration, 161
Export Credits Guarantee Department (ECGD), 215
Export insurance, 215

Factoring, 216
Fiduciary relationship, 92

Final demands, 211
Final letter, 219
Finance company deposits, 128
Financial cash flows, 10
Financial futures market, 83
Financial intermediation, 72, 73
Financial modelling package, 63
Financial Services Authority, 77
Fiscal policy, 84
Fixed charge, 107, 241
Float, 37
Floating charge, 107, 241
Forecasting, 57
Foreign banks, 78
Foreign exchange market, 83
Funding policy, 77

Garnishee order, 235
Gearing, 105, 187
General crossing, 96
Gilts, 130
Going concern, 17
Good faith, 92
Government bonds, 83
Government debt, 83
Government securities, 130
Guarantees, 108
Guarantees/bonds, 215

High Court, 234
High interest cheque/deposit accounts, 127
High risk, 174
High street bank deposits, 127
Hire purchase, 117

Index numbers, 59
Index points, 60
Index-linked stocks, 131, 132
Inflation, 59
In-house credit ratings, 192
Injunction, 162
Inspection, 52
Insurance against non-payment, 107
Interest, 126
Interest cover, 188
Interest rate policy, 85
Interest yield, 129
International banks, 78
Internet, 73
Investment banks, 78
Investments, 75
Invoice discounting, 217
Irregular items, 8

Index

Key account customers, 212
Keynes JM, 122

Leading and lagging, 44
Leasing, 115
LIBOR, 82
Lien, 235
Liquidation, 242
Liquidity, 15, 74, 134, 185
Loans, 113
Local authority bills, 75
Local authority market, 81
Local authority stocks, 133
London Inter-Bank Offered Rate (LIBOR), 114
London International Financial Futures Exchange (LIFFE), 83
Long-term contracts, 213

Market loans, 75
Market risks, 215
Maturity transformation, 73
Merchant banks, 74, 78
Methods of payment, 167
Misrepresentation, 161
Mistake, 161
Monetary policy, 84
Money market, 137
Money markets, 79, 80
Mortgagor/mortgagee relationship, 92
Moving averages, 52, 54
Multiplicative model, 56

National Debt, 77
NCM Credit Insurance Ltd, 215
Net cash flow, 10
Nominal ledger, 28

On account payments, 212
One-off cash flows, 28
Open offers, 237
Operating cycle, 6
Operational cash flow, 10, 12
Opportunity cost, 168
Optimal cash balance, 123
Option deposits, 127
Ordinary risk, 174
Overdraft facility, 104, 109, 111, 122
Overtrading, 11, 112

Parallel markets, 80
Past consideration, 161
Payment into court, 237
Payment score report, 180

Payment terms, 166
Permanent Interest Bearing Shares (PIBS), 137
Personal customers, 229
Personal data, 194
Personal guarantee, 108
Petition for bankruptcy, 235
Political risks, 215
Portfolio, 139
Post-dated cheques, 96
Potential slow payer, 174
Precautionary motive, 122
Price index, 59
Primary banks, 73
Primary money market, 81
Principal/agent relationship, 91
Prior charge capital, 187
Priority cash flows, 10
Profit margin, 182
Profitability, 14, 74
Profits and cash flows, 12
Proportional model, 56
Public board loans, 133
Public sector, 126
Public Sector Borrowing Requirement (PSBR), 85
Pull to maturity, 129

Quantity index, 60
Quantum meruit, 162
Quick ratio, 186

Random variations, 51
Ratio analysis, 105, 181
Receiver, 244
Redemption yield, 130
References, 175
Regression analysis, 52
Regular items, 8
Regular trading cash flows, 28
Reminder notices, 211
Repayment terms, 107
Repurchase of a company's own shares, 122
Rescission, 162
Reserve requirements, 84
Residual, 58
Retail banking, 73
Retail Prices Index, 59
Retailing business, 7
Retention of title, 235
Return on capital employed, 182
Revenue items, 8
Revolving facility, 104
Risk, 16, 138, 174

Safe custody, 143

Index

Safe deposit service, 91
Safety, 15
Sale and leaseback, 116
Sale of Goods Acts, 159, 164, 235
Seasonal variations, 51
Secondary banks, 73
Security, 137
Security for a loan, 107
Sensitivity analysis, 63
Settlement discounts, 167
Share buy-back, 122
Shares, 82
Short-term money markets, 80
Sight bill, 135
Sight deposits, 74
Slow payers, 229
Small Claims Court, 234
Solicitors, 233
Special crossing, 96
special dividend payment, 122
Specific account policies, 215
Specific guarantees, 215
Specific performance, 162
Speculative motive, 122
Spreadsheet model, 63
Stale cheques, 96
Standing orders, 98
Statement, 211
Statute barred debt, 244
Stock turnover, 183
Summary judgment, 234
Swinging account, 110
Syndicated loan, 118

Term bill, 135
Term loan, 104
Termination, 162
Terms and conditions of sale, 166
Time deposits, 74
Time series, 50
   additive model, 56
   finding the seasonal variations, 54
   finding the trend, 52
   multiplicative model, 56
   proportional model, 56
   residuals, 58
Trade creditors, 118
Trade credits, 150
Trade Protection Societies, 232
Trade references, 177
Transactions motive, 122
Treasury bills, 75
Treasury management, 19
Trend, 51
Turnover periods, 183

Unacceptable risk, 174
Uncertainty analysis, 50
Uncommitted facility, 104
Unenforceable contract, 160
Unexceptional items, 8
Unfair Contract Terms Act 1977, 159
Unsecured loan stock, 118

Void contract, 159
Voidable contract, 159
Volatility of cash flows, 50
Voluntary arrangements, 248

Warrant of execution, 235
Whole turnover policies, 214
Wholesale banking, 74
Window dressing, 10
Without prejudice offer, 237
Working capital, 4, 104, 183
Writ of fi fa, 235

Yearlings, 133

Zero or negligible risk, 174
Z-scoring, 230

AAT – Unit 15 Cash Management and Credit Control (5/00)

ORDER FORM

Any books from our AAT range can be ordered by telephoning 020 8740 2211. Alternatively, send this page to our address below, fax it to us on 020 8740 1184, or email us at **publishing@bpp.com**. Or look us up on our website: www.bpp.com

We aim to deliver to all UK addresses inside 5 working days; a signature will be required. Order to all EU addresses should be delivered within 6 working days. All other orders to overseas addresses should be delivered within 8 working days.

To: BPP Publishing Ltd, Aldine House, Aldine Place, London W12 8AW

Tel: 020-8740 2211   **Fax: 020-8740 1184**   **Email: publishing@bpp.com**

Mr / Ms (full name): _____

Daytime delivery address: _____

_____

Postcode: _____   Daytime Tel: _____

Please send me the following quantities of books.

	5/00 Interactive Text	8/00 DA Kit	8/00 CA Kit
FOUNDATION			
Unit 1 Recording Income and Receipts	☐		
Unit 2 Making and Recording Payments	☐		☐
Unit 3 Ledger Balances and Initial Trial Balance	☐	☐	
Unit 4 Supplying information for Management Control	☐		
Unit 20 Working with Information Technology (8/00 Text)	☐		
Unit 22/23 Achieving Personal Effectiveness	☐		
INTERMEDIATE			
Unit 5 Financial Records and Accounts	☐		☐
Unit 6 Cost Information	☐	☐	
Unit 7 Reports and Returns	☐	☐	
Unit 21 Using Information Technology	☐		
Unit 22: see below			
TECHNICIAN			
Unit 8/9 Core Managing Costs and Allocating Resources	☐		☐
Unit 10 Core Managing Accounting Systems	☐	☐	
Unit 11 Option Financial Statements (Accounting Practice)	☐		☐
Unit 12 Option Financial Statements (Central Government)	☐		
Unit 15 Option Cash Management and Credit Control	☐	☐	
Unit 16 Option Evaluating Activities	☐		
Unit 17 Option Implementing Auditing Procedures	☐		
Unit 18 Option Business Tax FA00(8/00 Text)	☐		
Unit 19 Option Personal Tax FA00(8/00 Text)	☐		
TECHNICIAN 1999			
Unit 17 Option Business Tax Computations FA99 (8/99 Text & Kit)	☐	☐	
Unit 18 Option Personal Tax Computations FA99 (8/99 Text & Kit)	☐	☐	
TOTAL BOOKS	☐ +	☐ +	☐ = ☐

@ £9.95 each = £ ____

Postage and packaging:
UK: £2.00 for each book to maximum of £10
Europe (inc ROI and Channel Islands): £4.00 for first book, £2.00 for each extra
Rest of the World: £20.00 for first book, £10 for each extra

P & P   £ ____

► Unit 22 Maintaining a Healthy Workplace Interactive Text (postage free)   ☐ @ £3.95   £ ____

GRAND TOTAL   £ ____

I enclose a cheque for £ _____ (cheques to BPP Publishing Ltd) or charge to Mastercard/Visa/Switch

Card number ☐☐☐☐ ☐☐☐☐ ☐☐☐☐ ☐☐☐☐ ☐☐☐☐

Start date _____   Expiry date _____   Issue no. (Switch only)___

Signature _____

AAT - Unit 15 Cash Management and Credit Control (5/00)

REVIEW FORM & FREE PRIZE DRAW

All original review forms from the entire BPP range, completed with genuine comments, will be entered into one of two draws on 31 January 2001 and 31 July 2001. The names on the first four forms picked out on each occasion will be sent a cheque for £50.

Name: _____ Address: _____
_____
_____

How have you used this Interactive Text?
(Tick one box only)
☐ Home study (book only)
☐ On a course: college _____
☐ With 'correspondence' package
☐ Other _____

Why did you decide to purchase this Interactive Text? *(Tick one box only)*
☐ Have used BPP Texts in the past
☐ Recommendation by friend/colleague
☐ Recommendation by a lecturer at college
☐ Saw advertising
☐ Other _____

During the past six months do you recall seeing/receiving any of the following?
(Tick as many boxes as are relevant)
☐ Our advertisement in *Accounting Technician* magazine
☐ Our advertisement in *Pass*
☐ Our brochure with a letter through the post

Which (if any) aspects of our advertising do you find useful?
(Tick as many boxes as are relevant)
☐ Prices and publication dates of new editions
☐ Information on Interactive Text content
☐ Facility to order books off-the-page
☐ None of the above

Have you used the companion Assessment Kit for this subject? ☐ Yes ☐ No

Your ratings, comments and suggestions would be appreciated on the following areas

	Very useful	*Useful*	*Not useful*
Introductory section (How to use this Interactive Text etc)	☐	☐	☐
Chapter topic lists	☐	☐	☐
Chapter learning objectives	☐	☐	☐
Key terms	☐	☐	☐
Assessment alerts	☐	☐	☐
Examples	☐	☐	☐
Activities and answers	☐	☐	☐
Key learning points	☐	☐	☐
Quick quizzes and answers	☐	☐	☐
List of key terms and index	☐	☐	☐
Icons	☐	☐	☐

	Excellent	*Good*	*Adequate*	*Poor*
Overall opinion of this Text	☐	☐	☐	☐

Do you intend to continue using BPP Interactive Texts/Assessment Kits? ☐ Yes ☐ No

Please note any further comments and suggestions/errors on the reverse of this page.

Please return to: Nick Weller, BPP Publishing Ltd, FREEPOST, London, W12 8BR

REVIEW FORM & FREE PRIZE DRAW (continued)

Please note any further comments and suggestions/errors below

FREE PRIZE DRAW RULES

1. Closing date for 31 January 2001 draw is 31 December 2000. Closing date for 31 July 2001 draw is 30 June 2001.

2. Restricted to entries with UK and Eire addresses only. BPP employees, their families and business associates are excluded.

3. No purchase necessary. Entry forms are available upon request from BPP Publishing. No more than one entry per title, per person. Draw restricted to persons aged 16 and over.

4. Winners will be notified by post and receive their cheques not later than 6 weeks after the relevant draw date.

5. The decision of the promoter in all matters is final and binding. No correspondence will be entered into.